Benedikt Linse

Data Integration on the (Semantic) Web with Rules and Rich Unification

Benedikt Linse

Data Integration on the (Semantic) Web with Rules and Rich Unification

Paving the Way for the Web of Data

Südwestdeutscher Verlag für Hochschulschriften

Imprint
Any brand names and product names mentioned in this book are subject to trademark, brand or patent protection and are trademarks or registered trademarks of their respective holders. The use of brand names, product names, common names, trade names, product descriptions etc. even without a particular marking in this work is in no way to be construed to mean that such names may be regarded as unrestricted in respect of trademark and brand protection legislation and could thus be used by anyone.

Publisher:
Südwestdeutscher Verlag für Hochschulschriften
is a trademark of
Dodo Books Indian Ocean Ltd., member of the OmniScriptum S.R.L Publishing group
str. A.Russo 15, of. 61, Chisinau-2068, Republic of Moldova Europe
Printed at: see last page
ISBN: 978-3-8381-1956-4

Zugl. / Approved by: München, Ludwig Maximilians Universität, Dissertation, 2010

Copyright © Benedikt Linse
Copyright © 2010 Dodo Books Indian Ocean Ltd., member of the OmniScriptum S.R.L Publishing group

ABSTRACT

For the last decade a multitude of new data formats for the World Wide Web have been developed, and a huge amount of heterogeneous semi-structured data is flourishing online. With the ever increasing number of documents on the Web, rules have been identified as the means of choice for reasoning about this data, transforming and integrating it. Query languages such as SPARQL and rule languages such as Xcerpt use compound queries that are matched or unified with semi-structured data. This notion of unification is different from the one that is known from logic programming engines in that it (i) provides constructs that allow queries to be incomplete in several ways (ii) in that variables may have different types, (iii) in that it results in sets of substitutions for the variables in the query instead of a single substitution and (iv) in that subsumption between queries is much harder to decide than in logic programming.

This thesis abstracts from Xcerpt query term simulation, SPARQL graph pattern matching and XPath XML document matching, and shows that all of them can be considered as a form of rich unification. Given a set of mappings between substitution sets of different languages, this abstraction opens up the possibility for format-versatile querying, i.e. combination of queries in different formats, or transformation of one format into another format within a single rule.

To show the superiority of this approach, this thesis introduces an extension of Xcerpt called XCERPT^{RDF}, and describes use-cases for the combined querying and integration of RDF and XML data. With XML being the predominant Web format, and RDF the predominant Semantic Web format, XCERPT^{RDF} extends Xcerpt by a set of RDF query terms and construct terms, including query primitives for RDF containers collections and reifications. Moreover, XCERPT^{RDF} includes an RDF path query language called RPL that is more expressive than previously proposed polynomial-time RDF path query languages, but can still be evaluated in polynomial time combined complexity.

Besides the introduction of this framework for data integration based on rich unification, this thesis extends the theoretical knowledge about Xcerpt in several ways: We show that Xcerpt simulation unification is decidable, and give complexity bounds for subsumption in several fragments of Xcerpt query terms. The proof is based on a set of subsumption monotone query term transformations, and is only feasible because of the injectivity requirement on subterms of Xcerpt queries. The proof gives rise to an algorithm for deciding Xcerpt query term simulation. Moreover, we give a semantics to locally and weakly stratified Xcerpt programs, but this semantics is applicable not only to Xcerpt, but to any rule language with rich unification, including multi-rule SPARQL programs. Finally, we show how Xcerpt grouping stratification can be reduced to Xcerpt negation stratification, thereby also introducing the notion of local grouping stratification and weak grouping stratification.

ZUSAMMENFASSUNG

Über die letzten Jahre wurden eine Vielzahl von Datenformaten für das Web entwickelt, und fast monatlich kommen neue Datenformate hinzu. Nicht nur die Anzahl an verschiedenen Formaten, sondern auch die Anzahl der Dokumente innerhalb eines Formats steigt stetig und rapide an. Mit der Fülle an Information wächst der Bedarf an Mitteln zur einfachen Integration und Transformation dieser Daten, wie auch zur Kombination und zur Herleitung neuen Wissens aus den bestehenden Datensammlungen. Regelsprachen konnten sich als Mittel der Wahl für alle drei oben genannten Zwecke etablieren. Die semi-strukturierte Natur der Daten im Web stellt jedoch neue Herausforderungen an Regelsprachen; insbesondere müssen Anfragen in Regelrümpfen Konstrukte zur unvollständigen Beschreibung der gesuchten Daten bereitstellen, wie z.B. Suche in beliebiger Tiefe oder Breite des Dokumentbaumes, optionale Teilanfragen, negierte Teilanfragen, reguläre Pfadausdrücke, und weitere. Wir bezeichnen den Abgleich von solchen *reichen Anfragen* mit semi-strukturierten Daten im Web als *reiche Unifikation*, und Regelsprachen, welche sich einer reichen Unifikation im Rumpf zur Extraktion von Daten aus Webdokumenten bedienen, als *Regelsprachen mit reicher Unifikation*. Neben ausdrucksstarken Anfragekonstrukten unterscheidet sich die reiche Unifikation von der herkömmlichen Prolog-Unifikation durch ihre Assymetrie, unterschiedliche Typen von Variablen und der schwer-entscheidbaren Subsumptionsrelation zwischen Anfragen. Weiterhin ist das Ergebnis einer reichen Unifikation mit einem Dokument keine einzelne Substitution, sondern eine Substitutionsmenge.

Diese Arbeit abstrahiert von der XPath- und SPARQL-Anfrageauswertung und von Xcerpt Simulationsunifikation und zeigt auf, dass sie alle als eine Art der *reichen Unifikation* betrachtet werden können. Damit werden Regelsprachen mit SPARQL- oder XPath-Anfragen im Rumpf zur Regelsprachen mit reicher Unifikation. Legt man nun noch Abbildungen zwischen Substitutionsmengen verschiedener Regelsprachen fest, erhält man *vielseitige Regelsprachen mit reicher Unifikation*, welche sich hervorragend zur Datenintegration aus, und zur Datentransformation zwischen verschiedenen Webdatenformaten eignen. Zur Untermauerung dieser These wird eine Erweiterung von Xcerpt namens XCERPT^{RDF} vorgestellt, welche neben den bereits bekannten XML Anfrage- und Konstrukttermen, RDF Anfrage- und Konstruktterme bereitstellt, und die Simulationsunifikation auf diese Terme erweitert. Anwendungsfälle zur kombinierten Anfrage von RDF und XML mittels XCERPT^{RDF} werden präsentiert. XCERPT^{RDF} ist die erste Sprache, welche Sprachmittel zur Anfrage und Konstruktion von zusammengesetzten RDF Daten (RDF Container und Collections), und Reifikation nach einer wohldefinierten formalen Semantik unterstützt. XCERPT^{RDF} beinhaltet eine reguläre Pfadsprache names RPL, die sich unter anderem durch Pfadprädikate, Kleenesche Operatoren, Negation und Disjunktion, sowie durche ihre effiziente Auswertbarkeit auszeichnet.

Neben der Einbettung von Xcerpt in das Rahmenwerk der Regelsprachen mit reicher Unifikation trägt diese Arbeit auch zum besseren theoretischen Verständnis und zur Erweiterung der Semantik von

Xcerpt bei. Die Entscheidbarkeit und Komplexität der Subsumption zwischen Xcerpt Anfragetermen wird durch ein System von subsumptionsmonotonen Anfragetermtransformationen gezeigt. Weiterhin wird die zweiwertige Fixpunktsemantik von Xcerpt auf eine dreiwertige wohlfundierte Semantik erweitert, welche in Anlehnung an die wohlfundierte Semantik in der Logikprogrammierung definiert ist. Zwei Klassen von lokal-stratifizierten und schwach-stratifizierten Xcerpt Programmen werden identifiziert, für welche die wohlfundierte Semantik zweiwertig ist. Zuletzt wird die für Xcerpt bekannte Gruppierungsstratifikation auf die Negationsstratifikation reduziert, was zu einer einfacheren Definition von sowohl gruppierungs- wie auch negationsstratifizierten Programmen führt.

PUBLICATIONS

Some ideas and figures have appeared previously in the following publications:

[BEE+07] François Bry, Norbert Eisinger, Thomas Eiter, Tim Furche, Georg Gottlob, Clemens Ley, Benedikt Linse, Reinhard Pichler, and Fang Wei. Foundations of rule-based query answering. In Grigoris Antoniou, Uwe Aßmann, Cristina Baroglio, Stefan Decker, Nicola Henze, Paula-Lavinia Patranjan, and Robert Tolksdorf, editors, *Reasoning Web*, volume 4636 of *Lecture Notes in Computer Science*, pages 1–153. Springer, 2007.

[BFLL07] François Bry, Tim Furche, Clemens Ley, and Benedikt Linse. RDFLog—taming existence - a logic-based query language for RDF. Research report, University of Munich, 2007.

[BFL+08a] François Bry, Tim Furche, Clemens Ley, Benedikt Linse, and Bruno Marnette. RDFLog: It's like datalog for RDF. In *Proceedings of 22nd Workshop on (Constraint) Logic Programming, Dresden (30th September–1st October 2008)*, 2008.

[BFL+08b] François Bry, Tim Furche, Clemens Ley, Benedikt Linse, and Bruno Marnette. Taming existence in RDF querying. In Diego Calvanese and Georg Lausen, editors, *RR*, volume 5341 of *Lecture Notes in Computer Science*, pages 236–237. Springer, 2008.

[BFL06] François Bry, Tim Furche, and Benedikt Linse. Data model and query constructs for versatile web query languages: State-of-the-art and challenges for Xcerpt. In José Júlio Alferes, James Bailey, Wolfgang May, and Uta Schwertel, editors, *PPSWR*, volume 4187 of *Lecture Notes in Computer Science*, pages 90–104. Springer, 2006.

[BFL08c] François Bry, Tim Furche, and Benedikt Linse. Simulation subsumption or déjà vu on the Web. In Diego Calvanese and Georg Lausen, editors, *RR*, volume 5341 of *Lecture Notes in Computer Science*, pages 28–42. Springer, 2008.

[BFLP08] François Bry, Tim Furche, Benedikt Linse, and Alexander Pohl. XcerptRDF: A pattern-based answer to the versatile web challenge. In *Proceedings of 22nd Workshop on (Constraint) Logic Programming, Dresden, Germany (30th September–1st October 2008)*, pages 27–36, 2008.

[BFL+09a] François Bry, Tim Furche, Benedikt Linse, Alexander Pohl, Antonius Weinzierl, and Olga Yestekhina. Four lessons in versatility or how query languages adapt to the web. In *Semantic Techniques for the Web, The Rewerse Perspective*, volume 5500 of *Lecture Notes in Computer Science*. Springer, 2009.

[BFLS06] François Bry, Tim Furche, Benedikt Linse, and Andreas Schroeder. Efficient evaluation of n-ary conjunctive queries over trees and graphs. In Angela Bonifati and Irini Fundulaki, editors, *WIDM*, pages 11–18. ACM, 2006.

[BFL09c] Francois Bry, Tim Furche, and Benedikt Linse. Model theory and entailment rules for RDF containers, collections and reification. forthcoming, 2009.

[BFL09d] Francois Bry, Tim Furche, and Benedikt Linse. The perfect match: RPL and RDF rule languages. In *Proceedings of the third international conference on Web reasoning and rule Systems*. Springer, 2009.

ACKNOWLEDGMENTS

Many people contributed to this thesis. Amongst others I would like to thank the following persons:

- François Bry for giving me the chance to work on this fascinating topic in an international team of researchers, and for his continous and abundant stream of interesting ideas, many of which had a great impact on the development of this thesis.
- Michael Kifer for proof reading my thesis and very valuable remarks.
- Norbert Eisinger for introducing me to the beauty of logic programming.
- Tim Furche for countless fruitful discussions and support in the area of XPath and Xcerpt query evaluation, RDF Semantics, RDF query languages, complexity classes, Xcerpt query term subsumption, and for interesting research ideas.
- Alexander Pohl for the common work on XCERPT^{RDF}, Clemens Ley for the common work on RDFLog, Olga Poppe for countless discussions about the semantics and evaluation of rich unification languages and Harald Zauner for his great implementation of RPL. Sacha Berger for discussions about programming languages and type systems.
- The unknown reviewers of my publications for giving valuable feedback which has also been integrated into this thesis.
- My family for their support and for always being there when I need them.

CONTENTS

I INTRODUCTION 1
1 MOTIVATION 3
  1.1 Rule languages with Rich Unification 6
  1.2 Substitution Sets as the result of Rich Unification 9
  1.3 Asymmetry of Rich Unification 10
  1.4 Rich Unification and Subsumption 11
  1.5 Rich Unification and Types 13
  1.6 Outline and Contributions of this Thesis 14
2 PRELIMINARIES 15
  2.1 Introduction to Xcerpt 15
  2.2 RDF and the Semantic Web Vision 17
    2.2.1 RDF Abstract Data Model 19
    2.2.2 RDF/XML 21
    2.2.3 Notation 3 24
  2.3 The RDF/S Model Theory 24
  2.4 RDF Extensions 29
  2.5 Critique of the RDF/S Model Theory 31
3 RELATED WORK: DATA INTEGRATION ON THE (SEMANTIC) WEB 33
  3.1 State of the Art: The SPARQL Query Language 33
    3.1.1 SPARQL graph patterns 34
    3.1.2 Blank nodes in SPARQL graph patterns 36
    3.1.3 Testing RDF Graphs for Equivalence in SPARQL 38
    3.1.4 Semantics and Complexity of SPARQL 39
  3.2 Extensions of SPARQL 41
    3.2.1 nSPARQL 41
    3.2.2 SPARQLeR 42
    3.2.3 XSPARQL 44
    3.2.4 SPARQL update 46
    3.2.5 SPARQL and Rules 47
  3.3 Flora-2 49
  3.4 RQL 52
  3.5 Triple 53
  3.6 SWRL 55
  3.7 Metalog 56
  3.8 The Rule Interchange Format 57

II VERSATILE QUERYING WITH XCERPT^{RDF} 61
4 VERSATILE USE CASES 63
  4.1 Querying XML with Xcerpt: Examples and Patterns 66
    4.1.1 Xcerpt^{XML} Data and Rules. 67
    4.1.2 Xcerpt^{XML} Queries: Pattern-based Filtering of Search Results 69
    4.1.3 Mining Semantic data from Microformats embedded in personal profiles. 70
  4.2 Querying RDF with Xcerpt: Examples and Patterns 72
    4.2.1 Representation of RDF Graphs as XCERPT^{RDF} Data Terms 72
    4.2.2 XCERPT^{RDF} Query Terms 76

xv

        4.2.3 XCERPT^{RDF} Construct Terms and Rules   79
    4.3 Glueing RDF and XML with Rules   84
        4.3.1 Versatile Rules   84
        4.3.2 Transforming LinkedIn embedded Microformat information to DOAC and FOAF   86
5 XCERPT^{RDF} SYNTAX AND SIMULATION   89
    5.1 Compound RDF data structures in XCERPT^{RDF} 89
    5.2 A Model Theory for RDF Containers, Collections and Reification   92
        5.2.1 RDFS$^+$ Model Theory and Entailment Rules   92
        5.2.2 RDFCC Model Theory and Entailment Rules   94
        5.2.3 RDFR Model Theory and Entailment Rules   100
    5.3 Abstract Syntax of XCERPT^{RDF} 102
    5.4 XCERPT^{RDF} Declarative Semantics: Term Simulation   109
    5.5 XCERPT^{RDF} Queries, Facts, Rules and Programs   116
6 THE XCERPT^{RDF} REGULAR PATH LANGUAGE RPL   119
    6.1 Design Goals of RPL   119
    6.2 RPL by Example   120
    6.3 Syntax of RPL   123
    6.4 Compositional Semantics of RPL   124
    6.5 Restrictions and Extensions of RPL   127
    6.6 RPL compared to Lorel, SPARQLeR and nSPARQL   129
    6.7 Further Complexity Results   132
    6.8 Compilation of RPL to Prolog   135

III XCERPT MULTI-RULE SEMANTICS AND TERM SUBSUMPTION   139
7 XCERPT TERM SIMULATION AND MULTI-RULE SEMANTICS   141
    7.1 Simulation as the Foundation for Versatile Querying   141
    7.2 Simulation and Negation: Local Stratification   146
    7.3 Well-Founded Semantics for Xcerpt   150
    7.4 Grouping versus Negation Stratification   156
        7.4.1 Elimination of Single Grouping Constructs   157
        7.4.2 Elimination of Nested Grouping Constructs   159
8 XCERPT QUERY TERM SUBSUMPTION   163
    8.1 Xcerpt^{XML} Query Terms and Simulation   165
    8.2 Simulation Subsumption   165
    8.3 Simulation Subsumption by Rewriting   167
    8.4 Properties of the Rewriting System   170
        8.4.1 Subsumption Monotonicity and Soundness   170
        8.4.2 Completeness   172
        8.4.3 Decidability and Complexity   173
    8.5 Complexity for Xcerpt Fragments   174
    8.6 Future Work in the Area of Xcerpt Query Term Subsumption   185
9 SUMMARY AND FUTURE WORK   187

IV APPENDIX   189
A PROOFS RELATED TO XCERPT QUERY TERM SUBSUMPTION   191
    A.1 Non-ground Simulation between Xcerpt^{XML} Query Terms   191
    A.2 Proof of Completeness of the Rewriting System   193

BIBLIOGRAPHY   197

LIST OF FIGURES

Figure 1   Example terms for the illustration of blank node simulation.   113
Figure 2   An example RDF graph   121
Figure 3   Relationships among subexpressions of RPEs   124
Figure 4   Reduction from the Hamilton Cycle Problem to $RPL^{\rightarrow,/,\{\}}$ evaluation   135
Figure 5   Social graph corresponding to the facts in Listing 7.1   147
Figure 6   Local stratification for Listing 7.1   148
Figure 7   Dependency graph for Listing 7.2   150
Figure 8   Weak stratification for Listing 7.6   154
Figure 9   Computation of the well-founded semantics for the program S in Listing 7.6   155
Figure 10   Dependency graph of the grouping-free transformation of Q   161
Figure 11   Embeddings from [Kil92] versus Xcerpt simulation   177
Figure 12   Homeomorphic and minor embeddings.   179
Figure 13   Representation of an undirected graph as an Xcerpt({}) data term for the proof of Theorem 18   183
Figure 14   Simulation for Xcerpt({{}})   184

LIST OF TABLES

Table 1   Syntax of XCERPT^{RDF} data terms   77
Table 2   Query term simulation with different scopes for without   78
Table 3   Query term simulation with variables for nodes, predicates, graphs and concise bounded descriptions.   79
Table 4   Syntax of XCERPT^{RDF} query terms   80
Table 5   Application of substitution sets to XCERPT^{RDF} construct terms   81
Table 6   Application of substitution sets to XCERPT^{RDF} construct terms with casting of variable bindings.   84
Table 7   Evaluation of the program T(P) in Example 34   158
Table 8   Complexity of Simulation and Subsumption for Xcerpt fragments. (m is the size of the query term; n is the size of the data for simulation and the size of the subsumed query term for subsumption.)   184

xvii

ACRONYMS

BLD Basic Logic Dialect (RIF)

EBNF Extended Backus Naur Form

FLD Framework for Logic Dialects (RIF)

FOL First Order Logic

GRDDL Gleaning Resource Descriptions from Dialects of Languages

NCMP Numbered Container Membership Property

OWL Web Ontology Language

RDF Resource Description Framework

RDFCC RDF Container and Collection

RDFR RDF Reification

RDFS Resource Description Framework Schema

RDF/S RDF and RDFS

RIF Rule Interchange Format

RPE Conditional RDF path expression

RPL Conditional RDF path language

RQL RDF Query Language

SeRQL Sesame RQL

SPARQL SPARQL Protocol and RDF Query Language

SWRL Semantic Web Rule Language

XML Extensible Markup Language

Part I

INTRODUCTION

1

MOTIVATION

With the amount and diversity of information on the Web rapidly and steadily growing, and with new data formats, flavors of microformats and methods for embedding semantic information in HTML emerging on a monthly basis, rules have been agreed upon as the method of choice for data integration and knowledge exchange on the Web [BHK+09]. In the last years we have witnessed the rise of Semantic Web data formats, most prominently the Resource Description Framework and Topic Maps, as well as the increasing use of Microformats (hCard, hCalendar, hResume, hReview, etc.), embeddings of semantic information in HTML (RDFa, eRDF, GRDDL), and wiki markup languages for collaborative online document creation. Due to their declarativity, rule languages have been found as a suitable means for transforming and integrating information from diverse sources (XSLT, XSPARQL, SPARQL Construct Rules, Xcerpt) as well as for inferring new knowledge.

Heterogeneity of data on the Web

Microformats and embeddings of semantic information in HTML

Considering that industrial software engineering is mostly dominated by the imperative and object-oriented programming paradigm, with increasing influence of functional techniques, it may be surprising that rules have such a strong foothold in business applications and on the (Semantic) Web. Taking a closer look, however, the advantages of rules become evident:

- *Ease of use*: With rules encoding simple pairs of conditions and consequences, they are rapidly explained even to users with limited programming experience. Facilitated by their relatively simple syntax, visual modelling tools for rules further lower the barrier of their adoption [LW06], [BBF+06], [BBB+04], [BBSW03].

    Benefits of rules for data integration

- *Context-independence*: Rules are, to a large part independent of the rest of the program they appear in and are thus ideal to be exchanged over the Web and reused in various different applications. To give an example, the pair of Datalog rules

$$t(X,Y) \leftarrow r(X,Y).$$
$$t(X,Z) \leftarrow r(X,Y), t(Y,Z).$$

    compute the transitive closure t of a finite relation r, irrespective of other rules in the program, the extension of the predicate r, and the types of elements in the relation, be it strings, integers, the names of cities, or the classes of an ontology. In the higher order rule language HiLog[CKW93], context independence – and thus potential reuse – is further increased by parameterizing predicate names. The following pair of HiLog rules from [CKW93] computes the transitive closure for an arbitrary predicate r with finite extension.

    Higher order logic programming

$$closure(R)(X,Y) \leftarrow R(X,Y).$$
$$closure(R)(X,Z) \leftarrow R(X,Y), closure(R)(Y,Z).$$

    Since RDF data can be seen as a single ternary relation over subjects, predicates and objects, the transitive closure can also be computed over arbitrary RDF properties with finite extensions, independent of the context by the following pair of RDFLog rules[BFL⁺08a, BFL⁺08b].

$$\forall x, y, p \; \exists p_t \; . \; (\\ (\mathsf{triple}(x, p_t, y) \leftarrow \mathsf{triple}(x, p, t)) \land \\ (\mathsf{triple}(x, p_t, z) \leftarrow \mathsf{triple}(x, p, y), \mathsf{triple}(y, p_t, z)) \\ )$$

Context independence of rules on the Web is sometimes partially sacrificed for more concise formulation of queries: Most RDF rule languages proposed thus far (e.g. SPARQL, RDFLog, Xcerpt, Triple) allow the use of qualified names instead of URIs for the sake of conciseness. With qualified names depending on namespace prefix declarations, the context-independence of rules is only maintained by expansion of qualified names to URIs. This is easily achieved by a simple search-and-replace query over a rule or rule program.

- *Strong theoretical foundation*: Rules have a straditionally been used for information integration systems, especially in the context of relational databases: A simple SQL view definition can be seen as a Datalog rule.

  Motivated by this wide-spread use, the complexity of evaluation and containment for single datalog rules (i.e. conjunctive queries [CM77]), single datalog rules with negation [LS93], datalog rules with safe negation and built-in predicates [WL03], datalog rules with arithmetic comparisons[Klu88a], datalog programs [Shm87], etc. has been extensively studied. For an overview, see [Ull00].

- *Declarative Semantics*: Rule languages are in general equipped with a declarative semantics that is independent of the chosen evaluation strategy, and easier to understand. For logic programs without negation the declarative semantics is given as the minimal model semantics, or a fixpoint procedure. This fixpoint procedure gives directly rise to bottom-up evaluation methods for rule programs mentioned below. For logic programs with negation, a wide range of semantics has been proposed, most of which coincide on the class of stratified logic programs. Some of these semantics for rule programs with negation are briefly discussed below. Stratification is discussed in Section 7.2.

- *Availability of evaluation algorithms*: A series of evaluation strategies have been proposed to evaluate rule programs. These evaluation strategies differ in the following points: (i) some of them only evaluate Horn logic rules, others support negation as failure. (ii) Rules may be allowed to contain function symbols or support predicates only (Datalog). (iii) Some evaluation strategies table (memoize) intermediate results, thereby improving time efficiency and termination, but sacrificing space efficiency, others do not table intermediate results, but adhere to a pure depth-first-search strategy. (iv) Rule programs may be evaluated bottom-up (forward chaining, data driven), or top-down (backward chaining, goal driven). For an overview see [BEE⁺07].

Categorization of evaluation algorithms for rule programs

The most famous backward chaining evaluation strategy for rule programs is arguably SLD resolution[Apt88] (linear definite resolution with selection function), which is employed in most logic programming engines. SLD resolution allows function symbols, does not table intermediate results and does not handle negation. An extension of SLD resolution to rules with negative body literals is SLDNF[Apt92]. SLDNF resolution implements the so-called *program completion semantics* for logic programs with negation. The program completion semantics has been criticized for not being intuitive, and for its weak reasoning ability[vRS91b]. Alternatives to the program completion semantics include the *stable model semantics*[GL88], the *well-founded model semantics*[vRS91b], and the *inflationary semantics*. The stable model semantics and the well-founded semantics coincide on the set of locally stratified logic programs (discussed in Section 7.2), and are commonly seen to adequately capture the intuitive semantics of programs with negation as failure.

Semantics of logic programs with negation

An extension of SLD resolution to support tabling is OLDT resolution[TS86]. OLDT does not handle negative body literals. It terminates and is complete for all programs that do not define infinite relations. A backward chaining algorithm that handles both negative body literals and performs tabling is SLG resolution [RC97]. SLG resolution computes the well-founded model semantics. SLG resolution differentiates between *solution goals* and *look-up goals*. Each look-up goal l is assigned to a solution goal s which is a variant of l. Whereas the answers to solution goals are saved in a table, the answers to look-up goals are retrieved from the table of the associated solution goal. SLG resolution performs variant checking instead of subsumption checking for the sake of efficient implementation. Subsumption checking may further reduce redundant computations and is therefore employed in *subsumption based resolution* (SBR) [Pop].

For all the reasons given above, rule languages are ideal candidates for information integration on the Web. Information on the Web is, however, quite different from the information found in relational databases, or other kinds of databases employed in organizations:

Data on the Web does not adhere to a particular schema. Although there are schemas available for large parts of the information on the Web, such as the XML schema for XHTML 1.0 documents published by the W3C [Isho2], the RELAX NG schema for RDF/XML serializations of RDF graphs[Beco4], or the RELAX NG schema for XML Topic Maps[1], there is no guarantee that all data published on the Web validates against these schemas. Moreover, even in case of validation, knowledge about the structure of documents remains incomplete, since XML schema languages provide means for very loose data description (e.g. the XML schema and DTD any keywords). In particular, XML elements may have an arbitrary (but finite) number of children and may be deeply nested, nodes within an RDF graphs may have an arbitrary (but finite) number of incoming or outgoing edges, and RDF ontologies may be very large.

Why rule languages must adapt to the Web

There are (at least) two ways of bringing rule languages and semi-structured data on the Web together: (i) the data must be transformed

Bringing rule languages and semi-structured data together

---

1 http://www.isotopicmaps.org/sam/sam-xtm/#sect-relaxng

in a way such that it can be processed by rule languages, or (ii) the rule languages must adapt to the data. The first approach is taken by rule languages such as RDFLog, Triple, and to some extend also by SPARQL, the second approach is taken by rule languages such as Xcerpt, nSPARQL, rule languages based on XPath such as XPathLog [Mayo4] and the nameless language proposed in [VDo3]. Traditionally, the first approach has been taken by rule languages for RDF data, and the second approach has been more popular for rule languages dealing with XML, nSPARQL being a notable exception. This is mainly due to the fact that the decomposition of RDF graphs into RDF triples is a well-defined and intended way of dealing with RDF data, whereas the decomposition of XML trees into relational data is almost exclusively considered for the formal specification of XML query languages and the study of their complexity. This thesis takes the second approach and highlights the challenges faced when extending rule languages with rich unification in order to query semi-structured data.

As a result of the semi-structured nature of data on the Web, web query languages provide so-called *incompleteness constructs* for partially specifying the structure of documents that the query author is interested in. Examples of these incompleteness constructs include the XPath transitive closure axes descendant, ancestor, following-sibling, etc, the SPARQL OPTIONAL and UNION keywords, and double curly braces or square brackets in Xcerpt. Xcerpt is a rule language that makes intense use of incompleteness constructs in the body of rules. This thesis is inspired by Xcerpt, at the same time extending the language to allow other types of terms in rule bodies (e.g. for querying RDF data) and heads, and abstracting from it by introducing the notion of rule languages with *rich unification*.

1.1 RULE LANGUAGES WITH RICH UNIFICATION

To give the reader a better feeling about the notion of *rich unification*, this section outlines the commonalities and differences between Prolog (*poor*) unification on the one hand and SPARQL graph pattern matching over RDF graphs and XPath query evaluation over XML documents on the other. Moreover, we introduce the notion of rule languages with rich unification and show that SPARQL and Xcerpt fall into this category. Paying attention to the separation of data querying and result construction, one can also see XQuery as a rule language with rich unification.

Based on these observations, this thesis proposes to use *versatile rules* with *rich unification* for data integration on the Web. A versatile rule is a rule of the form

$$H \leftarrow L_1, \ldots, L_n$$

where H is the head of the rule, and $L_1, \ldots, L_n$ are its body literals. H may be a SPARQL construct pattern, an Xcerpt or $\textsc{Xcerpt}^{RDF}$ construct term, an XQuery expression involving element constructors and variables only, and $L_1, \ldots, L_n$ are possibly negated XPath 2.0 queries, SPARQL graph patterns, or Xcerpt or $\textsc{Xcerpt}^{RDF}$ query terms. In this way, data may be extracted by evaluating body literals over (semantic) web data and transformed into some other format using a suitable construction mechanism. With new web data formats being frequently invented, this framework of data integration with versatile rules is extensible to other formats such as Microformats, Topic Maps and wiki pages. The common ground that versatile rules build upon is the concept of *rich unification*, which is explained below.

Although versatile rules allow querying of different data formats in a single body of a rule, and construction of data in a format that is distinct from the formats queried, they do not have to. On the contrary, most SPARQL rules already fit into the framework of versatile rules, and even many XQuery programs can be thought of as versatile rules. The SPARQL rule in Listing 3.1 from [SP08] is a versatile rule with a single body literal consisting of a conjunction of unions of triple patterns, and a SPARQL construct pattern as the head. SPARQL is introduced in more detail in Section 3.1.

Listing 1.1: A SPARQL program consisting of a single construct rule

```
PREFIX foaf:    <http://xmlns.com/foaf/0.1/>
PREFIX vcard:   <http://www.w3.org/2001/vcard-rdf/3.0#>

CONSTRUCT { ?x  vcard:N _:v .
            _:v vcard:givenName ?gname .
            _:v vcard:familyName ?fname }
WHERE
{
   { ?x foaf:firstname ?gname } UNION
     { ?x foaf:givenname    ?gname } .
   { ?x foaf:surname    ?fname } UNION
     { ?x foaf:family_name ?fname } .
}
```

To see that also some XQuery programs can be considered as rules, consider Listing 1.2 from the XQuery recommendation [SCF+07]. It is essentially partitioned into three parts: Lines 1 and 2 extract data from XML documents, lines 3 and 4 operate on the selected variable bindings by selecting only the relevant ones and reordering them, and lines 5 to 10 construct the result. Omitting lines 3 and 4 from Listing 1.2, one obtains still a valid and useful XQuery program, which is a syntactical variant of a versatile rule. However, this example (and many others) shows that in practice it is often necessary to do more than simple querying and result construction; in particular data aggregation, filtering, grouping and reordering. Often, some of these tasks such as aggregation, ordering and grouping, can be, as in Xcerpt, accomplished during result construction. This thesis considers rule programs that are limited to data querying and result construction, and, to some extent, grouping.

Listing 1.2: An XQuery FLWOR expression

```
  for $d in fn:doc("depts.xml")/depts/deptno
2 let $e := fn:doc("emps.xml")/emps/emp[deptno = $d]
  where fn:count($e) >= 10
  order by fn:avg($e/salary) descending
  return
     <big-dept> {
7       $d,
        <headcount>{fn:count($e)}</headcount>,
        <avgsal>{fn:avg($e/salary)}</avgsal>
     } </big-dept>
```

8   MOTIVATION

Prolog unification versus matching of XPath and SPARQL queries

PROLOG UNIFICATION   With Prolog being the most famous rule language up to now, the notion of *unification* in Prolog deserves special attention also in the context of the Web. Unification is Prolog's sole way of binding variables to terms and is similar to the notion of matching a query with data. Often, unification is distinguished from matching in that in unification both terms may contain variables, but in matching, only the query may contain variables. During a forward chaining evaluation of a Prolog program with range restricted rules, unification of queries with ground terms (i.e. matching) is sufficient. In contrast, a goal-directed or backward evaluation of a Prolog program generally requires real unification between body literals and rule heads.

Given two first-order terms t_1 and t_2, unification is an algorithm that computes a *most general unifier* between t_1 and t_2.

Definition 1 (Unifier). *Given two first-order terms t_1 and t_2, a unifier for t_1 and t_2 is a mapping σ from the variables in t_1 and t_2 to terms such that the application of σ to t_1 is syntactically equal to the application of σ to t_2, written $\sigma(t_1) = \sigma(t_2)$.*

A unifier is also often called a substitution for the variables in t_1 and t_2. Before being unified, the terms t_1 and t_2 are *standardized apart*. Standardization apart is the renaming of variables within t_1 (or t_2) such that t_1 and t_2 are *variable-disjoint*, i.e. do not have any common variables. If there exists a unifier for t_1 and t_2, then t_1 and t_2 are called *unifiable*.

Roughly speaking, a unifier σ is a most *most general unifier* of two terms, if it instantiates as little as possible. For a precise definition of most general unifier see [BEE$^+$07][Definition 50]. For two unifiable first-order terms t_1 and t_2 the most general unifier is unique up to variable renaming.

Example 1. *Let $t_1 = f(g(X,Y),a)$ and $t_2 = f(g(V,a),Z)$. Then*

$$\sigma = \{X \mapsto b, V \mapsto b, Y \mapsto a, Z \mapsto a\}$$

is a unifier of t_1 and t_2, because $\sigma(t_1) = \sigma(t_2) = f(g(b,a),a)$. σ is not a most general unifier of t_1 and t_2, since for the unifier

$$\mu = \{X \mapsto V, Y \mapsto a, Z \mapsto a\}$$

there is no mapping τ such that $\mu = \tau \circ \sigma$. In contrast, μ is a most general unifier of t_1 and t_2, because it instantiates as little as possible. It does not instantiate the variables V and Y by ground terms, since this would be unnecessary.

RICH UNIFICATION VERSUS PROLOG UNIFICATION   Rich unification differs from Prolog unification in the following points.

- Unification of two Prolog terms yields a substitution. In contrast, rich unification yields *sets of substitutions*.

- Prolog Unification is symmetric. If term μ is a unifier for the pair of terms (t_1, t_2), then it is also a unifier for the pair (t_2, t_1). This does not hold languages with rich unification. *Rich unification is asymmetric.*

- Whereas subsumption between Prolog terms can be reduced to variable instantiation, *subsumption for languages with rich unification is more involved*, sometimes even at the verge of decidability.
- Due to the different data formats on the Web and the more complex nature of semi-structured data, *types and type coercion play important roles in rich unification*.

In the rest of this section, these properties of rich unification are elaborated upon and illustrated by example.

1.2 SUBSTITUTION SETS AS THE RESULT OF RICH UNIFICATION

Matching a SPARQL graph pattern P with an RDF graph G does not result in a substitution, but a so-called *solution set*. A solution set is a *set* of mappings from the free variables P to the vocabulary of G. Each mapping μ in the solution set is a *unifier* of P and G in the sense that μ(P) is a *subgraph* of G. In contrast to Prolog unification, there may be more than one valid mapping for P and G.

Example 2. *Consider the SPARQL pattern P and the RDF Graph G:*

$$P = \{ (?X, name, "Bill"), (?X, knows, ?Y) \}$$

$$G = \{ (\_:B, name, "Bill"), (\_:B, knows, anna), (\_:B, knows, chuck) \}.$$

Matching P with G yields the solution set S:

$$S = \{ \{ ?X \mapsto \_:B, ?Y \mapsto anna \}, \{ ?X \mapsto \_:B, ?Y \mapsto chuck \} \}$$

The evaluation of XPath queries over XML trees results in *sets of nodes*, not substitution sets. This is due to the fact that XPath queries can be considered as *unary* queries (i.e. Datalog queries with a single distinguished variable) over tree structured data. The distinguished variable in XPath is left implicit, and is determined by the last step expression outside of any predicate of the XPath expression.

Example 3. *Consider the XPath query* $q = a/b[c//a]$ *over the XML document D below. Evaluation of q over D yields the two nodes* `<b><c><c><a/></c></c></b>` *and* `<b><c><a/></c></b>`.

```
<a>
  <b><c><c><a/></c></c></b>
  <b><c><a/></c></b>
</a>
```

D can be encoded as the binary relations label, child and desc as follows: (i) each node in the document is assigned an unique id, (ii) the tuple (i, l) is in the relation label iff the label of the node with id i is l, (iii) the tuple (i_1, i_2) is in the relation child (desc) iff the node with id i_2 is child (descendant) of the node with id i_1. Then q can be written as the unary Datalog query

$$\begin{aligned}
q(x_2) \leftarrow\ & child(x_1, x_2), label(x_1, "a"), label(x_2, "b"), \\
& child(x_2, x_3), label(x_3, "c"), \\
& desc(x_3, x_4), label(x_4, "a").
\end{aligned}$$

Hence also for an XPath query over an XML document, there is no single solution, but many embeddings of the query in the data.

1.3 INCOMPLETE QUERIES AND ASYMMETRY OF RICH UNIFICATION

Unification between terms in logic programming is, by definition, symmetric. Unification in rule languages with rich unification, on the other hand, is asymmetric, which is an immediate consequence of the asymmetry of matching queries with data in these languages. Asymmetry of matching in languages such as SPARQL, XPATH or Xcerpt is due to the inherent incompleteness of queries, which in turn is necessitated by the semi-structured nature of data on the Web. Whereas for ground terms t_1 and t_2 in logic programming it holds that t_1 matches with t_2 if and only if t_1 and t_2 are syntactical equal, this is not true for matching web queries with web data. XPath expressions and SPARQL queries are inherently incomplete, in that they only specify what *must* be present in the data. They do not specify what *must not* be present. Additionally SPARQL supports optionality and blank nodes in queries acting as undistinguished variables, and XPath supports transitive closure axes for querying at arbitrary depth and breadth. Similarly, Xcerpt supports optionality and incomplete specification of queries in breadth, depth (descendant) and with respect to order. For a more detailed explanation of these concepts see Section 2.1.

FROM GROUND MATCHING TO TWO-WAY RICH UNIFICATION Rule languages with rich unification all agree in the way they base non-ground query matching on ground query matching. From an abstract point of view, the ground matching relationship between SPARQL queries and RDF graphs, as well as between XPath expressions and XML documents and between ground Xcerpt query terms and Xcerpt data terms is an infinite binary relation $R = \{(q_1, d_1), \ldots, (q_n, d_n)\}$, containing all pairs of queries and data items (q_i, d_i) such that q_i matches with d_i. Given this relation R, non-ground matching is defined in the very same way in all these languages: a not necessarily ground query q matches with data d if and only if there is a substitution μ such that $(\mu(q), d)$ is in R.

Example 4 (Ground and non-ground matching in SPARQL). *The ground matching relationship of basic SPARQL graph patterns is the relation*

$$R = \{(S, G) \mid G \text{ is an RDF graph}, S \subseteq G\}$$

The matching relationship between non-ground basic SPARQL graph patterns and RDF graphs is

$$R_V = \{(S, G) \mid \exists \mu \text{ such that } (\mu(S), G) \in R\}$$

where μ is a mapping from the variables in S to the vocabulary of G.

Non-ground matching is sometimes termed one-way unification, since only the query contains variables, which are bound to parts of the data. One-way unification is sufficient for a forward chaining evaluation of logic programs, but backward chaining requires two-way unification, i.e. the computation of mappings from variables in both the query, and in the construct pattern.

As a single-rule query language, SPARQL is not meant to be evaluated in a forward or backward chaining manner, and therefore does not define any kind of two-way unification. Nevertheless, SPARQL rule chaining may already take place on the Web today. Most popular RDF toolkits with support for SPARQL, such as Sesame [BKvH02] and Jena [CDD+04], also implement SPARQL's construct query form. It is thus easy to publish RDF documents on the Web that are views of other RDF data sources, and these documents may themselves be queried by other SPARQL (or RQL or SeRQL) engines. Hence, rule chaining on the Semantic Web most likely already takes place today, although we may not be aware of it yet.

Rule chaining on the Web

Since SPARQL rules are scattered over different query engines on the Web working independently of each other, most of them probably not even exposing the rules they evaluate, but only publishing their results, rule chaining on the (Semantic Web) takes place in an unsynchronized, and forward-chaining manner only. For a backward chaining evaluation, real unification is necessary, and can be consistently defined for all rule languages with rich unification as follows: Given a query q and a construct pattern p (e.g. a SPARQL construct pattern, an Xcerpt construct term or an XQuery expression composed of element constructors and variables only) $\sigma : vars(p) \cup vars(q) \rightarrow voc(p) \cup voc(q)$ is a most general unifier of q and p, if for all substitutions τ holds $((\tau \circ \sigma)q, (\tau \circ \sigma)p) \in R$, where R is the ground matching relation. Two-way unification aids backward chaining in the following way: If the unification of a body literal l_1 of a rule r_1 with the head h of a rule r_2 yields a non-empty substitution set, then r_2 is relevant in answering l_1, and other queries that unify with the head of r_1.

The necessity for two-way rich unification

Example 5 (Two-way unification in SPARQL). *Consider the SPARQL construct pattern P and the SPARQL query Q*

$$P = \{(a, b, ?X), (?X, c, ?Y), (?Y, a?X)\}$$

$$Q = \{(?V, b, ?W), (?S, c, a)\}$$

with $\mu = \{?V \mapsto a, ?W \mapsto ?X, ?S \mapsto ?X, ?Y \mapsto a\}$ *being the most general unifier of Q and P,*

$$\mu(P) = \{(a, a, a), (a, b, ?X), (?X, c, a)\}$$

and

$$\mu(Q) = \{(a, b, ?X), (?X, c, a)\}$$

and for any substitution τ *holds* $((\tau \circ \mu)q, (\tau \circ \mu)p) \in R$ *where R is the ground SPARQL matching relationship from example 4.*

1.4 SUBSUMPTION IN RULE LANGUAGES WITH RICH UNIFICATION

Query containment between web queries is much harder to decide than containment between Prolog terms. Subsumption or query containment has played a crucial role in database systems and research for a long time. [Scho4b] distinguishes binary XPath containment ($\subseteq_2$), unary XPath containment ($\subseteq_1$) and boolean XPath containment (subseteq$_0$). In binary XPath containment, XPath expressions are evaluated *relatively* over the entire XML tree to sets of *pairs* of nodes, and these sets are

Subsumption between Prolog terms compared with subsumption for languages with rich unification

tested for set inclusion. In unary XPath containment, XPath expressions are evaluated *absolutely* – i.e. with respect to the document root – to *sets of nodes*, which are subsequently tested for set inclusion. Boolean XPath containment simply tests if an XPath expression matches with a document or not, and does not consider the result of the queries. All three versions of containment can be reduced to each other. Analogous notions of containment can be defined for Xcerpt^{XML} query terms, for Xcerpt^{RDF} query terms and for SPARQL queries. In this thesis we consider only *boolean query term containment*, i.e we say that a query q_1 subsumes a query q_2 if and only if for all data d holds if q_2 matches d, then also q_1 matches d.

The subsumption relationship between two SPARQL graph patterns, between two XPath expressions or between two Xcerpt query terms is much more complex and harder to decide than between two Prolog terms. Still, deciding subsumption between queries is crucial for the efficient evaluation of rule programs, since it may be used in tabling engines to memoize intermediate results and avoid recomputation of solutions. Tabling evaluation engines for Prolog rule systems have already been developed, but not – to the best of the author's knowledge – for SPARQL rule programs or other rule programs with rich unification.

Deciding subsumption between Prolog terms can be seen as a one way unification between Prolog terms. Unification is an algorithm that computes the most general unifier between two generally non-ground Prolog terms. In Prolog it holds that a term t_1 subsumes another term t_2 if and only if t_2 is an instance of t_1.

Example 6. *The term* $t_1 = p(f(X), X)$ *subsumes the term* $t_2 = p(f(g(Y)), g(Y))$, *but it does not subsume the term* $t_3 = p(f(g(Y)), Y)$. *The substitution* $\{X \mapsto g(Y)\}$ *shows that* t_2 *is an instance of* t_1. *In contrast there is no substitution* ϕ *such that* $\phi(t_1) = t_3$.

The instance relationship (and thus the subsumption relationship) between Prolog terms can be checked in time linear in the size of both terms by a parallel depth first traversal of both terms.

SPARQL query evaluation and containment

In contrast, subsumption for queries in other rule languages are much harder to decide. For example, evaluation of a basic SPARQL graph pattern P possibly containing filter expressions over an RDF graph G is in $O(|P| \cdot |G|)$, evaluation of a basic SPARQL graph pattern with filter expressions and the union keyword is NP-complete, and adding the optional keyword makes evaluation PSPACE complete [PAG06]. Here, the evaluation problem is *not* finding all mappings μ from the variables in P to nodes in G, such that $\mu(P) \subseteq G$. Instead, the evaluation problem takes P, G and a mapping μ as input, and the output is to decide if $\mu(P) \subseteq (G)$. In contrast, given a simple SPARQL graph pattern P (even without filter expressions) and an RDF graph G, deciding if P matches G is already NP-complete, since it is exactly the graph coloring problem (see e.g. [Kub04]). Containment for SPARQL queries has, to the best of the author's knowledge, not yet explicitly been studied, but containment is obviously harder to decide than matching, i.e. already NP-hard.

XPath query containment

Unlike SPARQL, XPath query containment has extensively been studied [NS02, Scho4b, MS02, tL07]. Already the small fragment XPath$^{\{/,//,*\}}$, i.e. XPath with the descendant axis and label wild cards has been shown to be CONP-complete. XPath version 2.0 [BBC$^+$07], the current version of the XPath recommendation, is more expressive than

XPath 1.0 in that it allows variable references. XPath query containment under an existential semantics (i.e. not given a variable mapping to check, but testing for the existence of a variable mapping such that the query q matches with an XML tree t) has been studied in [DT01]. It turns out that already for the comparatively small fragments XPath$^{\{/,//,[],*,|,vars\}}$, XPath$^{\{/,[],vars,\neq\}}$, and XPath$^{\{/,//,[],|,vars,\neq\}}$ containment is Π_2^p-complete, whereas for the fragment XPath$^{\{/,//,[],*,|,vars,\neq\}}$ it is undecidable.

In Section 8 we show that Xcerpt query term subsumption is in $O(n!^n)$ by a system of subsumption monotone transformations transforming the subsuming query term into the subsumed one.

1.5 TYPES AND TYPE COERCION IN RULE LANGUAGES WITH RICH UNIFICATION

Types play a much more crucial role in rule languages with rich unification than they do in conventional rule languages. SPARQL variables may be bound to IRIs, literals, blank nodes or even entire subgraphs of an RDF graph. Blank nodes are only allowed to appear as subjects or objects in an RDF graph, and literals as objects only. Thus, when constructing graphs by filling variable bindings into SPARQL construct patterns, one must take care to not construct invalid RDF graphs. This is most easily and most elegantly met by the introduction of variables with different types. Variables of type IRI may appear anywhere in a construct pattern, variables of type blank node must not appear in predicate position, and variables of type literal may only appear in object position. Note that SPARQL, as of today, does not support variables with different types. Instead, invalid triples that are constructed by SPARQL construct-query rules are simply omitted from the result. By the introduction of types for variables, SPARQL rules could already be checked for type-safety, i.e. to not construct invalid RDF triples, at compile time.

Xcerpt already knows three different kinds of variables: label variables, XML term variables and XML attribute variables. Term variables may not appear at the place of attributes or labels in Xcerpt construct terms, and analogous constraints apply for attribute and label variables. The type of a variable is derived from the position it appears at within query terms. For example, the variable HREF in the first rule of Listing 1.3 is an attribute variable, since it appears within round parentheses in the query term. In the construct term of the same rule, however, it appears as a term variable. Thus this rule is unsafe and can be rejected at compile time. Similarly, in the second rule, an element variable is used at the place of an attribute in the construct term, the third rule uses a label variable at the position of an element, and only the fourth rule is type safe. XCERPT^{RDF}, which is introduced in Section 5, provides node, predicate, graph, arc and concise bounded descriptions.

Listing 1.3: "Type safety in Xcerpt"

```
CONSTRUCT link[ var HREF ] FROM desc a(( var HREF )) END
CONSTRUCT link(var Div) FROM desc var Div → div{{ }} END
CONSTRUCT label[ var Label ] FROM desc var Label{{ }} END
CONSTRUCT label[ var Term ] FROM desc var Term END
```

1.6 OUTLINE AND CONTRIBUTIONS OF THIS THESIS

The contributions of this thesis are as follows:

- We extend the XML query language Xcerpt to Xcerpt^{RDF}, thereby allowing combined and native querying of XML and RDF data. In this way Xcerpt^{RDF} becomes a versatile rule language with rich unification.

- Based on Xcerpt and Xcerpt^{RDF}, we describe versatile use-cases for querying RDF and HTML data enriched with micro formats.

- With Xcerpt^{RDF} providing query constructs aimed at querying RDF containers and collections and RDF reification, we formalize the intuitive semantics of these modeling primitives provided by [MM04] and [Hay04]. Formalization of these concepts is an indispensable prerequisite for their consistent treatment across all query languages. Furthermore, we identify a complete set of entailment rules for a syntactical characterization of the RDF containers, collections and reification semantics.

- We provide the syntax, semantics and complexity RPL, a novel and expressive RDF path query language for incorporation into RDF rule languages such as SPARQL and Xcerpt^{RDF}. Supporting path negation and regular string expressions for matching qualified names, URIs and literals, RPL is more expressive than previously proposed RDF path query languages. Despite of this surge in expressivity, it can still be evaluated efficiently.

- We show the decidability of Xcerpt query term subsumption at the aid of a system of subsumption monotone transformation rules, that allows the transformation of a term t_1 into a term t_2 if and only if t_1 subsumes t_2. By appropriate pruning of the search tree, we show that Xcerpt query term subsumption is in $O(n!^n)$. Additionally we identify complexity bounds for subsumption in several less expressive fragments of Xcerpt query terms.

- We adapt the well-founded semantics of logic-programming to rule languages with rich unification. The particular challenge that must be overcome in this context is that ground queries in rule languages with rich unification are generally not part of the Herbrand Universe. In addition, we identify two classes of locally and weakly stratified programs that have a two-valued model in the well-founded semantics for rule languages with rich unification, analogous to the locally and weakly stratified fragment of logic programs.

2

PRELIMINARIES

Contents

2.1 Introduction to Xcerpt   15
2.2 RDF and the Semantic Web Vision   17
    2.2.1 RDF Abstract Data Model   19
    2.2.2 RDF/XML   21
    2.2.3 Notation 3   24
2.3 The RDF/S Model Theory   24
2.4 RDF Extensions   29
2.5 Critique of the RDF/S Model Theory   31

This chapter introduces the design principles of Xcerpt (Section 2.1), the Semantic Web Vision and its basic data format RDF (Section 2.2), the model theoretic semantics of RDF and RDF Schema (Section 2.3), some extensions of RDF (Section 2.4) and some well-known criticism of the RDF model theory (Section 2.5).

2.1 INTRODUCTION TO XCERPT

Xcerpt is a versatile, declarative language which was primarily designed for XML querying. Xcerpt as described in [Sch04a] has been extended to the reactive rule language XChange in [Pö5]. A type system based on regular rooted graph grammers for Xcerpt is described in [Ber08]. XChangeEQ [Eck08] is a pattern-based language inspired by Xcerpt for querying streams of XML events with both formal and operational semantics. Efficient algebraic evaluation of Xcerpt query terms and single-rule queries is described in [Fur08b, BFLS06]. Processing of RDF data with Xcerpt by a translation to a relational representation is described in [Bol05], challenges for *native* RDF querying are outlined in [BFL06], a syntactic extension called XCERPT^{RDF} for native RDF querying is presented in [BFLP08] and [Poh08]. XCERPT^{RDF} simulation and XCERPT^{RDF} use-cases are described in this thesis and in [BFL$^+$09a]. An extension of XCERPT^{RDF} with the path language RPL is described in [BFL09d]. As a formal foundation for the XCERPT^{RDF} query primitives for RDF containers, collections and reifications, the model theoretic of these compound RDF modelling mechanisms is specified in [BFL09c]. Xcerpt query term subsumption has been studied in [BFL08c] and is further refined in Chapter 8.

Xcerpt and its extensions

The design principles of Xcerpt as layed out in [BS02] and [BFB$^+$05] are valid for querying all kinds of semi-structured data and thus Xcerpt is an ideal language to be extended to query new semistructured data formats appearing on the Web such as RDF, Microformats, topic maps, etc and to act as an intermediary between these formats. Among these design principles are the following:

Design principles of Xcerpt

- *Positional, or pattern based querying*: Contrasting the navigational approach of XPath and XQuery where each path expression yields at most one variable binding (unary queries), Xcerpt takes a positional one, returning multiple variable bindings for patterns representing trees (and sometimes even graphs) (n-ary queries). These patterns, which are used to extract variable bindings from semistructured data, are called query terms and are informally discussed in Section 4 and formally defined in Section 5 for RDF and Section 8 for XML.

- *Clear separation of querying and construction*: A further characteristic of Xcerpt is the clear separation of construct and query parts in Xcerpt programs. This is achieved by the introduction of substitution sets, which may be considered as an interface between the querying and construction of data. Substitution sets are generated by matching query terms with semistructured data and consumed by their application to so-called *construct terms*. Construct and query terms are connected via Xcerpt *construct-query-rules*.

- *Goal directed reasoning on the Web*: Several construct query rules make up an Xcerpt program and are evaluated using forward or – similar to Prolog programs – backward chaining. While forward chaining evaluation of rules is sensible in the case of restricted amounts of data, the open nature on the Web requires backward chaining – or goal directed reasoning – to write programs that query an a priori unknown amount of data such as Web crawlers or Semantic Web agents [Hen01].

- *Strong answer closedness*: Reusability of code fragments is enhanced by so-called answer closedness. We call a query language answer closed, if (i) data in the queried format can be used as a query, and (ii) answers to queries can again be used as queries. A query language is called *weakly answer closed*, if condition (ii) is true only for some queries, and *strongly answer closed*, if condition (ii) holds true for any query in the language.

- *Reasoning capabilities*: Being a rule-based language, Xcerpt is ideally suited for deriving new knowledge from exisiting Web data, or detecting inconsistencies between data published on the Web.

- *Versatility*: From the beginning, Xcerpt was conceived to be versatile, supporting XML, bibtex and RDF querying. When querying RDF, however, Xcerpt had to rely on *syntactic* processing of serializations of RDF data and on a conversion of the nested RDF graph structure to sets of triples. This thesis extends Xcerpt to Xcerpt^{RDF} which is able to natively query RDF graphs, thereby respecting the semantics of RDF containers, collections and reifications.

SET ORIENTED PROCESSING CAPABILITIES IN XCERPT   In the same way as the logic programming language Prolog offers set-oriented constructs such as findall, bagof, setof and coverof, and as SQL provides group by, order by and aggregate functions such as count, Xcerpt offers the set-oriented grouping constructs all and some and set-based aggregation operations such as count and sum.

As pointed out by [GP91] the choice of including set oriented constructs in rule-based query languages is motivated by the fact that the "ability of a single rule to directly access all of the data to be manipulated eliminates the need for unwieldy control mechanisms and marking schemes". Furthermore, the "division of a rule into LHS[1] and RHS[2] breaks up the specification of a relation from the actions to be performed on it" and prevents a rule from accessing "the entire relation that its LHS defines".

[GP91] further highlight that set-oriented constructs may be added to the left hand side (i.e. the query part) of rules as well as to the right hand side (i.e. the construct part). Since Xcerpt not only separates querying from construction, but also querying from filtering, set-oriented constructs are not necessary in Xcerpt query terms. As might be expected, and as the need for expressive web query languages dictates, grouping constructs are allowed in Xcerpt construct terms and filter expressions. For details on how to use Xcerpt's set-oriented constructs the reader is referred to [Sch04a].

The availability of set-oriented constructs in a logic programming language has an important impact on the evaluation methods employed by the language. In this case, tuple-based processing is simply not feasible, but sets of substitutions must be memorized during the evaluation. While the linearity of SLD resolution often pays off in terms of low memory consumption for programming languages without set-oriented constructs, it is inconvenient in their presence. Instead, set-oriented evaluation mechanisms, that memorize computed extensions of predicates naturally fit with these languages. This thought has been considered in the optimization of the rule chaining in Xcerpt, which is described in Section 8.

2.2 RDF AND THE SEMANTIC WEB VISION

> "The Semantic Web is an evolving extension of the World Wide Web in which the semantics of information and services on the web is defined, making it possible for the web to understand and satisfy the requests of people and machines to use the web content. It derives from W3C director Tim Berners-Lee's vision of the Web as a universal medium for data, information, and knowledge exchange". [Wikipedia]

While the World Wide Web is, today, only comprehensible for human beings, the Semantic Web has the aim of giving Web content also a semantics for machines, or to be more precise, to be understandable for software agents that crawl and query Web content on the behalf of human users.

Imagine a software agent that is given the task of making an appointment for some person called Anna living somewhere in Munich with a dentist nearby. There are several sources of information that the software agent must gather and process:

A semantic Web use case

- Anna's calendar information
- the location of Anna's working or living place
- a list of dentists in Munich and their addresses

---
1 left hand side
2 right hand side

- geographic information about the distance between Anna's address and the one of the dentist.

- the dentists' calendar information

Already today, many people manage their calendars online (such as with Google calendar or within some social networking site), or they manage their calendars with some desktop application such as Lotus Notes or Microsoft Exchange, which can be easily exported into some serialization format such as CSV (comma separated values) or some more standardized format such as iCalendar.

Lists of dentists in a particular region can be found online using yellow pages or a directory service such as the Yahoo! directory. A human being can easily find out the distance between two addresses online using mapping services such as Google Maps or Live Search Maps.

Although all necessary information for fulfilling the task of the software agent could be already put online today, the implementation of the software agent is still a very challenging task, since the information is scattered over a variety of places, in a variety of different formats, and more importantly not intended to be understood by computers.

The role of RDF in the Semantic Web

This is where RDF comes into play. Together with the Web ontology language (OWL), RDF is the first data format with a model-theoretic semantics, that has achieved considerable popularity on the Web. The availability of a model theoretic semantics for a Web data format allows the derivation of new knowledge from existing knowledge in a clearly defined way. Thus, given the information that John Doe is a dentist in Schwabing, and that Schwabing is a district of Munich, one can derive by a simple rule that John Doe is a dentist in Munich.

Already today, RDF is used for describing persons and their relations (FOAF[3]), Software Projects (DOAP[4]), biological data (e.g. the UniProt database[5]), for exporting Wikipedia metadata, metadata about music (MusicBrainz[6]), etc.

All of the above information could be converted to RDF, and for many standardized formats such as iCal, tools for translating them to RDF format are already available. The next step in the development of the Semantic Web is the establishment of suitable RDF vocabularies for the application domains mentioned above (calendar information, geographic positions, directions, distances, extensions, maps of cities, entries in white and yellow pages). Once these vocabularies have emerged and been agreed upon, and once there are tools for translating the information, which is already available today, into these vocabularies, query, reasoning and transformation languages will help to write truly intelligent software agents that can indeed solve problems as complex as the one described above. I.e. the scheduling of an appointment with an a-priori unknown dentist that is compatible with the calendars of the persons involved and that complies with geographic constraints.

---

3 http://xmlns.com/foaf/spec/
4 http://trac.usefulinc.com/doap
5 http://dev.isb-sib.ch/projects/uniprot-rdf/
6 http://musicbrainz.org/

2.2.1 RDF Abstract Data Model

Before taking a closer look at the syntax and serializations of RDF, i.e. the form in which the programmer encounters RDF data on the Web, we first explore the abstract data model of RDF, i.e. the concepts in which RDF is thought of, the way we should think about RDF data. These "Concepts and Abstract Syntax" are defined in [Kly04]. Arguably the most important concepts of RDF are *RDF Graphs* and *RDF Triples* as defined in [Kly04]:

> "The underlying structure of any expression in RDF is a collection of triples, each consisting of a subject, a predicate and an object. A set of such triples is called an RDF graph [...]. This can be illustrated by a node and directed-arc diagram, in which each triple is represented as a node-arc-node link (hence the term "graph").
>
> Each triple represents a statement of a relationship between the things denoted by the nodes that it links. Each triple has three parts:
>
> - a subject,
> - an object, and
> - a predicate (also called a property) that denotes a relationship.
>
> The direction of the arc is significant: it always points toward the object. The nodes of an RDF graph are its subjects and objects.
>
> The assertion of an RDF triple says that some relationship, indicated by the predicate, holds between the things denoted by subject and object of the triple. The assertion of an RDF graph amounts to asserting all the triples in it, so the meaning of an RDF graph is the conjunction (logical AND) of the statements corresponding to all the triples it contains."

While RDF statements[7] always consist of exactly three components – the subject, the predicate and the object – each of these components may be – up to some restrictions – of one of three different types: *URI references*, *RDF literals* or *RDF blank nodes*. The restrictions are: the subject must not be a literal and the predicate must be a URI reference. There are no restrictions for the type of the object.

URI REFERENCES IN RDF GRAPHS   URI references are used to refer to concepts or real world objects one would like to make a statement about. Assuming that a person called Anna would like to introduce herself on the Web and make some statements about herself in RDF format, such that these statements can be processed by software agents or Semantic Web search engines, she would first have to come up with some URI reference for herself, for the Person Anna. To avoid name conflicts Anna could pick a URI belonging to a domain that belongs to her (e.g. http://www.anna.org/me. Note that RDF makes no assumption about the content of the web page located at http://www.anna.org/me. In fact it does not even demand that at there is a

---

[7] we use the terms *RDF statement* and *RDF triple* synonymously

web page at the given URI. The URI has the sole purpose of identifying the concept of the Person Anna for software applications that reason about RDF data.

RDF LITERALS   The use of RDF literals is motivated by the following scenario: Assume that Anna would like to state that her first name is "Anna". As the subject of the RDF statement she would pick the URI http://www.anna.org/me. Choosing the predicate, she could make use of the popular friend-of-a-friend (FOAF) vocabulary, that was specified to describe persons and their interrelationships. The predicate designated for this purpose has the URI http://xmlns.com/foaf/0.1/firstName and is commonly abbreviated by foaf:firstName using the namespace prefix foaf associated with http://xmlns.com/foaf/0.1/. Picking the object of the statement, Anna could come up with a namespace URI for the string "Anna", but since all information about the string "Anna" is already conveyed by simply writing it as a sequence of characters, a special type of node was introduced for Strings, which is called an *RDF Literal*. Thus the statement that Anna would like to make in RDF is the following triple:

(http://www.anna.org/me, foaf:firstName, "Anna").

Plain and typed literals

Language tags for plain literals

As mentioned above, literals may only occur in object position of RDF triples. The RDF recommendation [Klyo4] distinguishes *plain* and *typed* literals. The string "Anna" from above is called a plain literal, since it does not have any associated datatype. Plain literals may have an optional language tag such as "en", "fr", "de" that determines the natural language the string is written in. The literal "Anna@en" is a plain literal with a language tag. Typed literals are associated with a datatype, usually one of the simple datatypes defined by RDF Schema [BGo4]. The type of the literal is separated from the literal itself by "^^". An example for a typed literal is 27"|http://www.w3.org/2001/XMLSchema#integer>.

RDF BLANK NODES   The last type of node that can be found in RDF triples, and which can only occur in subject or object position, are RDF blank nodes, often abbreviated as b-nodes. Blank nodes are used whenever one would like to make statements about a concept without giving it a URI reference, because the exact nature of the concept is unknown or because there is no need to identify the concept. The use of blank nodes in RDF triples thus only asserts the existence of a resource that satisfies the relationships asserted by the triples, without identifying this resource (by giving it a URI reference). Blank nodes use the empty namespace prefix "_" followed by a colon and an identifier. Anna might want to state that she knows some person called Bob, by making use of the FOAF vocabulary and by picking the blank node identifier "_:bob" with the following triples:

http://www.anna.org/me, foaf:knows, _:bob
_:bob, foaf:firstName, ''Bob''

Scope of URIs and blank node identifiers

While RDF is only a data representation language, the role of blank nodes and URIs in RDF can be compared to the notion of local and global variable identifiers in programming languages. The scope of local variable declarations is limited to the method, module or class they are defined in, while global variable declarations are valid in the entire program or even software package. Similarly, the scope of blank node identifiers is restricted to the document they occur in, and the scope of URI references is unlimited, i.e. the same URI reference is supposed to denote the same concept in all RDF documents ever published. This means that URI references have to be carefully picked, and that the same blank node identifier may denote different resources in different RDF documents.

While the same URI denotes the same resource across all RDF documents, two different URIs might very well denote the same resource, that is, the *unique name assumption* does not hold in RDF. Under the unique name assumption, which underlies many description logic dialects, and has been investigated thoroughly in classical logics, different identifiers always denote different resources. Enforcing the unique name assumption would simply be impossible in a distributed environment such as the Web.

Unique name assumption

A closely related design decision of many RDF query languages is the adoption of the *open world assumption*. Under the open world assumption, the relevant information is assumed to be only partially known. This means that from the pure inability to prove some statement, this statement cannot be assumed to be false – thus, the open world assumption does not allow *negation as failure*. Since RDF does not provide *strong negation* (and neither any other means for deriving the falsity of a statement), RDF query languages based on the open world assumption do not provide a negation operator at all. The *closed world assumption*, on the other hand, assumes total knowledge of the relevant data, and thus allows to derive negative conclusions simply by failing to derive their positive counterparts. The open world assumption can, however, be combined with *scoped negation as failure*, as proposed in [PFH06]. This approach is also taken in Xcerpt.

Open and closed world assumption; (Scoped) Negation as failure

LEAN RDF GRAPHS   The presence of blank nodes in RDF graphs introduces the possibility of specifying redundant graphs. One RDF statement may assert that there is a person that is president of Germany, another statement may state that the person represented by the URI http://example.org/Horst is president of Germany. Since the first statement is a logical consequence of the second statement, the RDF graph made up of both statements is *redundant*, or in RDF terminology *non-lean*. Note that redundancy in RDF graphs cannot be determined by simply comparing single triples, but is instead a global attribute of the entire RDF graph, since the same blank node may appear in multiple RDF statements. Since RDF is a logical language, which is formally specified by a model theory, the notion of redundancy or non-leanness of RDF graphs can be specified in terms of logical entailment. Given an arbitrary RDF graph, computing a lean version of the graph, i.e. a graph which is logically equivalent, but non-redundant, is an NP-hard problem [GHM03].

Redundancy in RDF graphs and leanness

2.2.2   *RDF/XML*

Since RDF data is not only a data format for describing – among others – resources on the Web, but is also exchanged over the Web, it is unsurprising that its primary serialization format RDF/XML is an XML application. The RDF/XML specification [Bec04] builds upon the XML

Information Set[CT04] and upon Namespaces in XML[BHLT06] and the XML Base recommendation [MT08] for abbreviating URI references within RDF graphs in their RDF/XML serialization.

In order to encode the graph in XML, the nodes and predicates have to be represented in XML terms – element names, attribute names, element contents and attribute values. RDF/XML uses XML QNames as defined in Namespaces in XML [BHLT06] to represent RDF URI references. All QNames have a namespace name which is a URI reference and a short local name. In addition, QNames can either have a short prefix or be declared with the default namespace declaration and have none (but still have a namespace name).[Bec04][Section 2.1]

This quote is clarified by Listing 2.2.2, which gives an example for the serialization of an RDF graph as an RDF/XML document.

```xml
<?xml version="1.0"?>
<rdf:RDF xmlns:rdf="http://www.w3.org/1999/02/22-rdf-syntax-ns#"
    xmlns:foaf="http://xmlns.com/foaf/0.1/"
    xml:base="http://www.anna.org/">
  <rdf:Description rdf:ID="anna">
    <foaf:firstName>Anna</foaf:firstName>
    <foaf:knows>
      <rdf:Description rdf:about="http://bob.org/bob">
        <foaf:firstName>Bob</foaf:firstName>
      </rdf:Description>
    </foaf:knows>
  </rdf:Description>
</rdf:RDF>
```

ENCODING OF URIS IN RDF/XML In the above RDF/XML document, URIs are encoded in three different manners: The URI `http://www.anna.org/#anna` is encoded using the RDF base declaration `xml:base="http://www.anna.org/"` together with the `rdf:ID` attribute and the local name anna. The URI `http://xmlns.com/foaf/0.1/knows` is encoded by defining the namespace prefix `foaf` and making use of it in an element name (`foaf:knows`), which represents the knows-relationship between Anna and Bob. Finally the URI for Bob is simply given as the value of an `rdf:about` attribute of a `rdf:description` element. The `rdf:about` attribute could also have been omitted, in which case there would be no URI representing the person Bob, but only a blank node.

STRIPED SYNTAX OF RDF/XML The basic pattern for serializing RDF graphs within RDF/XML is a *striped* nesting of elements within the `rdf:RDF` root element: XML elements with an odd depth within the XML document tree represent nodes in the RDF graph, whereas XML elements occurring on an even level represent edges of the RDF graph. The outermost `rdf:RDF` element contains one or more `rdf:Description` elements, which are the entry points into the RDF graph. Each `rdf:Description` element is a subject of an RDF statement in the graph, and for each node in the RDF graph – with some exceptions – there is an `rdf:Description` element in its RDF/XML serialization. Note that since RDF graphs, in contrast to XML trees, may not have a single root from which all other nodes are reachable, it may be unavoidable to have more than one rdf:Description element directly within the rdf:RDF document root. An RDF graph that has n nodes without incoming edges will have at least n outermost rdf:Description elements in its RDF/XML serialization.

BLANK NODES IN RDF/XML Besides the implicit representation of RDF blank nodes in RDF/XML mentioned above, one can also use the rdf:nodeID attribute provided by the RDF/XML specification. Moreover, if a blank node only occurs in object position the empty rdf:description element can be omitted:

> "Blank nodes (not RDF URI reference nodes) in RDF graphs can be written in a form that allows the <rdf:Description></rdf:Description> pair to be omitted. The omission is done by putting an rdf:parseType="Resource" attribute on the containing property element that turns the property element into a property-and-node element, which can itself have both property elements and property attributes. Property attributes and the rdf:nodeID attribute are not permitted on property-and-node elements."[Beco4][Section 2.11]

LITERALS IN RDF/XML Literals of an RDF graph can be represented as XML text nodes of its RDF/XML serialization – just as the text node "Bob" of the RDF/XML document above represents the literal "Bob" of the corresponding RDF graph. Literals may also be encoded as attribute values. The statement that the first name of Chuck is "Chuck", where the person Chuck is represented by a blank node can be encoded in RDF/XML as <rdf:description foaf:firstName="Chuck"/>. Here foaf:firstName is called a property attribute.

FURTHER SYNTACTIC SUGAR FOR ABBREVIATING RDF/XML The above mentioned alternative encodings for URIs, literals and predicates are all abbreviations for the strictly striped RDF/XML syntax in which every URI, literal or blank node, be it in subject, predicate or object position is represented by an XML element or text node. But RDF/XML features many more syntactic variations, of which the most common ones are the following:

- empty property elements by usage of the rdf:resource attribute
- abbreviation of rdf:type statements
- using rdf:li as container membership properties instead of rdf:_1, rdf:_2, ...
- using rdf:parseType="collection" instead of implicit blank node construction
- usage of the rdf:id attribute on properties as an abbreviation for rdf reification.
- specification of the type of a literal with the rdf:datatype attribute
- usage of rdf:parseType="Literal" for inclusion of XML-literals

2.2.3 *Notation 3*

Notation 3[BL98], often also called N3, is not a formally specified RDF serialization format but only available as an ordinary HTML document on the W3C domain, which may be put into the form of a working group note or even a W3C recommendation in the future. Notation 3 must be distinguished from the RDF serialization format NTriples, which is a subset of Notation 3.

Notation 3 is meant to be "a language which is a compact and readable alternative to RDF's XML syntax, but also is extended to allow greater expressiveness. It has subsets, one of which is RDF 1.0 equivalent, and one of which is RDF plus a form of RDF rules."[BL98]. For space limitations this section gives only a brief introduction to Notation 3 by examples. The interested reader is referred to [BL98] for the complete documentation.

[:firstname "Ora"] dc:wrote [dc:title "Moby Dick"] .

The above Notation three fragment is equivalent to three rdf statements, the first one asserting that there is someone (represented by a blank node) who has the first name "Ora", the second asserting that there is something with the title "Moby Dick" (represented by another blank node) and the third one asserting that the first blank node is in dc:wrote relationship with the second blank. The example shows how statements containing literals, blank nodes and URIs, possibly abbreviated by using namespace prefixes and default namespaces can be expressed in N3. Blank nodes can be conveniently expressed with square brackets without the use of blank node identifiers (blank node identifiers are still necessary to encode multiple statements containing the same blank node). The prefix dc must certainly be declared and in this case refers to the dublin core vocabulary for RDF. Also a default namespace must be declared to ensure that :firstname can be expanded to form a URI. Finally literals are distinguished from URIs by enclosing them in double quotes.

Notation 3 introduces several shorthand notations for frequently used RDF properties such as rdf:type and allows to make statements about RDF graphs themselves, thereby introducing a new concept which is similar to RDF reification. Moreover, Notation 3 extends the expressivity of plain RDF by providing universal quantification of variables besides the existential quantification which is present as soon as blank nodes are used.

2.3 THE RDF/S MODEL THEORY

RDF and RDFS being logical knowledge representation languages, their semantics is formally specified by a model theory [Hay04]. This model theory allows to decide which conclusions can or cannot be drawn from RDF data published on the Web. The following definition of RDF graphs is similar to the definition of conjunctions of logical atoms in classical logic, and formalizes the notion of RDF data.

Definition 2 (RDF triple, RDF graph). *Let U be a set of URIs, L a set of literals and B a set of blank node identifiers. An RDF triple over U, B, L is a triple (s, p, o) of subject, predicate and object, where $s \in U \cup B$, $p \in U$ and $o \in U \cup B \cup L$. An RDF graph over U, B, L is a set of triples over U, B, L. An RDF graph is called* ground, *if it does not contain any blank nodes.*

There are two increasingly restrictive model theories for RDF, and two more for RDFS, an extension of RDF which extends RDF by – among others – a subclass relationships, the specification of domains and ranges of predicate, and typing of RDF properties. These four model theories are specified based on *simple RDF interpretations, RDF interpretations, RDFS interpretations* and *RDFS datatyped interpretations*.

For space reasons, only simple RDF interpretations and RDFS interpretations and the corresponding model theory are introduced here. (Non-simple) RDF interpretations extend simple RDF interpretations by giving a semantics to the RDF vocabulary rdf:type, rdf:Property and rdf:XMLLiteral. Given a *datatype map*, RDFS datatyped interpretations specify a minimal semantics for the typed literals in an RDF graph. A *datatype map* is a set of pairs of URI references and datatypes. A *datatype* in this context is defined as a mapping from a set strings (called the lexical space) to a set of values (called the value space).

In a very similar fashion to classical logic entailment, *simple entailment* is defined based on the concepts of *simple RDF interpretations* and *simple RDF denotations* and the model relationship between simple RDF interpretations and RDF graphs. RDF interpretations in turn make use of the notion of an *RDF vocabulary*:

Definition 3. *An RDF vocabulary V is a set of names, i.e. a set of URIs $\mathcal{U}$ plus a set of literals[8]. The vocabulary of an RDF graph are all the URIs and literals that occur in it.*

Definition 4 (Simple RDF interpretation [Hay04]). *A Simple interpretation of an RDF vocabulary* $V = \mathcal{U} \cup L$ *is a six-tuple* $(IR, IP, IEXT, IS, IL, LV)$ *where*

- $IR \neq \emptyset$: *the* domain *or* universe *of* I.
- IP: *the* set of properties *of* I.
- $IEXT : IP \rightarrow \mathcal{P}(IR \times IR)$.
- $IS : \mathcal{U} \rightarrow IR \cup IP$.
- IL : *a mapping from typed Literals in V into* IR.
- $LV \subseteq IR$: *the* set of literal values

The most obvious difference of simple RDF interpretations to interpretations of classical logic is that property names are also interpreted as elements of the domain. This is necessary, since the same URI may both appear in predicate position of an RDF triple and in subject and/or object position of another (or even the same) RDF triple. Note that for *simple* RDF interpretations, IR and IP are *neither* required to be disjunct *nor* is it demanded that $IP \subseteq IR$. But if a URI u appears within an RDF graph G both in predicate and in subject or object position, then for a simple interpretation $I = (IR, IP, IEXT, IS, IL, LV)$ that is a model of G, $IS(u)$ must be in the intersection of IR and IP, thus for such graphs, IR and IP must *not* be disjunct. Non-simple RDF interpretations (see Definition 8) require $IP \subseteq IR$.

While RDF interpretations give meaning to URIs and typed literals, RDF *denotations* give meaning also to untyped literals, and assign truth values to ground RDF triples and ground RDF graphs based on an interpretation:

Relationship between simple RDF interpretations and first-order interpretations

Relationship between IR and IP

---

8 blank node identifiers are – as variables in predicate logic – not considered part of the vocabulary

Definition 5 (Denotation of ground RDF graphs). *Given an RDF interpretation* I = (IR, IP, IEXT, IS, IL, LV) *over a vocabulary* V, *the denotation of a ground RDF graph is defined as follows:*

- *if* E *is a plain literal "aaa" in* V *then* I(E) = aaa
- *if* E *is a plain literal "aaa"@ttt in* V *then* I(E) = <aaa, ttt>
- *if* E *is a typed literal in* V *then* I(E)=IL(E)
- *if* E *is a URI reference in* V *then* I(E)=IS(E)
- *if* E *is a ground triple* (s, p, o) *then* I(E) = *true iff* s, p, o *are in* V, I(p) *is in* IP *and* (I(s), I(o)) *is in* IEXT(I(p)).
- *if* E *is a ground RDF graph then* I(E) = *false if* I(E') = *false for some triple* E' *in* E, *otherwise* I(E) = *true.*

By the above definition it is easy to see that the denotation of the empty RDF graph is always true, just as an empty conjunction is often considered true in first-order logic. Moreover, if some name in an RDF graph G is not in the vocabulary V of the interpretation I, then the denotation of G is false under I. Definition 5 already allows to decide entailment between ground RDF graphs. We say that an interpretation I is a model of a ground RDF graph G, if the denotation of G is true under I. A ground RDF graph G_1 *entails* a ground RDF graph G_2, if all models of G_1 are also models of G_2. Ground entailment between G_1 and G_2 can simply be reduced to testing the subset relationship between G_1 and G_2 and is thus decidable in linear time. Entailment between RDF graphs becomes more involved when blank nodes come into play. We therefore introduce denotations for non-ground RDF graphs:

Definition 6 (Denotation of arbitrary RDF graphs). *Let* G *be an RDF graph,* blank(G) *the set of blank nodes in* G, I *an interpretation and* A *a mapping from* blank(G) *to* IR.

Then [I + A] *denotes an* extended interpretation *which is like* I, *but maps any blank node* B *to* A(B). I(G) = true *if* [I + A'](G) = true *for some mapping* A' *from* blank(G) *to* IR.

The important clause in Definition 6 is that there must be *some mapping* A' from blank nodes to elements in the domain, such that the interpretation extended by this mapping makes the RDF graph true. Therefore blank nodes in RDF graphs can seen as existentially quantified variables.

Definition 7 (Model, simple entailment). *Let* G_1 *and* G_2 *be two not necessarily ground RDF graphs,* I *an intepretation.* I *is a* model *of* G_1, *if and only if the denotation of* G_1 *is true under* I. G_1 *simply entails* G_2, *if and only if every model of* G_1 *is also a model of* G_2.

Definition 8 (RDF interpretation (Adapted from [Hay04])). *RDF interpretations are simple RDF interpretations satisfying the following additional conditions:*

- $x \in$ IP *iff* (x, I(rdf : Property)) $\in$ IEXT(rdf : type)
- *For all literals* l, *which are typed as XML literals, and which are well-typed*[9] IL(l) *must denote the XML value of* l *(i.e. an XML fragment).*

---
9 An XML Literal is well-typed, if it the serialization of some well-formed fragment of XML. Otherwise it is called ill-typed.

- *For a well-typed XML literal l, IL(l) must be in LV.*

- *For a well-typed XML literal l, (IL(l), I(rdf : XMLLiteral)) is in IEXT(rdf : type).*

- *For an ill-typed XML literal l, IL(l) is not in LV, and (IL(l), I(rdf : XMLLiteral)) is not in IEXT(rdf : type).*

Definition 9 (RDFS interpretation [Hayo4])**.** *An RDFS interpretation is an RDF interpretation satisfying the following additional conditions:*[10]

- $x \in ICEXT(y)$ *iff* $(x, y) \in IEXT(I(type))$

- $IC = ICEXT(I(Class))$

- $IR = ICEXT(I(Resource))$

- $LV = ICEXT(I(Literal))$

- *If (x, y) is in IEXT(I(domain)) and (u, v) is in IEXT(x) then u is in ICEXT(y).*

- *If (x, y) is in IEXT(I(range)) and (u, v) is in IEXT(x) then v is in ICEXT(y).*

- *IEXT(I(subPropertyOf)) is transitive and reflexive on IP.*

- *If (x, y) is in IEXT(I(subPropertyOf)) then x and y are in IP and IEXT(x) is a subset of IEXT(y).*

- *If x is in IC then (x, I(Resource)) is in IEXT(I(subClassOf)).*

- *If (x, y) is in IEXT(I(subClassOf)) then x and y are in IC and ICEXT(x) is a subset of ICEXT(y).*

- *IEXT(I(subClassOf)) is transitive and reflexive on IC.*

- *If x is in ICEXT(I(ContainerMembershipProperty)) then (x, I(member)) is in IEXT(I(subPropertyOf)).*

- *If x is in ICEXT(I(Datatype)) then (x, I(Literal)) is in IEXT(I(subClassOf)).*

For RDF and especially for RDFS, so-called derivation rules have been identified, which can be used to derive additional knowledge from RDF graphs. While the definitions of (simple) RDF/S interpretations impose constraints on the valid interpretations of a graph only, derivation rules are *syntactical* transformations on RDF graphs, such that the model relationship between interpretations and the graphs to be transformed remain untouched. For simple RDF entailment, these derivation rules are very restricted. Given an RDF graph consisting of the single triple (a, b, c), one may add other triples to the graph in which the subject, the object or both are replaced by a blank node identifier. For RDFS entailment, these transformations include derivation rules for the transitivity of the subclass relationship, the subproperty relationship, derivation rules for the special predicates rdfs:domain and rdfs:range. The validity of these transformation rules can be checked by applying the following definition.

RDF/S derivation rules

---

10 The namespace prefixes rdf and rdfs are omitted for the sake of brevity.

Definition 10 (Valid and invalid transformations on RDF graphs (adapted from [Hay04])). *Let $\mathcal{G}$ be the set of all RDF graphs. A transformation $T : \mathcal{G} \to \mathcal{G}$ is valid, if g entails $T(g)$ for all RDF graphs $g \in \mathcal{G}$. Otherwise T is called invalid.*

Based on Definition 7, several lemmata have been derived, some of which are straight-forward. The *empty graph lemma* (Lemma 1) is analogous to the fact that the empty conjunction is equivalent to $\top$ in first order logic. The subgraph lemma 2 is analogous to the fact that in first order logic a conjunction c entails any conjunction c′ formed from a subset of the conjuncts of c. The instance lemma (Lemma 3) asserts that all graphs G which contain information about some resource r without identifying r, are entailed by all graphs G′ which identify r by some URI u, and are otherwise the same as G.

Lemma 1 (Empty graph lemma). *The empty set of triples is entailed by any graph.*

Lemma 2 (Subgraph lemma). *A graph entails all its subgraphs.*

Lemma 3 (Instance lemma). *A graph is entailed by any of its instances.*

The *merge* of a set of graphs $G_1, \ldots, G_n$ is the union of $G'_1, \ldots, G'_n$, where G'_i is obtained from G_i by consistent renaming of blank node identifiers, and $G'_1, \ldots, G'_n$ do not have any blank nodes in common. We say that $G'_1, \ldots, G'_n$ have been *standardized apart*. Lemma 4 says that if a set of RDF graphs is thrown accidentally together (without standardization apart), then the outcome may entail more than the merge of the graph, and that the taking the merge is the only right way of combining a set of RDF graphs on the Web. The *interpolation Lemma* (Lemma 3) shows that simple RDF entailment is decidable by giving a *syntactic* criterion for entailment. The model theoretic definition for entailment does not give an algorithm, since it requires the consideration of an infinite number of interpretations. Just as the interpolation lemma gives a syntactic criterion for deciding entailment, Lemma 6 gives a syntactic criterion for deciding the leanness of an RDF graph. Intuitively, an RDF graph is lean, if it does not contain any redundant information, that is, if it cannot be expressed by an equivalent (under bi-entailment) graph with a smaller set of triples.[11]

Lemma 4 (Merging lemma). *The merge of a set S of RDF graphs is entailed by S, and entails every member of S.*

Lemma 5 (Interpolation lemma). *S simply entails a graph E if and only if a subgraph of S is an instance of E.*

Lemma 6 (Leanness lemma). *An RDF graph G is lean with respect to simple entailment, if it has no instance, which is a proper subgraph of G.*

RDF graphs may *simply-entail* instances of themselves. For instance, the graph $G = \{(a, b, c), (a, b, \_ : X)\}$ entails $G' = \{(a, b, c)\}$, which is an instance of G. Lemma 7 states that this is only true for non-lean graphs. Lemma 8 is related to the Compactness Theorem of first order logic,

---

[11] In [Hay04], Lemma 6 is the *definition* of lean RDF graphs. The intuitive meaning of leanness, however, is the one of non-redundancy, and is better characterized in model theoretic terms as here. In this way, leanness not only applies for redundancy due to the presence of blank nodes, but also due to the presence of triples in the graph which are already contained under the RDFS semantics, or some other semantic extension of RDF. In fact, leanness under the RDFS semantics has already been considered in [GHM04].

which allows to draw conclusions from finite subsets S_i of an infinite set of formulas S to S itself. If RDF entailment were defined in terms of first order interpretations, Lemma 8 would be a direct consequence of the Compactness Theorem of FOL.

Lemma 7 (Anonymity Lemma). *Let E be a lean graph and E' a proper instance of E. Then E does not entail E'.*

Lemma 8 (Compactness Lemma). *If S entails E and E is a finite graph, then some finite subset S' of S entails E.*

2.4 RDF EXTENSIONS

In this section we briefly describe three extensions of the RDF/S model theory proposed by [ter05a] and [ter05a]. The RDF/S model theory explicitly encourages semantic extensions of RDF/S, and the extensions described in this section have been proven not to increase the complexity of checking ground and non-ground entailment between RDF graphs when compared to simple RDF entailment. In Sections 5.2.2 and 5.2.3 we propose two further extensions of the RDF/S model theory, that are orthogonal to the extensions D∗, pD∗ and R described in this section, in the sense that the semantic conditions layed on D∗, pD∗ or R interpretations do not interfere with the semantic conditions layed on RDFCC interpretations or RDFR interpretations. Put in another way, if an RDF graph is satisfiable under the D∗ semantics (or the pD∗, or the R semantics), and also under the RDFCC (or the RDFR semantics), then it is valid also if the conditions for D∗ (or pD∗ or R) and RDFCC (or RDFR) are combined.

D∗-ENTAILMENT   D∗ entailment is a minor extension of RDFS entailment, that deals with typed RDF literals, and that generalizes the notion of *XML clashes* to *D-clashes*. The only type known to RDF/S interpretations is the one of XML literals, but D∗ interpretations can be used with arbitrary RDF schema datatypes such as xsd:string and xsd:integer. An XML clash is present in an RDF graph when an RDF literal, which is not a well-formed XML fragment, is asserted to be of type XMLLiteral. Similarly, a D-clash occurs in an RDF graph G, whenever an RDF literal l in G is asserted to be of some XML Schema type t, and l does not belong the the lexical space of t.

When compared to ordinary RDF datatype entailment as described in [Hay04], which is also referred to as D-entailment, D∗ entailment is weaker, as the following example from [ter05a] illustrates: The set of triples $S = \{(a\ p\ \text{"true"}), (a\ p\ \text{"false"}), (b\ \text{rdf:type boolean})\}$ D-entails the triple $t = (a\ p\ b)$, but t is not D∗-entailed by S. This is best explained by the intuition that while D-entailment follows an 'iff-semantics' approach for entailment, D∗-entailment gets by with a 'if-semantics'. As a second example, an RDF graph G containing the triples (b rdf:type xsd:integer), (b rdf:type xsd:string), asserting that some blank node b in G is a surrogate for some literal that is both a string and an integer, has no D-interpretation, but it does have a D∗-interpretation. While D∗ entailment is in P for ground RDF graphs, and NP-complete for non-ground RDF graphs, the complexity of D-entailment has, to the best of the author's knowledge, not yet been determined.

PD* ENTAILMENT   pD*-Entailment[tero4] is a variant of OWL entailment, but weaker than OWL Full. In the pD* semantics there may be datatype clashes as well as P clashes. P clashes occur in two sets of circumstances: (a) for the same pair of resources it is asserted that they are the same (i.e. they are in the extension of the owl:same-as relation) and also different (i.e. in the extension of the owl:differentFrom relation), and (b) two classes a and b are defined to be disjoint (by using the relation owl:disjointWith) and at the same time non-disjoint by asserting that the same resource r is both of rdf:type a and b. Also RDF entailment under the pD* semantics is not harder than simple entailment.

R-ENTAILMENT   [tero5a] presents a straight-forward rule extension to RDF similar to RDFLog[BFL+08a, BFLL07], that can be used to describe other semantic extensions of RDF, such as the RDFS entailment rules, and the pD* entailment rules. This rule extension distinguishes proper rules for deriving new triples from an RDF graph, axiom rules for adding axiomatic triples to an RDF graph, and inconsistency rules for characterizing unsatisfiability of an RDF graph. Axiom rules have an empty body and a non-empty head, inconsistency rules an empty head but a non-empty body and proper rules have non-empty heads and bodies.

Definition 11 (RDF Rule Graph, RDF Rule). *An RDF rule graph is defined as a set of triple patterns, i.e. a subset of* $U \cup B \cup X \times U \cup B \cup X \times U \cup B \cup L \cup X$, *where* X *is a set of variables disjoint from* U, B *and* L.
An RDF rule is defined as a pair of rule graphs $\rho = (\rho_l, \rho_r)$ *with* $var(\rho_r) \subseteq var(\rho_l)$ *and* $bl(\rho_l) = \emptyset$.[12] ρ_l *is said to be the left hand side or the body of the rule, whereas* ρ_r *is the head, or right hand side of the rule. A rule* ρ *is said to introduce blank nodes iff* $bl(\rho_r) \neq \emptyset$.

In order to give a semantics to RDF rules, [tero5a] extends simple interpretations by a mapping from variables to elements of the domain:

Definition 12 (RDFR Semantics ([tero5a])). *Let* I *be a simple RDF Interpretation,* $Z : X \rightharpoonup R_I$ *a partial function from the set of variables* X *to the set of Resources of* I, *and* $A : B \rightharpoonup R_I$ *a partial function from the set of blank nodes to the set of resources in* R_I. I_Z *is defined as an extension of* I *such that* $I_Z(v) := Z(v)$ *for all* $v \in dom(Z)$, *and* I_{ZA} *is defined as an extension of* I_Z *setting* $I_{ZA}(v) := A(v)$ *for all* $v \in dom(A)$.
Let G *be a rule graph,* I *a simple interpretation and* $Z : var(G) \to R_I$ *a function.* I_Z *satisfies* G *iff there is a function* $A : bl(G) \to R_I$ *such that for each triple pattern* $(s\ p\ o) \in G$, $I_{ZA}(p) \in P_I$ *and* $(I_{ZA}(s), I_{ZA}(o)) \in IEXT(I_{ZA}(p))$.
Let I *be a simple RDF interpretation and* ρ *a proper rule.* I *satisfies* $\rho = (\rho_l, \rho_r)$ *iff for all* $(s\ p\ o) \in \rho_l \cup \rho_r$. $I(p) \in P_I$, *and for any function* $\mathcal{Z} : var(\rho) \to R_I$ *holds if* $I_{\mathcal{Z}}$ *satisfies* ρ_l, *then* $I_{\mathcal{Z}}$ *also satisfies* ρ_r.

In contrast to most other rule languages for RDF (except for RDFLog), the semantics for this rule extension is indeed based on (extensions of) RDF interpretations. In comparison to RDFLog, this rule extension does not consider quantifier alternations, i.e. grouping of resources in rule heads, but each instantiation of a rule is evaluated separately. In contrast, RDFLog and XCERPT[RDF] allow grouping of variable bindings by values,

---
[12] $var(\rho_r)$ and $var(\rho_l)$ denotes the set of variables in the rule head and rule body, respectively.

and construction of a single blank node for a set of substitutions. To see how XCERPT^{RDF} allows grouping of values consider Table 37 in Section 5.4.

[tero5a] shows that R-entailment is in P, if there is a bound on the number of rule bodies, and if the entailed graph is ground.

2.5 CRITIQUE OF THE RDF/S MODEL THEORY

The last section already made clear that the RDF and RDFS model theory is somewhat non-standard, when compared to first order model theories. For this reason it has been criticized by various authors (e.g. [PSF02, PH03a]). This section summarizes the criticism and outlines several possibilities for Semantic Web query languages to deal with this situation. Two directions have been followed by the W3C in the development of the Web Ontology Language OWL: OWL-DL simply breaks with RDFS in choosing a more standard model theory and redefining the semantics of RDFS vocabulary in a different way. OWL-Full on the other hand, builds upon the RDFS model theory, and must therefore deal with the consequences.

[PSF02] points out that a same-syntax and same-semantics extension of RDFS with a description logic (the OWL-Full way) leads to semantic paradoxes analogous to Russell's paradox in the set theory of Frege (See the problem of *contradiction classes* below). The idea of the Semantic Web tower is to have RDF as a fundamental building block on which more expressive ontology languages and rule languages are to be layered. There are several possibilities for extending RDF, and it turns out that not all of them are suitable. As described in the last sections, RDFS is a *same-syntax* and *same-semantics* extension of RDF. It is called a *same-syntax* extension, because all RDFS documents are syntactically valid RDF documents. Moreover it is called a *same-semantics* extension, because all entailments which can be derived by an RDF inference engine from an RDF database D can also be derived by an RDFS inference engine from the same database D. Just as RDFS is a same-syntax and same-semantics extension of RDF, one might expect that the Web Ontology Language OWL is a same syntax and same-semantics extension of RDFS. Unfortunately, such an extensions leads to semantic paradoxes (present in OWL-Full), which are due to the fact that RDFS defines classes extensionally, i.e. the members of a class are explicitely given by the rdf:type predicate, or derived by one of the RDFS inference rules. OWL, on the other hand, supports intentional class definitions. The following problems arise:

Same-syntax and same-semantics extensions of RDFS

The problem of *too few entailments* [PH03b] of the RDFS model theory is that not all entailments can be guaranteed. Adding a description logic language to RDFS gives rise to implicitly defined classes such as the intersection between two other classes: Assume that John is an instance of the class Student ⊓ Employee ⊓ European. Is John also an instance of Student ⊓ Employee? In the RDFS model theory any class or property is interpreted as an element of the domain itself, and thus the answer is no, because it cannot guarantee that an element in the domain exists for each intentionally defined class in a DL-extension of RDFS. The definition of classes in description logics is not limited to class intersection, but is also achieved by *class union* (e.g. A ⊔ B), class complementation (e.g. ¬A), existential restriction (e.g. ∃R.⊤) and universal restriction (e.g. ∀R.A). For all these intentional class deriva-

The problem of too few entailments

tions, RDFS interpretations must provide elements in the domain. To deal with this issue, OWL Full introduces comprehension principles to make sure that each OWL Full interpretation contains all the necessary classes.

The problem of contradiction classes

The problem of *Contradiction classes*: In RDF and RDFS resources can be defined as instances of themselves. With a description logic extension one could define a class C as an instance of itself and add a cardinality constraint $= 0$ on the rdf:type property. In a similar way (mentioned in [Pan04]), OWL Full allows the definition of a restriction class C that prohibits that the class C appears as the value of the its rdf:type property: $C := \forall \text{rdf}:\text{type} \neg C$. In pure description logics such a class is – of course – valid, since the rdf:type predicate does not have special semantics. In the combination with RDFS, on the other hand, the class membership of C cannot be determined. Given an arbitrary element e, assume that e is in C. Then e should have an outgoing rdf:type predicate with object C. This is, however, forbidden for elements in class C. Similar reasoning rules also out that e is *not* in C.

Different size of universes in OWL-DL and OWL-Full; Non-comparability of OWL-Full and OWL-DL entailment

[Pan04] mentions yet another problem, called *size of the universe*, which shows that the size of the universe of valid interpretations under the OWL-Full semantics differs from the size of the universe of valid OWL-DL interpretations. While this issue does not appear crucial at first glance, all three problems lead to the non-comparability of OWL-DL and OWL-Full entailment. For two ontologies $\mathcal{O}_1$ and $\mathcal{O}_2$, neither $\mathcal{O}_1 \models_{\text{full}} \mathcal{O}_2 \Rightarrow \mathcal{O}_1 \models_{\text{dl}} \mathcal{O}_2$ holds, nor $\mathcal{O}_1 \models_{\text{dl}} \mathcal{O}_2 \Rightarrow \mathcal{O}_1 \models_{\text{full}} \mathcal{O}_2$.

This section has shown that layering a first order language on top of RDFS is problematic. Xcerpt does not have to deal with these problems since it does not define derived classes as description logics do. Instead, Xcerpt considers XML documents and RDF graphs as *terms*. RDFS derivation rules are easily encoded as Xcerpt rules.

Description logics are an intensively studied area of research. Extensions of RDFS to description logics mostly aim at bringing the decidability of decision problems and the complexity bounds for these problems to the Semantic Web. These decision problems include checking the instance relationship for a given individual and a concept, the subsumption relationship between concepts, and the consistency of the description logic database.

In contrast, Xcerpt relies on the query author for writing programs that can be evaluated efficiently. Since Xcerpt supports recursion and value invention, i.e. the construction of new RDF fragments and new RDF graphs, Xcerpt is Turing-complete and thus undecidable.

3

RELATED WORK: DATA INTEGRATION ON THE (SEMANTIC) WEB

Contents

- 3.1 State of the Art: The SPARQL Query Language   33
  - 3.1.1 SPARQL graph patterns   34
  - 3.1.2 Blank nodes in SPARQL graph patterns   36
  - 3.1.3 Testing RDF Graphs for Equivalence in SPARQL   38
  - 3.1.4 Semantics and Complexity of SPARQL   39
- 3.2 Extensions of SPARQL   41
  - 3.2.1 nSPARQL   41
  - 3.2.2 SPARQLeR   42
  - 3.2.3 XSPARQL   44
  - 3.2.4 SPARQL update   46
  - 3.2.5 SPARQL and Rules   47
- 3.3 Flora-2   49
- 3.4 RQL   52
- 3.5 Triple   53
- 3.6 SWRL   55
- 3.7 Metalog   56
- 3.8 The Rule Interchange Format   57

3.1 STATE OF THE ART: THE SPARQL QUERY LANGUAGE

With the publication of the SPARQL W3C recommendation on January 2008, SPARQL has become the first RDF query language that has been standardized by a major standardization body. In contrast to most other languages that have been proposed for RDF querying, SPARQL is, due to its triple syntax, quite easy to understand and use for programmers familiar with relational query languages.

In this section, SPARQL is introduced by example, its semantics according to [PAG06] is recapitulated, and several extensions to SPARQL are presented. Throughout the presentation, the commonalities and differences to XCERPT^{RDF} are highlighted.

A SPARQL query consists of the three building blocks *pattern matching part, solution modifiers* and *output*. In addition there are four different kinds of query forms (identified by the keywords ASK, DESCRIBE, SELECT and CONSTRUCT). Arguably the most popular one is the *select* query form, which is inspired by SQL and returns so-called solution sets, the counterpart of Xcerpt substitution sets in SPARQL. An example of a *select* query is given in Listing 3.1. In case of a select query, the output part of the query is a selection of distinguished variables, i.e. the specification of the variables of interest in the query. If no variable bindings are of interest, the *ask* query form is to be used. It simply gives a yes/no answer to the question if a given query pattern is entailed by the RDF

Building blocks and query forms of a SPARQL query

graph being queried. A useful query form for RDF *graph transformations* is the *construct* query form, which does not return single values, but entire RDF graphs as a result. There are, however certain limitations to the blank node construction (in database theory termed *value invention*) in the SPARQL construct query form. Indeed, there is no possibility of expressing the RDFLog query in Example 7 as a SPARQL rule. In general, all RDFLog rules which contain a universal quantifier in the scope of an existential one are not expressible in SPARQL and most other RDF rule languages [1] proposed so far. Considering, that an extension of SPARQL in this direction does not increase the complexity of SPARQL query evaluation, this limitation may come as a surprise. An extension of SPARQL to allow arbitrary blank node construction as RDFLog and X<small>CERPT</small>^{RDF} is described in [BFL⁺09b].

Limitations to SPARQL blank node construction

Example 7 (An RDFLog rule not expressible in SPARQL).

$$\forall lt\ \exists pr\ \forall st((\text{triple}(st, \text{knows}, pr) \leftarrow \text{triple}(st, \text{attends}, lt))$$

The RDFLog rule above expresses that for each lecture lt *there is a professor* pr *such that all students* st *attending* lt *know the professor* pr.

A final query form is given by the *describe* key word which pays tribute to the fact that a blank node identifier returned as a variable binding in a SPARQL select-query is somewhat useless, since it only asserts the fact that something exists, and cannot be reused in a followup query to extract further information about the resource in question. When using the *describe* query form, not only single identifiers are returned as variable bindings, but also *descriptions* of resources. The exact nature of a resource description is left unspecified in the SPARQL recommendation, but a promising solution is the one of *Concise Bounded Descriptions* presented in [Stio5].

The SPARQL query form which is most similar to X<small>CERPT</small>^{RDF} rules is the *construct* query form. X<small>CERPT</small>^{RDF} does not distinguish between query forms, but is strongly answer closed in the sense that every X<small>CERPT</small>^{RDF} data term is also a X<small>CERPT</small>^{RDF} query, and in that every result of an X<small>CERPT</small>^{RDF} query is again an RDF graph. While SPARQL *construct* queries are answer closed, the remaining query forms are not. However, SPARQL *ask* and *select* queries can be simulated by *construct* queries. Similarly, boolean queries can be formulated in X<small>CERPT</small>^{RDF} by interpreting the empty RDF graph as false and all other RDF graphs as true, and tuple-generating queries can be expressed in X<small>CERPT</small>^{RDF} by wrapping the tuples within RDF containers or similar constructs. *Describe* queries are expressed in X<small>CERPT</small>^{RDF} by using concise-bounded-description variables.

All four SPARQL query forms make use of the pattern matching part, which is described next.

3.1.1 SPARQL graph patterns

SPARQL is weakly answer closed in the sense that any RDF graph is also a valid SPARQL graph pattern. But only in the case of the construct query form, also the result of a SPARQL query is again an RDF graph. The syntax of SPARQL graph patterns resembles the one

---

[1] The term *rule language* must be taken with a grain of salt here, since SPARQL is mostly considered as a query language, especially if a query form other than CONSTRUCT is used.

of Turtle [DB08], but is augmented with variables. Listing 3.1 (from [SP08]) shows a query to retrieve the name and email address of persons within an RDF graph using the FOAF vocabulary. With the term *graph pattern*, one refers to the set of triples within curly braces in lines 4 to 5. The select-clause serves to specify the *distinguished* variables of the query. Any variable appearing within the graph pattern, but not within the select-clause is called a *non-distinguished* variable. The terms *distinguished* and *non-distinguished* variables have thus the same meaning as in conjunctive queries in database theory.

Listing 3.1: A simple SPARQL query
```
PREFIX foaf:    <http://xmlns.com/foaf/0.1/>
SELECT ?name ?mbox
WHERE
   { ?x foaf:name ?name .
     ?x foaf:mbox ?mbox }
```

SPARQL allows the selection of variables that do not appear within the graph pattern as shown in Listing 3.2. The empty query pattern matches with any RDF graph, and the variable ?x in the select clause does not appear within the query pattern. In database theory, such rules are said to violate the principle of range-restrictedness. In fact the intuitive semantics of non-range-restricted rules is unclear and varies from one language to another. While according to [SP08] Listing 3.2 is supposed to return a single solution with no binding for the variable ?x, unbound variables are forbidden within construct clauses of SPARQL queries. In Prolog, on the other hand, the non ground fact p(X) simply remains uninstantiated and can be unified with ground bodies of other queries such as p(a).

Range-restrictedness in SPARQL

Listing 3.2: A non-range-restricted SPARQL query matching with arbitrary RDF graphs
```
SELECT ?x
WHERE {}
```

Since queries such as the one in Listing 3.2 can also be expressed with the SPARQL ask query form, and since SPARQL does not allow any kind of rule-chaining, non-range-restricted queries do not add to the expressive power of the SPARQL language, but cause the semantics of the language to be more complex than it needs to be.

The graph pattern in Listing 3.1 is termed a *basic graph pattern*. It consists of two *triple patterns*, which are ordinary RDF triples except that subject, predicate and object may be replaced by SPARQL variables. Basic graph patterns may contain *filter expressions* in addition to a set of triple patterns. Filter expressions use the boolean predicates '=', 'bound', 'isIRI' and others to construct atomic filters. Additionally the logical connectives '&&' for logical conjunction, '||' for logical disjunction and '!' for logical negation are used to construct compound filters from atomic ones. Atomic and compound filters are used to eliminate sets of variable bindings that do not fulfill the filter requirements.

Besides basic graph patterns, SPARQL provides group graph patterns that may either be *unions of graph patterns*, *optional graph patterns* or *named graph patterns*. Unions of graph patterns are similar to disjunctions in the bodies of rules in logic programming. For the query to succeed, only one of the graph patterns in the union must be successful, and the solution sets from all graph patterns in the union are collected to yield the solution set for the union. *Optional graph patterns* are patterns that may bind additional variables besides the ones present in the non-optional parts of a graph pattern, not causing the entire query to fail if the optional graph pattern fails. In contrast to unions of graph patterns, the non-optional part is obliged to match. *Named graph patterns* are introduced into the SPARQL language, because Semantic Web databases may hold multiple RDF graphs, each identified by a URI. To explain the concept of querying named graphs in SPARQL, the notion of a *dataset* must be introduced. A *dataset* is a pair (d, N) where d is the default graph to be queried, and N is a set of named graphs. Datasets are specified by the FROM and FROM NAMED clauses in SPARQL. Whereas the default graph is the merge of all RDF graphs specified in the FROM clause, the FROM NAMED clauses specify the set N of named graphs, and remain unmerged. The GRAPH key word must subsequently be used to refer to named graphs in a WHERE clause as Listing 3.3 (taken from [Pol07]) illustrates.

Listing 3.3: Querying named graphs in SPARQL
```
SELECT ?N WHERE { ?G foaf:maker ?M .
         GRAPH ?G { ?X foaf:name ?N } }
```

As [Pol07] points out, the query in Listing 3.3 is somewhat unintuitive, since SPARQL engines compliant with the W3C specification will search for answers to the triple pattern ?X foaf:name ?N only in named graphs, but not in the default graph. The notion of *named graphs* is discussed in more detail in [CBHS05a], and can be compared to grouping XML data in XML documents.

3.1.2 Blank nodes in SPARQL graph patterns

Blank nodes in SPARQL graph patterns act in the same way as non-distinguished variables, and therefore cannot be used to reference specific blank node identifiers within an RDF graph. Hence, one could substitute an arbitrary blank node for the variable ?x in Listing 3.1 and still obtain the same result.[2]

Before proceeding, we will quickly discuss this treatment of blank nodes in SPARQL. When issuing a query with a blank node, newcomers to the SPARQL language may have five different expectations in mind:

- *Syntactic equality:* The blank node in the query is supposed to match only with the data that uses exactly the same blank node identifier, as it is the case for URIs in graph patterns. While this is a valid desire, it would fall into the domain of syntactic processing of RDF data. A query on two equivalent RDF graphs should obviously return equivalent answers. But what is a sensible notion of equivalence in this context? As with all data items in information processing, one may introduce several equivalence relationships for RDF graphs. One such equivalence relationship is bi-entailment, and it is arguably the most sensible one for RDF graphs. In this thesis we adopt the following understanding of bi-entailment: two RDF graphs H and G are considered equivalent under bi-entailment, iff G RDF-entails H and H RDF-entails G. Of course, bi-entailment could also be based on simple RDF

Bi-entailment versus syntactic equivalence of RDF graphs.

---
[2] Note that one could *not* use a blank node at the place of the other two variables in Listing 3.1, since they are distinguished.

entailment, RDFS entailment, datatype entailment, or other extensions of RDF entailment. Another quite different equivalence relationship would be syntactic equality, and there is certainly the necessity to compare RDF graphs for syntactic equality, but then we could also simply consider them as plain text files and run a UNIX diff command to test them for equality. With the decision for *syntactic equality* for blank nodes in queries, one would obtain different results for equivalent RDF graphs (under bi-entailment), and for this fact the decision of SPARQL not to use *syntactic equality* is a sensible one.

- *Treatment as non-distinguished variables:* The blank node is supposed to act as a non-distinguished variable as explained above.[3] One minor problem with this understanding is that there are two alternative ways of specifying the same query, which may be confusing for new-comers to the language. Another more important issue with this solution is that while SPARQL remains answer closed in the sense that any RDF graph can be used as a SPARQL query, the answer to such a query would not only be graphs that are equivalent or contain an equivalent graph, but also graphs that are more specific. The simple SPARQL graph pattern $\{(\_ : X, b, c)\}$ will also return true on the RDF graph $\{(a, b, c)\}$. This behavior can, however, be consistently explained by stating that an RDF graph G matches with a ground SPARQL graph pattern P, if and only if G simply entails P.

- *Banning of blank nodes within queries*: As the inclusion of blank nodes within queries does not add expressive power to SPARQL graph patterns, an obvious approach is to ban blank nodes from graph patterns. This approach has the advantage that SPARQL users cannot be fooled to assume a different semantics of blank nodes in graph patterns other than non-distinguished variables. On the other hand, this approach has the obvious drawback that SPARQL is not answer closed in the sense that an RDF graph containing blank nodes cannot be viewed as a SPARQL query.

- *Treatment as ordinary variables:* Since blank nodes are viewed as existentially quantified variables in RDF graphs, one might view them as plain variables in queries as well, and specify in the select-clause if they are to be treated as distinguished variables or non-distinguished variables. This solution has the plain advantage that any RDF graph can be viewed as a query. Still, this approach is similar to treating blank nodes as non-distinguished variables (see above): An RDF graph pattern containing blank nodes (such as $\_:X$ b c) not only matches with RDF graphs that are equivalent or contain an equivalent RDF graph (such as $\{(\_ : X, b, c), (c, d, e)\}$) but also with RDF graphs that are more specific (such as $\{(a, b, c)\}$). Clearly this approach would mean that there is no longer the necessity for SPARQL variables.

- *Matching blank nodes only:* A final intuition query authors may have in mind is that blank node identifiers in queries must be mapped to blank node identifiers in the data only. None of the above approaches can express this semantics. The graph pattern $\{\_:X$ b c$\}$ would thus return true when evaluated on the

---

[3] This expectation is in fact the one SPARQL implements.

graphs $\{(\_: X, b, c)\}$ and $\{(\_: Y, b, c)\}$, but it would not match with $\{(a, b, c)\}$. Thus with answer closedness in mind, this approach ensures that an RDF graph q considered as a SPARQL query only matches with RDF graphs that are equivalent or have a subgraph equivalent to q. The major drawback of this solution is, however, that the same query may once return true for an RDF graph g_1 and false for an equivalent (under bi-entailment) RDF graph g_2. To see this, consider again the query pattern $\_:X$ b c and the graphs $g_1 := \{(\_: Y, b, c), (a, b, c)\}$ and $g_2 := \{(a, b, c)\}$. Under the light of this deficiency and with the availability of the filter predicate isBlank in SPARQL that can be used for imitating this blank node semantics, it is a good choice not to adopt this treatment of blank nodes in SPARQL graph patterns.

3.1.3 Testing RDF Graphs for Equivalence in SPARQL

None of the above solutions are completely satisfactory in that they do not allow the specification of a query q that returns true on exactly the equivalence class $\Sigma_{\Leftrightarrow}(g)$ induced by RDF bi-entailment for an arbitrary graph g containing a blank node.

Note that SPARQL query patterns cannot express the above query even in the absence of blank nodes. Consider the RDF graph $g := \{(a, b, c)\}$ consisting of a single triple. Evaluating g as a SPARQL query pattern will yield all RDF graphs that *contain* g, but there is no way of expressing a query that will find all *equivalent* graphs.

In other words, a SPARQL basic graph pattern q returns true on an RDF graph g iff g RDF-entails[4] n(q) where the normalization operator n replaces variables in q by blank nodes (multiple occurrences of the same variable by the same blank node identifier, and distinct variables by distinct blank nodes, that do not occur anywhere else in q). Hence, with basic SPARQL graph patterns it is only possible to demand that something *be entailed* by the graph g to be queried, but not to restrict the entailments of g. The development of the language XCERPT^{RDF}, on the other hand, is influenced by the assumption that query authors would like to both demand some entailments from a graph as well as demand that something is *not* entailed by it.

There is, however, the possibility to express such queries in SPARQL at the aid of optional graph patterns, SPARQL filter constructs, and the SPARQL unbound keyword. The query in Listing 3.4 only returns true for the one-triple graph {(eg:a, eg:b, eg:c)}, where the namespace prefix eg is bound as indicated in Listing 3.4. For all other graphs it returns false. The graph pattern first ensures that the triple (eg:a, eg:b, eg:c) is in fact contained in the RDF graph. Secondly it uses an optional pattern to find other triples in the graph. The filter inside the optional pattern makes sure that the optional pattern matches with a triple other than (eg:a, eg:b, eg:c). The second filter expression makes sure that the optional graph pattern was unsuccessful by testing for a binding of the variable ?x.

Negation as failure in SPARQL

---

[4] As outlined in Section 2.3, there are different variants of RDF entailment. In this section we mean simple RDF entailment when when speaking of RDF entailment only.

Listing 3.4: A query that only matches with a graph consisting of a single triple (a b c)
```
PREFIX eg: <http://eg.org/>
ASK
WHERE   { eg:a eg:b eg:c .
    OPTIONAL { ?x  ?y  ?z
      FILTER ( ?x != eg:a  ||  ?y != eg:b  ||  ?z != eg:c )
    }
    FILTER (!bound(?x))
  }
```

Before proceeding to the study of the complexity and semantics of SPARQL, we will quickly discuss how to test for equivalence with RDF graphs containing blank nodes. Consider the graph

$$G = \{(eg:a, eg:b, eg:c), (?X, eg:b, eg:d)\} \qquad (3.1)$$

consisting of two triples only with a single occurrence of a single blank node. When formulating a SPARQL query to return true on exactly the set of RDF graphs equivalent to g, one first needs to test for the presence of the two triples and then for the absence of triples that are different from the two ones given in the graph. While the query in Listing 3.5 is not trivial to figure out, testing graphs for equivalence in SPARQL becomes even more complex in the presence of multiple occurrences of the same blank node identifier, since in this case it does not suffice to test for the absence of single triples only, but one has to test for the absence of multiple triples connected via blank nodes – i.e. concise bounded descriptions [Sti05].

Listing 3.5: A query that only matches the graph G in Equation 3.1
```
PREFIX eg: <http://eg.org/>
ASK
WHERE {
    eg:a eg:b eg:c .
    ?blank eg:b eg:d .
    OPTIONAL { ?x  ?y  ?z
      FILTER ( ( ?x != eg:a  ||  ?y != eg:b  ||  ?z != eg:c ) &&
               ( !(isBlank(_?x))  ||  ?y != eg:b  ||  ?z != eg:d ) )
    }
    FILTER (!bound(?x))
  }
```

Obviously the queries in Listing 3.4 and 3.5 are much more complicated than they need to be. This is due to the absence of explicit negation in SPARQL, a design decision that is supposed to make implementation easier and to circumvent the non-monotonicity of negation as failure.[5] In Section 5 we show how the query in Listing 3.4 can be expressed by the single XCERPT[RDF] term RDFGRAPH { a { b → c } }.

3.1.4 Semantics and Complexity of SPARQL

[PAG06] recursively defines the semantics of SPARQL query patterns in terms of relational algebra operators as follows:

---
[5] Since negation as failure still is expressible in SPARQL, as shown above, both of these goals are missed.

- The semantics $[\![t]\!]_G$ of a possibly non-ground triple t evaluated over an RDF graph G is the set of mappings µ such that the domain of µ is the set $Var(t)$ of variables in t and the application $\mu(t)$ of the mapping µ to t is a triple in G. Here, $\mu(t)$ is simply the triple pattern with the variables in t replaced by their bindings in µ.

- The semantics $[\![(P_1 \text{ AND } P_2)]\!]_G$ of a conjunction of query patterns evaluated over the RDF graph G is defined as the set $\{[\![P_1]\!] \bowtie [\![P_2]\!]\}$ $= \{\mu_1 \cup \mu_2 \mid \mu_1 \in [\![P_1]\!], \mu_2 \in [\![P_2]\!], \mu_1 \text{ and } \mu_2 \text{ are compatible}\}$ of unions of compatible pairs of mappings of P_1 and P_2. In this context two mappings are termed *compatible* if they coincide on the bindings of their common variables. The semantics of the conjunction can thus be thought of as the natural join over the relations defined by the conjuncts.[6]

  In [Polo7] the notion of compatibility of pairs of mappings is refined to *brave compatibility, cautious compatibility* and *strict compatibility*. While in the absence of unbound variables within mappings, all three notions of compatibility coincides, in the presence of unbound variables, only the brave compatibility coincides with compatibility as understood by [PAG06].

   - Two mappings σ_1 and σ_2 are *bravely compatible* if they coincide on the bindings of their common bound variables. Brave compatibility hence does not restrict the bindings of variables that are unbound in either σ_1, σ_2 or both.
   - σ_1 and σ_2 are *cautiously compatible* if for all common variables – no matter if bound or unbound – the bindings coincide.
   - σ_1 and σ_2 are *strictly compatible* if they are cautiously compatible and if additionally there is no common variable of σ_1 and σ_2 which is unbound in both.

- The semantics of a graph pattern $[\![P_1 \text{ OPT } P_2]\!]_G$ including an optional construct over an RDF graph G is defined as the left outer join between $[\![P_1]\!]$ and $[\![P_2]\!]$.

- Finally the semantics $[\![P_1 \text{ UNION } P_2]\!]$ of a union of two graph patterns is defined as the union of $[\![P_1]\!]$ and $[\![P_2]\!]$.

[PAG06] extend the semantics to SPARQL queries including filter expressions and show some important properties of SPARQL queries:

- Generally the expressions `(P1 AND (P2 OPTIONAL P3))` and `(P1 AND P2)OPTIONAL P3))` are not semantically equivalent, but they are equivalent for the class of *well-defined* graph patterns introduced in the same work.

- In the presence of optional patterns, AND is only commutative for well-designed graph patterns.

Some results on the complexity of query evaluation in SPARQL from [PAG06] are the following:

---

6 Note that the terms *relation* and *sets of mappings* can be used interchangeably here.

- The combined complexity of SPARQL graph patterns involving only AND and FILTER expressions is in $O(|P| \cdot |D|)$ where $|D|$ is the size of the data and $|P|$ is the size of the query. This result is based on the assumption that the application of a mapping μ to a triple t is achieved in a constant amount of time, independently of the number of variables in μ.

- The combined complexity of SPARQL graph patterns involving AND, FILTER and UNION is NP-complete. The proof is by polynomial reduction of the satisfiability problem of propositional logic formulas in conjunctive normal form to SPARQL queries.

- The combined complexity of SPARQL graph patterns including AND UNION and OPTIONAL is PSPACE-complete, independently of the presence or absence of FILTER expressions.

- The data complexity of SPARQL graph patterns is in LOGSPACE.

3.2 EXTENSIONS OF SPARQL

SPARQL being the most popular RDF query language and the only one which has been standardized by some standardization organization such as the W3C, it has received considerable attention from the research community. Its expressiveness and complexity has been formally studied, and as a result of its limited expressiveness, extensions of SPARQL in different directions have been proposed. With the absence of path expressions in SPARQL, nSPARQL[PAG08] has been suggested to enhance the expressive power of SPARQL into this direction. The necessity of combined processing of XML and RDF has been acknowledged by XSPARQL[AKKP08], an extension of XQuery to RDF processing at the aid of SPARQL WHERE and CONSTRUCT clauses. Just as SQL allows the deletion and insertion of data and creation of new tables, SPARQL update [SMB+08] and SPARQL+[7] extend SPARQL with facilities to manipulate and create RDF graphs. Finally [CP06], [Pol07] and [SS04] eliminate the restriction of SPARQL to single rules by allowing possibly recursive multi-rule programs.

3.2.1 nSPARQL

nSPARQL[PAG08] is an extension of SPARQL to support arbitrary-depth navigation in SPARQL queries. It arose from the need to answer queries for finding all nodes reachable from a given node via a given predicate name, a disjunction of predicate names or simply for finding all transitively connected nodes. The RDF path language employed in nSPARQL remains unnamed in [PAG08], but is constructed from nested regular expressions. We thus adopt the name NRE for the nSPARQL path language.

The syntax of NRE is heavily influenced by the syntax of XPath, and NRE borrows the notions of axes, node tests, reverse axes, step expressions, and path predicates from XPath. While path expressions in XPath evaluate to a set of nodes of an XML document, path expressions in nSPARQL evaluate to a set of *pairs* of nodes within an RDF graph. This is due to the fact that XPath expressions are always evaluated

---

[7] http://arc.semsol.org/home

with respect to a context node, while this is not necessarily the case for nSPARQL expressions.

Although the terms *axis* and *node* tests are borrowed from XPath, the function quite differently in NRE. While a node test n following an axis specification a in an XPath expression a :: n returns true if and only if the node reached by the axis has label n, node tests in nSPARQL do not test the label of the navigation end. For example, if the next axis is used, the corresponding node test does not test the label of the node reached, but the label of the edge traversed from the source node to the sink node. Even more confusing are node tests paired with the node axis. Although the node axis is used to navigate from an edge within an RDF graph to an adjacent node, a node test on this axis applies to the node the edge originates from. While this design decision allows for a brief description of the semantics of NRE, it is unintuitive for users familiar with XPath.

The following examples illustrate the syntax and semantics of nSPARQL path expressions evaluated over an RDF graph G:

- next::a allows the navigation from one node in an RDF graph to another node via an edge labelled a in a composed nSPARQL path expression. It evaluates to all pairs of nodes connected via a predicate labeled a: $\{(x,y) \mid (x,a,y) \in G\}$. The axis next^{-1} can be used to navigate in the reverse direction.

- edge::a allows the navigation from a node x to an edge y within an RDF graph, if the graph contains the triple (x,y,a). It evaluates to $\{(x,y) \mid (x,y,a) \in G\}$. The axis edge^{-1} is used to navigate from predicates of triples to their subjects.

- node:a allows the navigation from an edge x to a node y if the corresponding triple has subject a. It evaluates to $\{(x,y) \mid (a,x,y) \in G\}$. node^{-1} is used for navigating in the reverse direction.

- nSPARQL path expressions are combined just like XPath step expressions by the / sign: The nSPARQL expression next::a/next::b finds pairs of nodes connected via two triples with predicate names a and b over an arbitrary intermediate node. The URI of the intermediate node can be checked by using the self axis: next::a/self::c/next::b.

- The evaluation of nested nSPARQL path expressions is more complex. The semantics of edge::[exp] is given by $\{(x,y) \mid \exists z, w. (x,y,z) \in G \wedge (z,w) \in [\![exp]\!]_G\}$, where $[\![exp]\!]_G$ is the semantics of exp over G. Nested path expressions including the axes self, next and node are similarly involved.

3.2.2 SPARQLeR

A different approach for extending SPARQL with regular path expressions is taken by the language SPARQLeR described in [KJ07]. In contrast to nSPARQL, entire paths are bound to so-called path variables, which are distinguished from ordinary SPARQL variables in that they are prefixed by % instead of ?. The bindings of path variables are themselves represented as RDF sequences, which allows to put further restrictions on the bindings in SPARQL WHERE clauses, as the following example from [KJ07] demonstrates:

Listing 3.6: A simple SPARQLeR path query

```
CONSTRUCT %path
WHERE { r %path s . %path rdfs:_1 p . }
```

The query in Listing 3.6 finds all directed paths between a resource r and a resource s that have p as the first predicate. Bindings for the path variable %path in the above query are of the form $p_1, n_1, p_2, n_2, \ldots, p_i, n_i, p_{i+1}$, such that the triples $(r, p_1, n_1), (n_1, p_2, n_2), \ldots, (n_{i-1}, p_i, n_i)$ and (n_i, p_{i+1}, s) are in the queried graph. Since these bindings are represented as RDF sequences (as exemplified in Listing 3.7), triples in the same WHERE clause can be used to put restrictions on the bindings to path variables.

Listing 3.7: The RDF representation of bindings to SPARQLeR path variables

```
_:Path1 rdfs:_1 p1,
_:Path1 rdfs:_2 n1,
_:Path1 rdfs:_3 p2,
...
```

Since bindings to SPARQLeR path variables are represented as RDF sequences represented by blank nodes, the use of path variables within SELECT query forms hardly makes sense. Imagine Listing 3.6 with the SELECT keyword at the place of the CONSTRUCT keyword. The result of this query is a list of blank nodes generated by the SPARQLeR query generator, which means that the only information returned is the number of paths found within the queried graph. To deal with this inconvenience, SPARQLer introduces a list operator that extracts all resources from the paths. In the case of multiple bindings for a path variable, however, the application of the list operator merges the resources from all paths into a single list, thereby preventing the user from recognizing the actual paths.

SPARQLeR provides a second method for constraining paths at the aid of a ternary regex method to be used within FILTER clauses of SPARQLeR queries. The first argument to this method is the name of the path variable whose bindings are to be constrained, the second one is a regular path expression, and the third are options specifying whether the path must be directed, if it must be made up of schema classes, instances, or literals, and if rdfs:subPropertyOf inferencing is to be considered. SPARQLeR regular path expressions allow alternatives, concatenation, Kleene's star, wildcards, negations and reverse predicates. The SPARQLeR length method is used to find paths of a minimal, maximum or exact length.

While SPARQLeR seems to be a sensible suggestion for an extension of SPARQL, there are two obvious points of criticism:

- The fact that predicate names can be specified within path expressions, but subjects and objects cannot, seems to be an arbitrary design choice which is not motivated in [KJ07].

- Representing bindings to variables as RDF sequences that are not part of the original RDF graph and allowing these RDF sequences to be queried within the SPARQLeR WHERE clause may be confusing for novices in that the WHERE clause is successfully evaluated on a graph which does not entail every single triple of the clause.

3.2.3 XSPARQL

[AKKP08] advocates the reuse of plain XML and HTML data of the Web as RDF data on the Semantic Web, and vice versa and introduces the notions of *lifting* – i.e. transforming "syntactic" XML data into "semantic" RDF data – and lowering – transforming RDF data into XML. Starting out from the insight that current tools and languages are not adequate for translating between syntactic and semantic web data, they propose an integration of SPARQL into XQuery, which they dub XSPARQL, together with use-cases and a formal semantics. Since it aims at being data-versatile in the same sense as Xcerpt does, we take a closer look at XSPARQL in this section.

Listing 3.8: XML example data

```
<relations>
  <person name="Alice">
    <knows>Bob</knows>
    <knows>Charles</knows>
  </person>
    <knows>Charles</knows>
  </person>
  <person name="Charles"/>
</relations>
```

Listing 3.9: RDF example data

```
@prefix foaf: <...foaf/0.1/> .
_:b1 a foaf:Person;
     foaf:name _:b2;
     foaf:knows _:b3 .
_:b2 a foaf:Person;
     foaf:name "Bob";
     foaf:knows _:b3 .
_:b3 a foaf:Person;
     foaf:name "Charles" .
```

Listing 3.10 shows how the lifting task is solved in XSPARQL for the example data given in Listings 3.8 and 3.9. In line 3 all element nodes of the XML input file that represent persons are selected. Names are either given as the name attribute of a person element or as XML text nodes within knows elements. In order to make sure that the list $persons contains each name exactly once, duplicates are elminitated in the where clause by testing the absence of elements on the following axis that contain the same name. In this way duplicates are eliminated and only the last occurrence of a name is selected. In line 6, a numeric identifier is computed for each person which serves to construct unique blank nodes in the SPARQL construct pattern starting at line 8. The construct keyword is not part of the XQuery syntax, but newly introduced in XSPARQL to mark the beginning of a SPARQL construct pattern. Inside of SPARQL construct patterns, XQuery code is embedded within curly braces. In this way nested XSPARQL queries are constructed. While the outer XSPARQL query (lines 3 to 10) serves to represent the persons found in the XML source as RDF blank nodes with associated names and type, the inner SPARQL query translates the acquaintance relationships. Note that the triples constructed in line 18 are duplicates of the ones constructed in line 10, i.e. this line is superfluous.

Listing 3.10: Lifting in XSPARQL

```
  declare namespace foaf="...foaf/0.1/";
  declare namespace rdf="...-syntax-ns#";
3 let $persons := //*[@name or ../knows] return
  for $p in $persons
  let $n := if ( @p[@name] ) then $p/name else $p
6 let $id := count($p/preceding::*) + count($p/ancestor::*)
  where not(exists($p/following::*[@name=$n or data(.)=$n]))
  construct
9   _:b{$id} a foaf:Person;
            foaf:name { data($n) }.
    { for $k in $persons
12    let $kn := if ( $k[@name] ) then $k/@name else $k
      let $kid := count($k/preceding::*) + count($k/ancestor::*)
      where $kn = data(//*[@name=$n/knows) and
15         not(exists($kn/../following::*[@name=$kn or data(.)=$kn])
           )
      construct
        _:b{$id} foaf:knows _:b{$kid} .
18      _:b{$kid} a foaf:Person .
    }
```

XSPARQL does not set out to be a query language that natively supports XML and RDF querying in an intuitive and coherent way. Instead it explores how SPARQL can be integrated into XQuery, how the semantics of this integration can be defined and proposes an implementation on top of existing XQuery and SPARQL engines. XSPARQL succeeds in its coherent treatment of schema heterogeneous RDF/XML files, and due to the large expressiveness of XQuery it allows the formulation of many queries not expressible in SPARQL alone. On the other hand it suffers from the following deficiencies:

- *Intertwined querying and construction.* As can be observed in Listing 3.10, there is no clear separation of querying and construction in XSPARQL queries, a deficiency which is inherited from XQuery. While it is clear that there are queries that cannot be expressed by a single rule with a single query and construction pattern, this is not the case for the query above.

- *Complicated blank node construction.* An RDF query language should support automatic construction of blank nodes without the need of computing blank node identifiers within a program. Since blank node construction is essentially the same as the introduction of skolem terms within logic programs, languages such as RDFLog and Xcerpt achieve the same result in a much easier and straightforward way.

- *Absence of path patterns.* While XSPARQL inherits the complexity of XQuery, it suffers also from the limitations of SPARQL such as no support for containers, collections and reification, and limited support for negation. Above all, XSPARQL lacks rich path patterns to navigate RDF graphs at arbitrary depth, such as the ones proposed by nSPARQL and SPARQLeR.

- *Jumbling of query paradigms.* Due to the popularity of XQuery as an XML query language and SPARQL as an RDF query language, Listing 3.10 is easy to understand for most people familiar with

(Semantic) Web querying. For people unfamiliar with one or both of these languages, it may be confusing that a functional language such as XQuery is intermingled with a rule based language such as SPARQL. With XCERPT^{RDF} we introduce a purely rule based language based on the clear design principles of Xcerpt.

3.2.4 SPARQL update

Similar as for the XML query language XQuery, SPARQL has been conceived primarily as a data *selection* language, not as a data *manipulation* language. In fact, the SELECT, DESCRIBE and ASK query forms of SPARQL can only be used to *extract* parts of a graph, not to manipulate data or construct new data. The SPARQL CONSTRUCT query form allows limited transformations between one RDF dialect to another, but cannot be used to modify existing RDF stores. The W3C member submission *SPARQL update* sets out to eliminate this restriction.

SPARQL update consists of two sets of directives – one for updating graphs and the other for graph management. The set of directives for updating existing RDF graphs with SPARQL update constsits of the following seven commands:[8]

- The DELETE DATA FROM directive is used to delete a set of ground triples from a named or the default graph. In the latter case, the FROM keyword is omitted.

- The INSERT DATA INTO statement is used to insert a new set of ground triples into an existing graph identified by a URI. If the triples are to be inserted into the default graph, then the INTO keyword is omitted.

- The MODIFY operation consists of a delete and an insert statement (see below) issued on the same graph.

- The DELETE FROM ... WHERE operation is used to delete a set of triples from a graph. In contrast to the DELETE DATA operation discussed above, this command may specify the triples to be deleted in a non-ground form, i.e. with SPARQL variables bound in the WHERE clause. If the WHERE clause consists of the empty graph pattern, this command is indeed equivalent to the DELETE DATA operation above. In case the FROM keyword is omitted, the default graph is manipulated.

- INSERT FROM ... WHERE is the non-ground version of the INSERT DATA command. Its relationship to INSERT DATA is analogous to the relationship from DELETE FROM ... WHERE to the DELETE DATA operation. Together with the DELETE FROM ... WHERE operation, this operation can be used to move data from one RDF graph to another.

- The LOAD primitive copies all RDF triples from one named graph to another named graph or the default graph.

- The CLEAR primitive removes all triples from the default graph, or a named graph. It can be simulated by a DELETE FROM ... WHERE operation selecting all triples of a graph.

---

8 We only briefly sketch the commands for the sake of brevity.

Graph management in SPARQL update is achieved by the two operations CREATE GRAPH and DROP GRAPH which have the exact same semantics as the SQL operations CREATE TABLE and DROP TABLE. Only when a graph has been created by the CREATE GRAPH operation it is available for modification by one of the seven above mentioned manipulation directives.

To sum up, SPARQL update is a straight-forward extension of SPARQL to include mechanisms for creating new and changing existing RDF graphs, much inspired by SQL. The difference between the Web considered as a huge database and ordinary databases is, however, that the Web is open and generally readable and processable by any person or computer connected to the Internet. As a result RDF graphs will more likely to be reasoned with and transformed than updated. Write access to RDF graphs is restricted to the content provider, but deriving new knowledge from existing one, which is the fundamental use case for Semantic Web use-cases, is possible for all Web users and will be achieved with rule languages, not update languages. Under these considerations, update primitives have been excluded from XCERPT^{RDF}.

3.2.5 SPARQL and Rules

[Polo7] defines translation rules for SPARQL rules to datalog rules and thus opens up the possibility to rule chaining, i.e. the translation of multiple SPARQL rules to Datalog and the combined evaluation of the resulting rule set by a logic programming engine, thus allowing intermediate results to be constructed and queried. This extension gives SPARQL an obvious boost in expressivity (recursion) and affects its termination properties. In the following, the translation procedure from SPARQL to Datalog given in [Polo7] is quickly illustrated by an example, as it opens up the possibility for easy implementations also of single rule SPARQL queries on top of existing logic programming engines.

For this purpose reconsider the SPARQL query in Listing 3.11 and the RDF graph in Listing 3.12 available via the URL http://www.example.org/bob. The result of the translation is given in Listing 3.13.

Listing 3.11: A simple SPARQL select-query
```
PREFIX foaf:    <http://xmlns.com/foaf/0.1/>
SELECT ?name ?mbox
FROM http://example.org/bob
WHERE
  { ?x foaf:name ?name .
    ?x foaf:mbox ?mbox }
```

Listing 3.12: RDF Graph with some FOAF information
```
_:B foaf:name bob .
_:B foaf:nick bobby .
_:B foaf:mbox bob@example.org .
```

Listing 3.13: Translation of the SPARQL query in Listing 3.11 to Datalog with external predicates

```
triple(S, P, O, default) :- rdf(http://example.org/bob, S, P, O) .
answer_1( (Name, Mbox), default) :-
  answer_2(vars(Name, X), default),
  answer_3(vars(Mbox, X), default) .
answer_2(vars(Name, X), default) :- triple(X, foaf:name, Name,
    default) .
answer_3(vars(Mbox, X), default) :- triple(X, foaf:name, Mbox,
    default) .
```

The translation makes use of the external predicate rdf that takes four arguments: the graph to be queried as input, and the subject, predicate and object of triples as output. The external predicate rdf can thus be used to enumerate all triples within an RDF graph given by the input URI. The first rule in Listing 3.13 defines the 4-ary relation triple. In the case of multiple FROM or FROM NAMED clauses in the original SPARQL query, the relation triple will obviously be defined by the corresponding number of clauses. Since Listing 3.11 only contains conjunctions of triple patterns, but no UNION, OPTIONAL or FILTER expression, the translation remains of manageable size, and we focus the discussion of the tranlsation procedure on conjunctive triple patterns.

As can be observed in Listing 3.13, each triple pattern in the SPARQL query translates to a single Datalog rule, and each conjunction of triple patterns translates to a rule with body atoms referencing the rules obtained by the translation of its conjuncts. As expected, disjunctions (UNION) of triple patterns are translated to sets of rules. For details on the tranlsation procedure, involving more complex SPARQL queries with FILTER and OPTIONAL, the interested reader is referred to [Pol07].

While reusing existing rule languages together with the enormous body of knowledge about their semantics, evaluation methods and complexity is certainly a sensible way for designing a rule language for the Semantic Web, the approach taken in [Pol07] is not completely satisfactory for the following reasons:

- Blank node construction in rule heads has been largely ignored, especially the different modes of blank node construction as pointed out by [BFL+08a].

- This approach inherits the weakness of SPARQL concerning negation: implicit negation as failure is provided by the combination of the OPTIONAL directive and the unbound predicate. For newcomers to the language this feature is hard to discover, and should be better declared as what it is.

- The expressivity of SPARQL graph patterns is limited when compared to languages that allow possibly recursive path expressions such as Versa on RDF graphs or Conditional XPath[Mar05, Mar04b] and Xcerpt on XML documents. This limitation is obviously inherited by all rule extensions to SPARQL.

- Rule extensions of SPARQL remain pure RDF query languages and therefore cannot deal with the versatility requirements for modern Web query languages.

3.3 FLORA-2

Flora-2[YKZ03, Kif05] is a logic programming environment based on F-Logic[KLW95b] with features borrowed from HiLog[CKW93] and from Transaction Logic[BK93] and is developed at the State University of New York. Its applications range from ontology management over information integration to agent systems and it is supposed to be useful for doing "anything that requires manipulation of complex structured (especially semi-structured) data" [YKZ02].

The development of Flora-2 i is based on the following design principles:

Flora-2 design principles

- Knowledge *asserted* on the Web must be strictly separated from *inferred* knowledge, which is subject to change if the reasoning mechanism is non-monotonic, i.e. uses some form of negation as failure. Flora-2 is based on the assumption that non-monotonic negation is a valid requirement for Web reasoning languages.

- Knowledge gathered on the Web is assumed to be incomplete, and future changes to the knowledge should – as far as possible – not cause inconsistencies with earlier derivations. Thus, the specification that an object o has type t does not conflict with the specification that there is another class t' such that t' is subclass of t and o is of type t'. Likewise, the specification of the subclass relationship is not immediate. Both of these conventions are in line with the RDF/S model theory, which does not allow the derivation of inconsistencies.[9] Moreover, knowledge about any resource on the Web is assumed to be incomplete. Finding that eg:bob knows eg:anna in one RDF graph and later learning that eg:bob also knows eg:chuck from another resource on the Web, does not constitute a problem. Also this convention is in line with the open nature of the Web and the principles of RDF, but certainly differs from the nature of XML, which locally specifies all relations of one node to another. Finally, while logic-based programming or modelling languages generally assume that distinct ground terms denote distinct entities (the so-called *unique name assumption*), Flora-2 drops this convention due to the fact that the open nature of the Web hinders the adoption of unique names. Instead, Flora-2 provides an equality operator that can be used to state that two terms denote the same resource, corresponding to the owl:sameAs property in OWL[BvH+04]. All of the above conventions are subsumed under the notion *lazy knowledge assimilation* in [YKZ03].

Unique name assumption in logic-based programming and modelling languages

- Querying schema and reifications of triples should be naturally integrated into a Semantic Web query language.

FLORA-2 FEATURES FOR THE SEMANTIC WEB Although FLora-2 was not designed as a Semantic Web query language [YKZ03] argue that it provides many features that make it an appropriate rule language for the Semantic Web:

REPRESENTATION OF RDF GRAPHS RDF graphs can be represented by Flora molecules. When considering Flora-2 as a data representation

---

9 Apart from XML clashes for typed RDF literals

language, it shows similar features as RDF/XML: Several RDF statements sharing the same subject can be merged to a single molecule, and these molecules can be nested: In Listing 3.15 two statements about the blank node resource _# are merged into a single molecule. Furthermore the rdf:type statements can be implicitly written by appending a colon and a qualified name representing the class to the resource in question: In Listing 3.15 the statement _# rdf:type eg:mammal is abbreviated to read _#:'eg:mammal'.

Since RDF containers and collections are ordinary RDF graphs, they can also be represented as Flora-2 molecules (see Listing 3.14). Flora-2 does not implement the intuitive semantics for RDF containers and collections as presented in Section 5.2.2.

Listing 3.14: Flora-2 representation of an RDF container

```
_#[ 'rdf:type' ->> 'rdf:bag',
    'rdf:_1' ->> 'Huey',
    'rdf:_2' ->> 'Dewey',
    'rdf:_3' ->> 'Louie'
].
```

ANONYMOUS NODES   Whereas originally F-Logic was not designed to deal with anonymous resources, Flora-2 extends F-Logic to do so. It provides both an *unnumbered anonymous ID symbol* _# and a countable set of *numbered anonymous ID symbols* _#1, _#2, ... By convention, every occurrence of the unnumbered anonymous ID symbol refers to a distinct entity. In contrast, two occurrences of the same numbered anonymous ID symbol within the same Flora-2 clause refer to the same entity. Occurrences of the same numbered anonymous ID symbols distributed over distinct clauses refer to different entities of the universe. This semantics is equivalent to the semantics of many other RDF rule languages (e.g. RDFLog), in that blank nodes in rule heads are treated as skolem constants.

Listing 3.15: Blank nodes and typed data in Flora-2

```
_#:'eg:mammal'[
    'eg:lays_eggs' ->> literal('true'),
    'foaf:nick' ->> literal('puggle')
].

_#:'eg:mammal'[
    'foaf:nick' ->> literal('puggle')
]
```

The first molecule in Listing 3.15 states that there is an animal with nick name 'puggle' that is both a mammal and lays eggs. The second molecule in Listing 3.15 states that there is another (*different*) mammal also with nick name 'puggle'. Note that the same information cannot be expressed in RDF, since RDF provides no way for stating that two names must be interpreted as different elements of the domain. It is, however, expressible using the OWL owl:differentFrom vocabulary.

As a further remark, note that the RDF graph in Listing 3.16 is not expressible as a set of F-Logic atoms, since _:X and _:Y are neither required to be distinct, nor are they required to be interpreted as the same resource. Different RDF interpretations may map _:X and _:Y to the same element of the domain, or to different elements of the domain.

This subtle difference has, however, no effect on the result of queries, since Flora-2, as most other RDF query and rule languages does not support aggregates or negation.

Listing 3.16: An RDF graph with two blank nodes
```
_:X rdf:type eg:mammal.
_:X eg:lays_egss 'true'.
_:Y foaf:nick 'puggle'.
```

EXPLICIT AND IMPLICIT EQUALITY   In contrast to conventional logic programming languages, terms can be become equal in F-logic due to the availability of single valued predicates within terms. Consider the following example from [YKZ03]:

$$\text{mary}[\text{spouse} \rightarrow \text{joseph}].$$
$$\text{mary}[\text{spouse} \rightarrow \text{joe}].$$
$$\text{joseph}[\text{son} \twoheadrightarrow \text{frank}].$$

Since spouse is a single-valued predicate on mary, joe and joseph must be equal. In fact, Flora-2 can deduce from the above program that the term joe[son →» frank] holds. Besides this inferred equality, one may also state that two terms are equal with the built-in equality operator :=:. Both inferred equality and explicit equality are features which are important on the Web, because it is inherently distributed, and different actors may publish complementary information about the same resource, not knowing of each other. Therefore it must be possible for a third person to infer or explicitly assert the equality of the resources. This need is further acknowledged by the presence of the owl:sameAs predicate in the Web ontology language [BvH$^+$04].

PATH EXPRESSIONS FOR NAVIGATION IN RDF DOCUMENTS   Flora-2 inherits from F-Logic path navigation expressions. The F-Logic path expression

```
paper[authors → {author[name → john]}].publication..editors
```

from [YKZ03] finds all editors of papers which were co-authored by a person with name john. The predicate authors is called *multi-valued* or *set-valued* in F-Logic, in contrast to the *single-valued* predicate publication. Navigation along a single-valued predicate is written with a single '.', navigation along a multi-valued predicate by '..'. The use of path-expressions in Flora-2 circumvents the excessive use of conjunctions, which would have to be used in a query language without path navigation such as SPARQL. Path expressions in F-logic, and thus also in Flora-2 do not provide transitive axes such as the descendant or ancestor axis in XPath, RPL (see Section 6) and NRE (see also Section 6).

While we have presented many beneficial features of Flora when it comes to querying the semantic web, some more have not been touched in this overview. Among them is the support for querying reified statements, schema queries, and rules. Possible shortcomings of Flora-2 as an RDF query language are the absence of namespace declarations, transitivity within path expressions and support for RDF Literals. Namespace declarations and support for RDF literals could, however, be straight-forwardly added to the language.

3.4 RQL

RQL is an early RDF query language inspired by OQL, supporting *generalized path expressions*, variables, set-based queries, containers and collections, and aggregate functions. RQL differentiates between *schema queries, meta-schema queries* and *instance descriptions*.

Three layers of RDF graphs

[KMA⁺04] splits RDF graphs into an instance layer, a schema layer and a meta-schema layer. The schema layer contains information about classes, the subclass-hierarchy, the subproperty-hierarchy, and the domains and ranges or properties. In contrast, the instance layer contains information about individuals that are *members* of a class, but not classes themselves, and the relationships that hold between them. Finally the meta-schema layer includes the predefined RDF classes rdf:Property and rdf:Class and the corresponding instance relationships, and user-defined schema-information about the schema.

ORDINARY SCHEMA QUERIES The RQL schema queries subClassOf(Artist) and subClassOf^(Artist) find all transitive and direct subclasses of the class Artist, respectively. The RQL keywords subPropertyOf and subPropertyOf^ provide the same functionality for RDF properties. Superproperties and superclasses are determined with the vocabulary superPropertyOf, superPropertyOf^, superClassOf, and superClassOf^. Moreover, one can find all classes that are leaves in an RDF subclass hierarchy, and all properties that are leaves in an RDF subproperty hierarchy with the single keywords leafclass and leafproperty. topclass and topproperty achieve the same aim for the top most classes or properties of an RDF schema hierarchy. The keyword nca serves to find all nearest common ancestors of two classes or properties within an RDF Schema class or property hierarchy. The unary functions domain and range return the domains and ranges of properties.

All these queries (except for the nearest common ancestor query, which specifies a relation between three nodes) can be concisely expressed in the RDF path query language RPL introduced in Section 6 (See Example 30). A main difference between RQL and RPL queries is that RQL is explicitly geared at RDF schema querying, providing keywords for accessing the transitive subclass and subproperty hierarchies of RDFS. Since RDFS is certainly the RDF vocabulary in widest use, this seems to be a reasonable choice. On the other hand, the RPL method is not restricted to a single vocabulary extension of RDF, but is applicable to arbitrary RDF graphs, and is also more generally applicable to the RDFS vocabulary.

META-SCHEMA QUERIES Meta-schema queries in RQL are centered around the vocabulary Class, Property, Literal, and user-defined metaclasses such as RealWorldObject and SchemaProperty. While not explicitly mentioned in [KMA⁺04], a class M seems to belong to the meta-schema, if some class C of the schema is of type M.

The RQL queries Class, Property and Literal evaluate to all classes, properties, and literals of an RDF graph, respectively.

VARIABLES, SELECT-CLAUSES, CLASS AND PROPERTY INSTANCES
RQL provides three different kinds of variables: class variables, property variables and instance variables. Class variables and property variables are distinguished from instance variables in that they begin with a

dollar sign and at-symbol ('@'). Hence the query {$C1}creates{$C2} finds the domains and ranges of the property creates. In contrast, the query {C1}creates{C2} yields all pairs of individuals in an RDF graph that are connected via a creates property.

In contrast to the queries given above, queries involving variables must be contained within an RQL *select clause*, that tells distinguished and undistinguished variables apart. The notions of distinguished and undistinguished variables are used here in the same way as in SPARQL.

Example 8. *The query*

SELECT @P, range(@P) FROM {; Painter}@P

finds all pairs of nodes (p, r) *such that the domain of* p *is the class* Painter *or some of its superclasses, and such that* r *is one of the domains of* p.

Example 9. *The following RQL query consults the schema layer of an RDF graph to find classes* z *that are in the range of property* exhibited *and classes* x *that are in the range of property* creates. *Morever,* x *must be in the domain of property* exhibited.

SELECT $X, $Z FROM creates{$X}.exhibited{$Z}

Each class c and property p in an RDF graph is itself considered an RQL query, evaluating to the class extension of c and the property extension of p, respectively.

Besides the above-mentioned features, RQL provides also filter expressions, set based queries, aggregate functions, namespace queries, nested queries in the style of SQL, and quantifiers similar to the forall and exists quantifiers in XQuery.

CRITICISM RQL is a very expressive RDF query language, that fulfills almost all needs of query authors. In contrast to XCERPT^{RDF} it does not provide regular string expressions and recursion, and it lacks, to the best of our knowledge, a formal semantics. Integration with XML query languages for versatile data integration on the Web has not yet been attempted. Moreover it does not take into account the intuitive semantics of RDF containers, collections and reification. Finally, the distinction between instance, schema and meta-schema queries is based on the assumption that RDFS is the only important semantic extension to RDF, neglecting its extensions to datatypes and OWL.

3.5 TRIPLE

"TRIPLE is based on Horn Logic and borrows many features from F-logic, but is especially designed to querying and transforming RDF models."[SD01] Models in the TRIPLE terminology are similar to the idea of named graphs of SPARQL. Triple models (also called contexts in [DSN03]) are just a collection of RDF statements with an associated name which is used to refer to them. Besides these ordinary models, [DSN03] also introduces parameterized models, which can be seen as logic programs operating on RDF graphs (i.e. models in the terminology of [DSN03]). Cast in the nomenclature of logic programming, ordinary Triple models are sequences of facts (with an associated name, and each fact represents an RDF triple), and parameterized Triple models are sequences of rules.

The authors of [SD01] argue that most RDF query languages developed thus far have a static built-in semantics and are not flexible enough to adapt to different semantics. E.g. SPARQL does not care about RDF semantics at all, but considers the derivation of implied statements to be the task of an underlying data model. RQL in contrast implements the RDFS semantics, but cannot adapt to other semantic extensions to RDF such as RDFCC and RDFR (see Section 5.2) or RDF datatype semantics because it lacks user defined rules.

As most other query and transformation languages for the Web and the Semantic Web, TRIPLE supports namespace abbreviations and named graphs. Apart from this, TRIPLE features several characteristics which distinguish it from other languages for the Semantic Web:

- RDF statements are written in F-logic syntax – e.g. the RDFS axiomatic triple `rdf:type rdfs:domain rdf:Resource` is written as `rdf:type[rdf:domain ↦ rdf:Resource]`, assuming that the `rdf` and `rdfs` namespace prefixes are defined in the expected way.

- Resource abbreviations such as `isa := rdfs:subclassOf.` allow to write statements more briefly.

- Several statements with the same subject can be grouped by the subject in so-called *RDF molecules* and these groupings may be nested just as in RDF/XML.

- A brief syntax for reified statements allows for a significant reduction of the verbosity of RDF graphs. The RDF molecule `george[believes ↦ <osama[rdf:type ↦ deadPerson]>]` in fact represents five statements:
    - `george believes _:Statement1`
    - `_:Statement1 rdf:type rdf:Statement`
    - `_:Statement1 rdf:subject osama`
    - `_:Statement1 rdf:predicate rdf:type`
    - `_:Statement1 rdf:object deadPerson`

- path expressions in the extended dot notation

- Parameterized triple models consist of multiple rules with RDF molecules in the head. The application of such Triple models to an RDF graph is itself an RDF graph, which means that Triple is *answer closed*.

- *parameterized models* are defined in a so-called *model specification block* of the form

$$\forall Mdl@modelname(Mdl)\{\ldots\}$$

and consist of a model name, a parameter name for the RDF graph to be transformed, and contain a collection of facts and rules that are applied to the graph which is the parameter. Parameterized models are useful to enrich an RDF graph by axiomatic triples, the implied triples under the RDFS semantics – as the example in [SD01] shows – or other semantic extensions to RDF.

Parameterized models can be seen as view definitions on RDF graphs. Multiple rules may be present in the same rule, and the application of views to an RDF graph may be composed. This allows easy information integration across different RDF vocabularies.

The semantics of triple was first informally defined by a mapping from TRIPLE expressions to Horn Logic rules evaluated by an XSB Prolog system. In subsequent work [DSN03], a model theory was specified.

Compared to other Web query languages, Triple exhibits the following weaknesses:

- Very limited graph matching facilities. RDF molecules as the primary building blocks of Triple rule bodies do not support optional subqueries such as SPARQL, descendant constructs and arbitrary depth navigation within RDF graphs such as nSPARQL, different types of variables and support for RDF containers and collections as XCERPT^{RDF}.

- Complete support for blank node construction as in RDFLog remains unclear in Triple. The examples in [DSN03] suggest that blank node construction is not supported.

- Triple being a pure RDF query language, it is not format versatile as XSPARQL and XCERPT^{RDF}.

3.6 SWRL

SWRL [HPSB+04], an acronym for *Semantic Web Rule Language*, is a rule language for the Semantic Web built upon a combination of OWL DL and the Unary/Binary sublanguages of the Rule Markup Language [BW01].

RuleML is not a rule language itself, but a markup language for rules for the Semantic Web aimed at allowing easy and standardized interchange of rules between various applications on the Web. Nevertheless it is briefly introduced in this section because one of its sublanguages, namely the unary/binary datalog sublanguage, constitutes one of the building blocks of SWRL.

The RuleML initiative aims at standardizing a whole hierarchy of rule languages, which are potentially useful on the Web. At the very top of this hierarchy are *reaction rules*, meaning that all rules considered by the RuleML initiative are regarded as reaction rules. Two specializations of reaction rules are given by *integrity constraints* and *derivation rules*. All rule languages considered so far in this thesis fall into this last category of deriviation rules. Derivation rules are considered as reaction rules under the RuleML hierarchy since they may be regarded as reactive rules in which the only action allowed is the assertion of new facts.

A QUICK INTRODUCTION TO SWRL SWRL features four syntaxes: an abstract syntax, which is supposed to be used by parsers and other programs operating on rule programs, a human readable syntax which is primarily used in [HPSB+04] to explain how SWRL is supposed to be used, an XML syntax which allows to process rule programs with XML tools and finally an RDF syntax. In this overview of SWRL only the human readable syntax is needed and introduced by examples taken from [HPSB+04].

In contrast to RDF, the human readable syntax of SWRL uses prefix notation for atoms consisting of a predicate and two arguments. Being a rule language, it uses → for implication and ∧ for conjunction. With SWRL itself not providing disjunction and negation, an extension of SWRL in the direction of first order logic called SWRL-FOL [PS04] has been proposed. The following SWRL rule is used to derive the uncle relationship based on a hasParent and a hasBrother predicate.

```
hasParent(?x1,?x2) ∧ hasBrother(?x2, ?x3) → hasUncle(?x1,?x3)
```

SWRL has a direct model theoretic semantics which is based on the semantics of OWL, extending basic OWL interpretations by *bindings*. Bindings are mappings from *individual variables* and *datatype variables* to elements of the domain and the set of literal values, respectively. Recall the definition of OWL interpretations:

An abstract OWL interpretation is a six-tuple $I = <R, EC, ER, L, S, LV>$ with R being the domain of the interpretation, EC is the extension of classes and datatypes, ER is the extension of predicate symbols, $LV \subseteq R$ is a set of literal values, L is a mapping from typed literals to elements of LV, and S is a mapping from individual names to the extension of the class owl:thing.

The model theoretic semantics of SWRL rules is defined in the same way as for Datalog programs.[10]: A binding $B(I)$ satisfies the antecedent of a SWRL rule, iff it satisfies each of its atoms. $B(I)$ satisfies the consequent C of a rule, if C is non-empty, and $B(I)$ satisfies each atom in C.

3.7 METALOG

Metalog [Mar04a] is a logical language for the Semantic Web which aims to fill the gap present on the "People Axis" as described in [Mar04a]. Metalog aims at lowering the entrance level for authors of rule programs by providing a pseudo natural language interface.

It features two syntaxes: an RDF representation of logical formulae which is called *Metalog Model Level* (MML) and a natural language representation which is called *Pseudo Natural Language* (PNL). The semantics of the Metalog Model Level is defined by a mapping to the *Metalog Logic Level* (MLL), a subset of infinitary equational first order logic. MML is an extension of RDF by logical conjunction, disjunction, negation and implication, denoted by ml:and, ml:or and ml:imply, respectively, with the namespace prefix ml: referring to http://www.w3.org/1999/02/22-rdf-syntax-ns. Moreover, MML provides numerical comparison and the math operators $+$, $-$, $*$ and $/$. Instantiations of the operators are given an RDF representation using blank nodes and some reserved vocabulary. The simple RDFLog rule in Listing 3.17 is represented by Listing 3.18, where β_1 and β_2 denote the triples in the body of the rule in Listing 3.17, whose exact representation is left unspecified in [Mar04a].

Listing 3.17: A simple RDFLog rule

```
triple(ex:s₁, ex:p₁, ex:o₁), triple(ex:s₂, ex:p₂, ex:o₂)
   → triple(ex:s₃, ex:p₃, ex:o₃)
```

---

10 Except for the fact that SWRL rules may have conjunctions in rule heads. Since SWRL does not deal with explicit blank node quantification, conjunctions are straight-forwardly resolved by splitting a rule into muliple rules – one for each conjunct.

Listing 3.18: Metalog representation of a rule

```
_:Imp <ml:operator> <ml:imply>
_:Imp <rdf_1> _:Head
_:Imp <rdf_2> _:Body

_:Body <ml:operator> <ml:and>
_:Body <rdf_1> β₁
_:Body <rdf_2> β₂
```

The Pseudo Natural Language Interface operates on top of the logical layer, and is at the heart of the Metalog system. In this sense, Metalog is different from conventional rule languages for the Semantic Web, because the greatest part of the effort has been put in designing and implementing an easy to use pseudo natural language and into parsing of natural language.

Another distinguishing feature of Metalog is that it is one of the few RDF query languages that formalizes the semantics of RDF bags and alternatives. In the same way as the model theory for RDF containers and collections (RDFCC) presented in Section 5.2.2, Metalog assumes that an RDF bag entails any reordering of its members. The RDFCC model theory and Metalog disagree, however, in the way that RDF alternatives are formalized. While the RDFCC model theory treats all members of an RDF alternative equally, Metalog considers the first element in the alternative as a distinguished element – i.e. as the default value. The intuitive semantics provided by the W3C for RDF alternatives is not precise in this respect, and both semantics are conceivable. Metalog's treatment of RDF Containers is thus a further hint that a formalization of the RDF grouping constructs is in desperate need.

3.8 THE RULE INTERCHANGE FORMAT

The *rule interchange format* (RIF) is an effort of the W3C to standardize a family of rule languages serving as an exchange format for virtually all rule languages used on the Web. As mentioned in Section 1, the availability of rules and their interchange makes goal-directed evaluation of Web queries feasible. Moreover, it is in many cases more efficient to transmit rule sets instead of the views they define. The term "format" in RIF does not mean that RIF is only about syntax. On the contrary, the working group sets out to rigorously define the semantics of all the dialects within the framework.

With current rule languages not only differing in their syntax, but also in their expressivity and semantics, the invention of an interchange format for all available rule languages is a quite ambitious goal. The RIF working group has identified two major families of rules that must be representable in the RIF dialects: *logical rules* and *rules with actions*. The family of logical rules is outlined in the W3C working draft *Framework for Logic Dialects* (FLD) [BK09b], and the production rule dialect, a member of the family of rules with actions, is described in [dSMPH09]. The only completely specified member of the family of RIF logic dialects is the *basic logic dialect* (BLD) described in [BK09a]. [BK09b, dSMPH09, BK09a] are all W3C working drafts, and are complemented by the working drafts *RIF Core Dialect* [BHK⁺09], which is supposed to act as the basis for all RIF dialects, no matter if logic or reactive, *RIF RDF and OWL Compatibility* [dB09], which specifies the interoperation between

Families of RIF dialects

W3C specifications related to RIF

RIF rule languages and RDF data, and RDF/S or OWL ontologies, and *RIF Datatypes and Built-Ins 1.0* [PBK09], which lists the datatypes – to a large part adopted from XML Schema – and built in functions – partially adopted from XPath – that are expected to be supported by RIF dialects.

Syntactic and Semantic framework of FLD

Since the rules with action dialect is less related to the contents of this thesis, the focus of this section lies on the basic logic dialect and its embedding framework FLD. The framework for logic dialects defines a *syntactic framework* which is intended to be used as a starting point for deriving the syntax of a new rule language by specialization. Moreover FLD provides a *semantic framework* from which the semantics of a new dialect can be derived by the introduction of new datatypes, by fixing a partial or total order of truth values for the language, by defining the set of intended models for the rule language (such as minimal models, well-founded models, stable models, Herbrand models, etc) and by restricting the syntax of valid terms.

Terms within FLD

The syntactic framework of FLD is aware of 11 different types of terms: (a) constants and variables make up the set of *simple terms*, (b) *positional terms* generalize logic terms by allowing variables and entire terms to appear also in predicate position, (c) *terms with named arguments* give names to the arguments of a term, and therefore are agnostic of the order of the subterms, (d) *list terms* which may also be nested and open, (e) *equality terms*, (f) *classification terms* for specifying instance and subclass relationships, (g) *frame terms* for describing properties of objects, (h) *externally defined terms* for representing (among others) built-in functions treated as "black boxes", (i) *formula terms* for representing compound logical formulas, (j) *aggregate terms* aggregating information with functions such as Sum, Count, Max, Min, Avg, etc, (k) *remote terms* for querying external RIF resources, i.e. documents whose semantics is defined by RIF, and which – in contrast to external terms – are not treated as black-boxes.

FLD distinguishes between syntactically valid terms, and well-formed terms. The well-formedness of terms is expected to be specified by the RIF-dialects by the provision of signatures for the constant and variable symbols they use.

The *semantic framework* of FLD is based on the semantics of F-logic [KLW95a] and HiLog [CKW93], but adapted to deal with multiple truth values. FLD is parameterized by the set of allowed truth values. Moreover, FLD accomodates all kinds of semantics of logic programs – including minimal model semantics, stable model semantics and well-founded model semantics – by leaving open the set of *intended models*. Entailment is defined based on intended models as follows. A formula f_1 entails a formula f_2 if and only if all intended models of f_1 are also intended models of f_2. Again, the RIF dialect derived from FLD is expected to define which models are intended.

Relation between RIF and rich unification languages, XCERPT^{RDF}

The ambition of FLD being to encapsulate all RDF rule languages used on the Web, it is interesting to see if the syntax and semantics of Xcerpt can be encoded in terms of FLD, or, at least canonically be mapped to some (new) RIF dialect derived from FLD. Pure XCERPT^{RDF} (without XML querying capabilities) only uses simple terms and frame terms, but not positional terms, list terms, terms with named arguments or equality terms. Classification terms for XCERPT^{RDF} have been developed in [Poh08], but are not mentioned in this thesis. XCERPT^{RDF} allows formulas to be built from terms, but these are not considered as terms themselves. Externally defined terms, remote terms and aggregate terms could extend XCERPT^{RDF} in a natural and sensible manner, but are not introduced in this thesis, since the focus is on rich unification languages for versatile data integration. Rule languages with rich unification as introduced in Section 1 seem to not be derivable from FLD. SPARQL matching and XCERPT^{RDF} term simulation can, however, be translated to rules with negation, but without rich unification, e.g. to Prolog.

Part II

VERSATILE QUERYING WITH XCERPT^{RDF}

4
VERSATILE USE CASES

Contents

4.1 Querying XML with Xcerpt: Examples and Patterns 66
    4.1.1 Xcerpt^{XML} Data and Rules. 67
    4.1.2 Xcerpt^{XML} Queries: Pattern-based Filtering of Search Results 69
    4.1.3 Mining Semantic data from Microformats embedded in personal profiles. 70
4.2 Querying RDF with Xcerpt: Examples and Patterns 72
    4.2.1 Representation of RDF Graphs as XCERPT^{RDF} Data Terms 72
    4.2.2 XCERPT^{RDF} Query Terms 76
    4.2.3 XCERPT^{RDF} Construct Terms and Rules 79
4.3 Glueing RDF and XML with Rules 84
    4.3.1 Versatile Rules 84
    4.3.2 Transforming LinkedIn embedded Microformat information to DOAC and FOAF 86

With the rise of a plethora of different semi-structured Web formats, versatility [BFB+05] has become the central requirement for web query languages. Besides the well-known and ubiquitous formats HTML, XML and RDF, there are quite a lot of less familiar formats such as RDFa [AB07, Adi08] for embedding RDF information in HTML pages, the microformats [Kc06] geo, hCard, hCalendar, hResume, etc., the ISO-standard Topic Maps [GM06, Pep00]. We call a web query language *format versatile*, if it can handle, merge or transform data in different formats within the same query program. The need for integrating data from different formats has been acknowledged by partial solutions such as GRDDL [dav06, W3C07, Gan07], hGRDDL [Adi08] and XSPARQL [AKKP08]. All these solutions have in common that they try to solve the problem of web data integration by applying a mix of already established technologies such as XSLT transformations, DOM manipulations, and a combination of XML and RDF query languages such as XQuery and SPARQL. It is thus unsurprising that understanding these solutions requires a large background knowledge of the employed technologies, and that the methods are much more complicated than they could be if a format-versatile language particularly geared at integrating data from different web formats was employed.

Besides format versatility, we distinguish two other kinds of versatility: *schema* and *representational versatility*. A web query language is called *schema versatile*, if it can handle and intermediate between different schemata (i.e. schema heterogeneity) on the Web. Usage of different schemata for representing similar data is very common and well-studied in the field of data integration [Ull00, Len02]. Since the Web is being enhanced with structured and semantically rich data, data integration on the Web [KMA+98] has also received considerable attention and has spurred the growth of ontology alignment [NM00, EV03, EV04]

63

research. Schema heterogeneity on the Web is encountered whenever two ontologies describe the same kind of information on the Web, but employ different languages for this end.

Finally, *representational heterogeneity* is encountered in XML dialects such as RDF/XML, where the same information is represented differently due to the use of syntactic sugar notations – e.g. for rdf:type arcs or for the concise notation of literals, URIs or RDF containers. Moreover, representational heterogeneity is present in any XML dialect that does not enforce any order of the information that it provides, since for serialization an arbitrary order must be chosen. We call a language *representational versatile*, if it can query data agnostic of the representational variant chosen.

In this chapter, we show how the design of Xcerpt query terms, construct terms and rules has lead to a versatile language with respect to all three issues – format, schema and representation. This section starts out by looking at Xcerpt from an abstract point of view, its relationship to logic programming and the interface defined by Xcerpt terms. In Section 4.1, we introduce XML querying, construction and transformation at the example of harvesting search results and microformat information of personal profile pages of a social network. In Section 4.2, Xcerpt's RDF querying capabilities are presented with special emphasis on treating RDF specifies such as containers, collections and reifications. Finally, in Section 4.3, we present a use-case on combining microformat information harvested with Xcerpt^{XML} and RDF data queried with Xcerpt^{RDF}, thus combining versatile querying in XML and RDF.

XCERPT TERMS FROM AN ABSTRACT POINT OF VIEW: SIMULATION, SUBSTITUTIONS, AND APPLICATION OF SUBSTITUTION SETS.

Xcerpt is a rule and pattern based language inspired by logic programming, but with significantly richer querying capabilities that are necessitated by the semi-structured nature of data on the Web.

In contrast to Prolog unification, Xcerpt uses a more involved kind of unification called *simulation unification*[1] to extract bindings of logical variables from Web data.

While Prolog rules consist of possibly non-ground terms in the head and the body of a rule, Xcerpt distinguishes between *construct terms* and *query terms* to be used in the heads and the bodies of rules, respectively. This differentiation is necessary because the semi-structured nature of data on the Web requires expressive query constructs – such as descendant, subterm negation, optionality – only in the query part of a rule (i.e. in the query terms), and constructs for reassembling the data – such as grouping – only in the construction part (i.e. the construct terms). Additionally, Xcerpt offers data terms as an abstraction of XML (and thus also HTML) and RDF data. Xcerpt terms fulfill the following three properties: (i) any data term is also a query term, (ii) any data term is also a construct term, and (iii) the intersection between the set of construct terms and query terms is exactly the set of data terms, where some subterms may be substituted by variables.

Also Prolog differentiates between terms and ground terms and facts. In Prolog it holds that any ground term is a fact (i.e. data). In Xcerpt, however, a term may very well be ground, but still be only an incomplete description of data – i.e. a query. Xcerpt terms are formally – but, for the sake of brevity, not in their entirety – defined in Section 7.1.

---

1 The term *simulation* is derived from graph simulation as defined in [ABS00].

The differences between Prolog Unification and Simulation unification can be briefly summarized as follows:

- *Non-Symmetry of simulation unification.* Whereas Prolog unification is a symmetric operation on two generally non-ground terms, Xcerpt simulation unfication is a non-symmetric relation having a query term as the first argument, and a construct term as the second.

- *Different types of variables.* While Prolog Unification only allows for one single type of variable that will bind to any type of term, Xcerpt differentiates between different types of variables. Obviously the types of variables also differ with the data format that is being queried (XML, RDF, Topic Maps, Microformats, etc). When querying XML data, Xcerpt distinguishes between term variables, that bind to an entire XML fragment and label variables, that bind to a qualified or local name only.[2]

- *Notations for querying incomplete data.* Due to the almost schemaless nature of data on the Web, Xcerpt terms must be able to incompletely specify or describe the data that is being searched for. These notations include optionality of subterms, subterms at arbitrary depth and negated subterms and are introduced in detail in Section 4.1.

- *Substitution sets instead of substitutions.* While in Prolog one can find a single most general unifier for two terms t_1 and t_2 up to variable renaming, this is not true for Xcerpt. Simulation unification between two Xcerpt terms xt_1 and xt_2 results in a set of substitutions (that may very well contain only a single substitution or none at all), which is due to the richer kind of simulation and the deeper structure of data found on the Web. Imagine, for example, a biological database in XML format on the Web that contains data about enzymes and chemical reactions they catalyze. Although the database may be contained in a single XML document, the query for all pairs of enzymes and catalyzed reactions should, obviously, return more than a single tuple.

Feature unification [Kay84, Kay85], i.e. unification between feature terms, has been investigated in linguistics to aid automatic translation of natural language texts. Feature terms are used as an abstract representation of text, and are similar to semi-structured expressions as far as they can be arbitrarily nested as XML documents, may contain nodes that are entirely represented by their properties (just as RDF blank nodes), and in that the order of subterms may or may not be relevant. In contrast to simulation unification, feature unification is symmetric, and feature terms do not provide constructs for specifying incompleteness in depth or different types of variables. Finally, feature unification does not return sets of variable bindings but serves to translate text from one natural language to another.

Matching or – in Xcerpt terminology – simulating queries with data is only one of two steps in the transformation of semi-structured data. Just as Prolog, but more consequently (because of aggregation), Xcerpt clearly separates extraction of data (the data is bound to variables

---

[2] Variables for term identifiers and for XML attributes are not considered in this survey for the sake of brevity.

within *rule bodies*) and construction of new data (reassembling the data by application of substitution sets to *rule heads*).[3] This separation contrasts with XML query languages such as XQuery and XSLT, in which querying and construction is *intertwined*. Construction of new data with rule based languages is achieved by applying a substitution to a term. As mentioned above, however, Xcerpt does not deal with ordinary substitutions, but with *substitution sets*, and moreover, it differentiates between different kinds of terms. Therefore, we must be more specific: Construction of new data in Xcerpt is achieved by applying *sets* of substitutions to *construct* terms. The step from single substitutions to substitution sets allows the introduction of grouping constructs and aggregations to rule-based web querying. In the absence of grouping and aggregation constructs, application of substitution sets does not result in a single Xcerpt term, but in a set of terms (which may very well be unary or even empty).

The above discussion of Xcerpt terms can be summarized by the following interface (written as a functional type signature) of an Xcerpt term, where QTerm, CTerm and DTerm denotes the set of query, construct and data terms, respectively:

$$\text{simulates} :: \text{QTerm} \to \text{CTerm} \to \text{Bool}$$
$$\text{simulation\_unify} :: \text{QTerm} \to \text{CTerm} \to \text{SubstitutionSet}$$
$$\text{apply\_substitution\_set} :: \text{SubstitutionSet} \to \text{CTerm} \to [\text{DTerm}]$$

The function *simulates* returns true for a query term q and a construct term t if and only if the substitution set $\text{simulation\_unify}(q, t)$ is non-empty. In addition to the three above mentioned functions, a function which decides the subsumption relationship between two Xcerpt query terms is required if an optimized tabling algorithm for backward chaining evaluation of a multi-rule program is to be used. For more information about the subsumption relationship between Xcerpt query terms see Section 8.

In Section 4.1, we informally introduce the XML processing capabilities of Xcerpt, Xcerpt^{XML} terms, Xcerpt^{XML} simulation unification and the application of substitution sets to Xcerpt^{XML} terms. In Section 4.2 we do the same for XCERPT^{RDF}. Section 4.3 gives an intuitive introduction to Xcerpt multi-rule programs, and shows how Xcerpt programs are used for data integration between RDF and XML.

4.1 QUERYING XML WITH XCERPT: EXAMPLES AND PATTERNS

A large number of query languages for XML data have been proposed in the past. They range from navigational languages such as XSLT [Kay07] XQuery [SCF+07], their common subset XPath [BBC+07], and Quilt [CRF00] (the predecessor of XQuery) over pattern based languages such as XML-QL [DFF+98], UnQL [BFS00] and Xcerpt to visual query languages such as visXcerpt [BBB+04], XQBE [ABCC03] and XML-GL [CCD+98]. For a comprehensive survey over XML query languages, their expressive power and language constructs, see [BBFS05], for a comparison of Lorel, XML-QL, XML-GL, XSL and XQL see [BC99].

---

3 Queries against a single Prolog rule, such as the append rule, may indeed be used to achieve both: concatenation of lists and finding components of a list. Still, querying is performed by matching *rule bodies* with terms, and data construction by filling in bindings for variables in *rule heads*.

In this section, we introduce the XML processing capabilities of Xcerpt, taking Web search results, personal profile pages from the LinkedIn social network and FOAF documents as a running example. With this data, the following task will be accomplished:

- We will extract links to LinkedIn profile pages from search results of the Google search engine. LinkedIn is a popular social network for keeping track of business contacts. In principal, this use case could be applied to any other social network that makes parts of its pages available for indexing by search engines. We chose LinkedIn in this example since its HTML pages are well-structured and make at the time of this writing more and cleaner use of semantic markup. Unfortunately, Google search results are primarily intended for human consumption, and presentation by the browser, not for machine processing or even understanding. As a result, the relevant search results for a person name are wrapped within deeply nested HTML which primarily serves presentation purposes, and snippets of text extracted from the indexed pages. Still, Xcerpt's powerful querying constructs, such as optionality and the descendant axis, allow the concise formulation of query terms that extract only the relevant links by matching among others class and id attributes.

- From the profile pages relevant data of the curriculum vitae of the persons is identified and extracted by exploiting the microformat vocabularies hresume, hcalendar and hcard which LinkedIn has integrated into the HTML pages for semantic enrichment of the textual content.

- Finally, FOAF documents are queried to find additional information not present in the LinkedIn profile. Since FOAF is an RDF format that may be serialized in RDF/XML, we will discuss the syntactic XML structure of these documents and their correspondence to $\text{X{\scriptsize CERPT}}^{RDF}$ query terms in this section, but use $\text{X{\scriptsize CERPT}}^{RDF}$ to query their contents in Section 4.2.

4.1.1 $Xcerpt^{XML}$ Data and Rules.

This section introduces Xcerpt^{XML} data terms, that abstract from XML documents, ignoring XML specificities such as processing instructions, comments, entities and DTDs. Xcerpt^{XML} terms are introduced to allow a more concise representation of XML data that can be extended to form queries and construct patterns to be used in rules.

Rules are written in a similar fashion to Datalog or Prolog rules, and have the following general form:

```
CONSTRUCT <CONSTRUCTTERM> FROM <QUERY> END
```

Xcerpt queries are enclosed between the FROM and END keywords and are *matched* – in Xcerpt terminology *simulated* – with data. Due to Xcerpt's answer closedness (see Definition 13 for details), data may also be used as queries. To see how XML is represented as Xcerpt data, consider the FOAF document in Listing 4.1 and the corresponding Xcerpt data term in Listing 4.2.

FOAF is an acronym for "Friend-Of-A-Friend", which is a vocabulary for specifying relationships among people, their personal information such as adresses, education and contact information. FOAF is primarily an RDF vocabulary, and is therefore semantically richer than plain XML data, but most FOAF documents are serialized in RDF/XML. Therefore, FOAF documents serialized in RDF/XML can be queried or transformed *syntactically* (on the XML level) or *semantically* (on the RDF level). While this section deals with syntactic transformations of Web data, semantic queries, transformations and reasoning using XCERPT^{RDF} are discussed in Section 4.2.

Listing 4.1: A friend-of-a-friend document

```
<rdf:RDF xmlns:rdf="http://www.w3 ... rdf-syntax-ns#"
         xmlns:rdfs="http://www.w3 ... rdf-schema#"
         xmlns:foaf="http://xmlns.com/foaf/0.1/"
         xml:base="http://www.example.com/">
  <foaf:PersonalProfileDocument rdf:about="descriptions/Bill.foaf">
    <foaf:maker rdf:resource="#me"/>
    <foaf:primaryTopic rdf:resource="#me"/>
  </foaf:PersonalProfileDocument>
  <foaf:Person rdf:ID="me">
    <foaf:givenname>Bill</foaf:givenname>
    <foaf:mbox_sha1sum>5e22c ... 35b9</foaf:mbox_sha1sum>
    <foaf:depiction rdf:ID="images/bill.png"/>
    <foaf:knows>
      <foaf:Person>
        <foaf:name>Hillary</foaf:name>
        <foaf:mbox_sha1sum>1228 ... 2f5</foaf:mbox_sha1sum>
        <rdfs:seeAlso rdf:ID="descriptions/Hillary.foaf"/>
      </foaf:Person>
    </foaf:knows>
  </foaf:Person>
</rdf:RDF>
```

Listings 4.1 and 4.2 exhibit an overwhelming similarity. Therefore, we will only quickly discuss the points in which the data term representation deviates from the XML serialization. While attributes are given as name-value pairs inside of opening tags in an XML document, they are given in round braces following a qualified name in Xcerpt^{XML}. Moreover, the beginning and end of an element are specified by opening and closing brackets (or braces). Namespace prefixes are declared outside of the data terms, which disallows redefinition of namespace prefixes. Nevertheless all XML documents conforming to the Namespace recommendation [BHLT06] can also be represented as an Xcerpt^{XML} data term. Finally, text nodes are enclosed within quotation marks in order to be differentiated from empty element nodes.

Listing 4.2: A friend-of-a-friend-document written as an Xcerpt data term

```
declare namespace rdf "http://www.w3 ... rdf-syntax-ns#";
declare namespace rdfs "http://www.w3 ... rdf-schema#";
declare namespace foaf "http://xmlns.com/foaf/0.1/"
declare xml-base "http://www.example.com/"

rdf:RDF [
  foaf:PersonalProfileDocument (rdf:about="descriptions/Bill.foaf")
    [
      foaf:maker (rdf:resource="#me"),
      foaf:primaryTopic (rdf:resource="#me") ],
  foaf:Person (rdf:ID="#me") [
```

```
    foaf:givenname [ "Bill" ],
    foaf:mbox_sha1sum [ "5e22c ... 35b9" ],
    foaf:depiction (rdf:ID="images/bill.png"),
    foaf:knows [
      foaf:Person [
        foaf:name [ "Hillary" ],
        foaf:mbox_sha1sum [ "1228 ... 2f5" ]
        rdfs:seeAlso (rdf:ID="descriptions/Hillary.foaf") ] ] ]
```

4.1.2 Xcerpt^{XML} Queries: Pattern-based Filtering of Search Results

Consider the task of finding people and their curriculum vitae who study or have studied at the university of Munich. Searching for the term "LinkedIn" and "Munich" with a decent search engine returns among other search results links to pages of personal profiles of persons living in that city. The following Xcerpt query can be used to filter out other links in the search result page of Google.[4]

```
html{{
  desc div((id="res"))[[
    h2((class="hd")){ "Search Results" },
    desc h3((class="r")){{
      or(
        a((href=var Link as /.*linkedin\.com\/in\//)){{ }},
        a((href=var Link as /.*linkedin\.com\/pub\//)){{ }}
      )
    ]]
  }}
}}
```

The following features of Xcerpt must be explained to understand the above query: (in)completeness in breadth for elements and attributes, incompleteness in depth, logical variables, regular expressions and query term disjunction.

- Curly braces are used to specify subterm relationship between an element and another element or a text node. The query h2{ "Search Results" } finds h2 elements with an enclosed text node with text "Search results". Double curly braces signify that more subterms may be present than are specified. If more than one subterm is specified within double curly braces, they must be mapped in an injective manner, i.e. they may not match with the same subterm of the data. This injectivity requirement can be avoided by using triple curly braces {{{ }}}. Square parentheses may be used instead of curly braces, if the order of the subterms appearing in the query is relevant. In the presence of zero or one subterm only, using square brackets or curly braces has the same semantics. A query that uses double or triple braces or brackets is termed *incomplete in breadth*, a query with single braces or brackets only is termed *complete in breadth*.

- XML attributes and values are given in round parentheses directly following element names. Attribute names are followed by an "=" sign and by an attribute value in quotation marks.

---
[4] We make use of the fact that all LinkedIn profile pages start either with http://www.linkedin.com/pub/ or http://www.linkedin.com/in/.

Double parentheses may be used to state that there may be more attributes present in the data than specified in the query. Since XML attributes are always considered to be unordered, there is no way of expressing an ordered query on attributes in Xcerpt. In case of double parentheses, the attributes are said to be specified *incompletely in breadth*.

- The desc keyword has the same semantics as the XPath descendant axis: The subterm following the desc may either be a direct child of the surrounding term or nested at arbitrary depth within one of the children. A term using the desc keyword is termed *incomplete in depth*, the other terms are said to be completely specified in depth. As the example above shows, incompleteness significantly eases query authoring, since it requires only a very basic knowledge about the structure underlying the queried data.

- Logical variables are used to extract information from an HTML or XML document. In Xcerpt^{XML} terms, variables may bind either to entire XML elements, in which case they are called *term variables*, to the labels of elements only (*label variables*), to entire attributes (*attribute variables*) or to the values of attributes only (*label variables*). Variables may additionally feature a variable restriction initiated with the as keyword. Variable restrictions serve to lay a restriction on the possible bindings of variables.

- Regular expressions are delimited by the sign '/' and can be used at the place of labels to restrict the set of XML names that are matched by an Xcerpt^{XML} query term. The query term /ab*/, for example, will match with the labels a, ab, abb, etc. only.

- Queries may be composed using the boolean connectives and, or, and not which have the same intuitive semantics as in logic.

4.1.3 *Mining Semantic data from Microformats embedded in personal profiles.*

Let us now turn to the second task of our use case. Having identified relevant URIs from the results of a search engine query, we now exploit microformats as a semantic enrichment for HTML pages to gather additional knowledge from web pages.

LinkedIn uses the microformats hcalendar, hresume, hcard, hAtom, and XFN to semantically enrich the contents of their pages. Unfortunately, the use of microformats has not been standardized, but evolves over time. Moreover, there is no underlying formal data model for microformat data as in RDF or XML. Microformats primarily use the XML attribute names class and rel for semantic information. In contrast to RDF, microformats do not use namespaces or globally unique identifiers, which makes it hard or sometimes even impossible to find out the exact semantics of an HTML fragment enriched by microformats. For example, both the hresume and the hcalendar specifications make use of a tag called summary for specifying either the summary of one's experience gained during a professional career or the summary of an event description.[5] With this deficiency in mind, the importance of query

---

5 Consult the descriptions of these microformats available online http://microformats.org/wiki/hresume and http://microformats.org/wiki/hcalendar for details.

languages that transform semantic information embedded in HTML pages into a more precise RDF dialect becomes even more obvious. The fragment of a personal profile in Listing 4.3 pictures the use of microformats on LinkedIn and serves as further example data in this section.[6] One can observe that finding the semantic information within the HTML markup requires knowledge about the microformat standards, and that using the class attribute both for identifying elements to be formatted by stylesheets and for microformat predicate names is against the principle of separation of concerns coined by Dijkstra in [Dij82].

Listing 4.3: A simplified personal profile page with embedded semantic information.

```
<html xmlns="http://www.w3.org/1999/xhtml" xml:lang="en-US" lang="
    en-US">
<head><title>John Doe - LinkedIn</title></head>
<body>
<div class="hresume">
  <div class="profile-header">
    <div class="masthead vcard contact portrait">
      <h1 id="name">
        <span class="fn">
          <span class="given-name">John</span>
          <span class="family-name">Doe</span>
        </span>
      </h1>
    </div>
  </div>
  <div id="experience">
    <h2>John Doe Experience</h2>
    <ul class="vcalendar">
      <li class="experience vevent vcard">
        <h3 class="title">Research assistant</h3>
        <h4 class="summary">
          <a href="...">University of Munich</a>
        </h4>
        <p class="organization-details">(Research industry)</p>
        <p class="period">
          <abbr class="dtstart" title="2000-02-01">February 2000</
            abbr> until
          <abbr class="dtstamp" title="2008-11-24">Present</abbr>
          <abbr class="duration" title="P8Y10M">(8 years 10 months)
            </abbr>
        </p>
      </li>
    </ul>
  </div>
</body>
</html>
```

The following Xcerpt query extracts the first and last name of a Person, if she has some experience as a research assistant in some organization in Munich. Aside from that, the query extracts the duration of the working relationship between the person and the organization if present. Unlike other query subterms, the relevant subterm for the duration is marked optional, which means that the whole query is still successfull, if the optional subquery fails to match. Optional matching of subterms is only suitable if the subterm contains variables, and has also been proposed for SPARQL and other query languages. In contrast to SPARQL, however, the order of optional subterms within a query does not have any effect on the query result – see [FLB[+]06] for a more detailed discussion of this issue.

Listing 4.3 makes use of abbreviations for displaying information about the start, end and duration of an event. The actual date or

---

[6] The majority of the HTML markup serving presentation purposes and also most of the irrelevant content has been stripped out to shorten the presentation.

duration is hidden within an XML attribute value that is meant for computational processing. [7]

Listing 4.4: Finding research assistants from some organization in Munich.

```
html{{
  body{{
    desc{{
      desc /.*/((class="given-name")){ var FirstName },
      desc /.*/((class="family-name")){ var LastName }
    }},
    desc /.*/((class=/.*experience.*/")){{
      /.*/((class="title")){ "Research assistant" },
      /.*/((class="summary")){ /.*Munich.*/ },
      optional /.*/((class="period")){{
        /.*/((class="duration" title=var Duration)){{ }}
      }}
    }
  }}
}}
```

Listing 4.4 highlights the peculiarities of matching HTML documents with embedded microformat information. While element names have almost no relevance, the values of the class attributes are of primary importance. When querying plain HTML data, or XML dialects such as XMLSchema or DocBook, however, the role of attributes is less important, but element names occurr more often in the query. Another issue in extracting microformat information from documents is that the values of class attributes are often space separated lists of microformat predicate names such as vcard contact portrait. Up until now, Xcerpt has no specialized means for accessing these atomic strings in attribute values, which results in excessive use of regular expressions. Therefore, it may be beneficial to invent a domain specific language or at least a class of query patterns that are specifically suited for querying microformat information and which would allow a less verbose notation of the query in Listing 4.4. In the following Section, we introduce the class of XCERPT^{RDF} query terms, which are geared at native and concise RDF querying.

4.2 QUERYING RDF WITH XCERPT: EXAMPLES AND PATTERNS

In this section, the RDF processing capabilities of Xcerpt – united under the term XCERPT^{RDF} – such as data, query and construct terms particularly geared towards RDF are introduced by example. This section is structured in four parts. In Section 4.2.1 XCERPT^{RDF} data terms as a convenient way for representing RDF data are introduced. In Sections 4.2.2 and 4.2.3, XCERPT^{RDF} query and construct terms are introduced as syntactic extensions to data terms.

4.2.1 *Representation of RDF Graphs as* XCERPT^{RDF} *Data Terms*

Many serializations for RDF Data have been proposed (RDF/XML, Notation3, Turtle, NTriples, etc.), with their inventors pursuing a set of

---

[7] This convention was proposed by Tantek Çelik on his blog (http://tantek.com/log/2005/01.html#d26t0100) since humans prefer dates in a natural language description over a formal and concise notation, and may also deduce some information from the context.

partially competing goals: On the one hand, (i) RDF serializations are supposed to be as short as possible, on the other hand, (ii) an optimal serialization should have a canonical and unique representation for each RDF graph – put more formally, there should be an isomorphism between the set of RDF graphs and the set of RDF graph serializations. Moreover, RDF serializations should be (iii) interchangeable between software systems on the Web, and at the same time (iv) easy to author and read by humans.

RDF/XML was proposed by the W3C with the first and the third aim in mind. Due to the encoding of RDF in XML, RDF/XML is easily exchanged over the Web, and standard XML tools, such as XPath, XQuery, XSLT processors and XML Schema validators can be used to process this serialization. Furthermore, the RDF/XML syntax allows for a plethora of syntactic sugar notations that significantly reduce the verbosity of an XML encoding of data. Unfortunately, RDF/XML does not perform well in the second and fourth discipline, i.e. it is not canonical, and it is not easy to read and write by humans. Due the availability of the syntactic sugar notations, there are many different possibilities for encoding the same RDF graph, which makes parsing XML/RDF into a set of triples a major challenge, and also requires more background knowledge about the serialization format by the user than other serializations do.

Notation3 is a product of discussions in the Semantic Web Interest Group and performs well under the first and lasst criterion. [8] Due to its non-XML serialization format and some short hand notations, it is easier to read and write for human users, and is also quite dense in comparison with other serialization formats. Notation3 does not perform well, however, under the second and third design goal.

Turtle being a subset of Notation3, and NTriples being a minimal subset of Turtle (and thus also of Notation3), NTriples does not provide any short hand notations and is thus significantly more verbose and redundant than Notation3. Still, it is quite readable for human users and can be easily read into or serialized from a relational database containing only one single relation for all triples in an RDF graph[9]. Due to its simplicity, NTriples comes pretty close to fulfilling the second aim: An RDF graph being a set of triples, its possible NTriples serializations only differ in the order of the triples and in the naming of the blank nodes.

With $\text{Xcerpt}^{\text{RDF}}$ data terms, we introduce yet another format for serializing RDF graphs. Besides the common goals stated above, $\text{Xcerpt}^{\text{RDF}}$ data terms were invented with three other goals in mind: (a) compatibility with $\text{Xcerpt}^{\text{XML}}$ data terms, (b) extensibility to query terms involving variables and incompleteness constructs[10], and (c) support for RDF specificities such as containers and collections[11].

Consider the RDF graph displayed as an XML/RDF document in Listing 4.1 and as an $\text{Xcerpt}^{\text{XML}}$ data term in Listing 4.2. Its representation as an $\text{Xcerpt}^{\text{RDF}}$ data term is as follows:

Listing 4.5: A friend-of-a-friend-document written as an $\text{Xcerpt}^{\text{RDF}}$ data term.

```
declare namespace rdf "http://www.w3 ... rdf-syntax-ns#";
declare namespace rdfs "http://www.w3 ... rdf-schema#";
```

[8] Its specification can be found online at http://www.w3.org/DesignIssues/Notation3.
[9] This is a common schema for RDF stores
[10] any $\text{Xcerpt}^{\text{RDF}}$ data term is per se also an $\text{Xcerpt}^{\text{RDF}}$ query
[11] This last point has already been partially addressed by XML/RDF

```
declare namespace foaf "http://xmlns.com/foaf/0.1/"
declare namespace ex "http://www.example.org/"

ex:descriptions/Bill.foaf {
  rdf:type → foaf:PersonalProfileDocument,
  foaf:maker → ex:#me,
  foaf:primaryTopic → ex:#me {
    rdf:type → foaf:Person,
    foaf:givenname → "Bill",
    foaf:mbox_sha1sum → "5e22c ... 35b9",
    foaf:depiction → base:images/bill.png,
    foaf:knows {
      _:SomePerson {
        rdf:type → foaf:Person,
        foaf:name → "Hillary",
        foaf:mbox_sha1sum "1228 ... 2f5"
        rdfs:seeAlso → base:descriptions/Hillary.foaf
} } } }
```

As another example consider Figure 6 from the RDF Primer [MM04]. Its representation as an XCERPT^{RDF} term is as follows:

Listing 4.6: Example from the W3C RDF Primer in XCERPT^{RDF} notation.
```
declare namespace exterms "http://www.example.org/terms/"
declare namespace exstaff "http://www.example.org/staffid/"

exstaff:85740 {
  exterms:address → _:A {
    !http://www.example.org/terms/city → "Bedford",
    exterms:street → "1501 Grant Avenue",
    exterms:state → "Massachusetts",
    exterms:postalCode → "01730"
  }
}
```

Similarly to RDF/XML, Notation3, Turtle and SPARQL, XCERPT^{RDF} data terms can be abbreviated using namespace prefixes in qualified names. Full URIs are distinguished from qualified names by prefixing an exclamation mark, blank nodes by the prefix _:, and literals by quotation marks.

In the RDF graph above, multiple statements have the blank node _:A as their common subject, which is factored out in the XCERPT^{RDF} serialization. In many cases RDF statements do not only share the subject, but also the predicate, in which case also the predicate can be factored out:

```
declare namespace ex "http://www.example.org/"
declare namespace foaf "http://xmlns.com/foaf/0.1/"

ex:anna { foaf:knows → (ex:bob, ex:chuck) },
```

XCERPT^{RDF} also supports the factorization of properties only, objects only, predicate and object, subject and object, and of all three elements – subject, predicate and object, in which case there will be one XCERPT^{RDF} term for each RDF triple. Factoring out the predicate only could be used, for example, to represent a clique of friends, in which every member knows every other member and herself:

```
(ex:anna, ex:bob, ex:chuck) {
  foaf:knows → (ex:anna, ex:bob, ex:chuck) },
```

The RDF graph in Listing 4.6 has only a single node without incoming edges, and therefore the choice of the root of the Xcerpt^{RDF} term is trivial. RDF graphs may, however, have multiple nodes without incoming edges or none at all, or may even be entirely disconnected. In the case of no nodes without incoming edges, one can arbitrarily pick a root node for the Xcerpt^{RDF} term representation, but in the case of multiple nodes without incoming edges, and in the case of a disconnected RDF graph, the graph cannot be serialized as a single Xcerpt^{RDF} term, but only as a conjunction of terms. Therefore, the keyword RDFGRAPH is introduced:

```
RDFGRAPH {
  ex:anna { foaf:knows → ex:bob },
  ex:chuck { foaf:knows → ex:bob }
}
```

RDF Schema is a specification that "describes how to use RDF to describe RDF vocabularies" [McBo4]. It therefore provides a set of URIs, with a semantics defined by RDFS entailment rules, and which are in popular use for defining new RDF ontologies. Xcerpt^{RDF} provides shorthand notations for the most common ones among them: rdf:type, rdfs:range, rdfs:domain, rdf:Property and rdfs:Resource.

```
ex:name { is [ex:Person -> ex:Name] }
```

The Xcerpt^{RDF} term above is a shorthand for the following Xcerpt^{RDF} term:

```
ex:name {
  rdf:type → rdf:Property,
  rdfs:domain → eg:Person,
  rdfs:range → eg:Name
}
```

If the domain and/or the range of a predicate shall be left unrestricted, then the restricting classes can be simply omitted as in the Xcerpt^{RDF} term eg:name{ is [eg:Person ->] }. In Xcerpt^{RDF} this expands to the following term:[12]

```
ex:name {
  rdf:type → rdf:Property,
  rdfs:domain → eg:Person
}
```

Besides the RDFS vocabulary, RDF distinguishes a set of URIs for expressing reification of RDF statements and containers and collections of Resources in RDF bags, sequences, alternatives or lists. Xcerpt^{RDF} provides syntactic sugar notations both for reifications on the one hand and RDF containers and collections on the other hand. Consider the following Xcerpt^{RDF} term:

```
ex:bob { ex:believes →
  _:Statement1 { < ex:anna{ foaf:knows → ex:bob } >
}
```

---

[12] Note that under the RDFS entailment rules, also the triple ex:name rdfs:range --> rdf:Resource would be implied. Xcerpt^{RDF}, however, does not enforce the RDFS semantics, since RDF/S entailment rules can be easily encoded in Xcerpt^{RDF} itself.

The XCERPT^{RDF} term enclosed in angle brackets is a reified statement, and thus the entire term is equivalent to the following, significantly more verbose one:

```
ex:bob { ex:believes →
  _:Statement1 {
    rdf:type → rdf:Statement,
    rdf:subject → ex:anna,
    rdf:predicate → foaf:knows,
    rdf:object → eg:tim
  }
}
```

Whereas bags, sequences and alternatives are termed as RDF containers, and are considered to be open (i.e. there may be other elements in the container, which are not specified in the present RDF graph), RDF collections (i.e. RDF lists) are considered to be completely specified. However, this intuitive semantics is in no way reflected within the RDF/S model theory. When using only XCERPT^{RDF} shorthand notations for representing RDF graphs featuring RDF containers, collections or reification, one can be sure to respect this intuitive semantics. XCERPT^{RDF} provides the reserved words bagOf, seqOf, altOf and listOf to reduce the verbosity serializing RDF containers and collections. To represent a research group, one might chose the following XCERPT^{RDF} term, which would expand to the four triples in Listing 4.7.

```
_:Group1 { bagOf{ eg:anna, eg:bob, eg:chuck } }
```

Listing 4.7: An RDF bag written as an XCERPT^{RDF} data term without shorthand notation.

```
_:Group1 {
  rdf:type → rdf:Bag,
  rdf:_1 → eg:anna,
  rdf:_2 → eg:bob,
  rdf:_3 → eg:chuck
}
```

4.2.2 XCERPT^{RDF} Query Terms

Just as in Xcerpt^{XML}, XCERPT^{RDF} data terms are augmented with constructs for specifying incompleteness to yield XCERPT^{RDF} query terms. Such constructs include the use of logical variables, subterm negation, subterm optionality, incompleteness in breadth and qualified descendant. While originally invented for XML processing, these constructs are also beneficial for querying RDF graphs as exemplified in Example 4.8. The query extracts variable bindings for all Persons and their nick names within an RDF graph, who know some Person with nick name 'Bill', who in case do *not* know any other Person named 'Hillary'. As in Xcerpt^{XML}, the optional keyword is used to bind the nick name to the variable var Nick whenever possible, but does not cause the query to fail if the nick name is not present. Also the semantics of double curly braces and the without keyword is analogous to Xcerpt^{XML}. In Listing 4.8, the scope of the without and optional keyword is explicitly given by round parentheses. The scope of a without or optional does not have to be the entire subterm following the keyword, but may also

Table 1: Syntax of Xcerpt^{RDF} data terms

term	=	node | node '{' arc (',' arc)* '}' | reification
node	=	blank | uri | literal | qname
arc	=	uri '→' term | container | collection
blank	=	attvalueW3C
literal	=	'"' char* '"' | "'" char* "'"
uri	=	'!' uriW3C
qname	=	qnameW3C
collection	=	bag | sequence | alternative
container	=	'listOf' '{' '}' | 'listOf' '{' term (',' term)* '}'
bag	=	'bagOf' '{' '}' | 'bagOf' '{' term (',' term)* '}'
sequence	=	'seqOf' '{' '}' | 'seqOf' '{' term (',' term)* '}'
alternative	=	'altOf' '{' '}' | 'altOf' '{' term (',' term)* '}'
reification	=	'<' term '>'

be restricted to the edge only. Table 2 gives an intuition of the exact semantics of without with varying scopes by providing example data that does or does not simulate with the given query terms. The intuitive semantics for optional can be described by similar examples, but is left unspecified here for the sake of brevity. Note, however, that optional subterms are only useful if they contain variables for extracting data.

Listing 4.8: An Xcerpt^{RDF} query term.
```
var Person{{
  optional (foaf:nick → var Nick),
  rdf:type → foaf:Person,
  foaf:knows → _:X{{
    foaf:nick → 'Bill', rdf:type → Person,
    without (
      foaf:knows → {{ _:Y{{ foaf:nick → 'Hillary' }} }}
    )
  }}
}}
```

Although the Xcerpt^{XML} constructs for specifying incomplete queries mentionend above retain their semantics in Xcerpt^{RDF}, there are some different requirements in XML and RDF processing that are also reflected in the way that Xcerpt^{RDF} variables are used in Xcerpt^{RDF} query terms.

An obvious difference between matching RDF graphs and matching XML documents is that while extracting entire subtrees from an XML document is a very common task, extracting entire RDF subgraphs from an RDF graph is less frequently used, since this may often result in the whole RDF graph being returned. Therefore, the default variable binding mechanism in Xcerpt^{RDF} is not *subgraph extraction* but *label extraction*. Therefore, the most common form of variables used in Xcerpt^{RDF} query terms are *node* and *predicate* variables. Node and

Table 2: Query term simulation with different scopes for without

query term	simulating terms	non-simulating
a{{ without (b →) c }}	a{ d → c}	a{ b → c}
	a{ b → e, d →c }	a{ b → d, b → c }
		a{ b → d }
a{{ without (b → c) }}	a{ }	a{ b → c }
	a{ b → d }	a{ b → d, b → c }
a{{ b → without c }}	a{ b → d }	a{ b → c }
	a{ e → c, b → f }	a{ }
a{{ b → without c {{ d → e }} }}	a{ b → c }	a{ b → c{ d → e }}
	a{ b → c{ d → f }}	a{ }
a{{ b → (without c) {{ d → e }} }}	a{ b → f{ d → e }}	a{ b → f }
		a{ b → c }

predicate variables are written using the keyword var. A node (predicate) variable binds to a single node (arc) of the queried graph. *graph variables* are identified by the keyword graphVar and bind – similarly to Xcerpt^{XML} term variables – to entire subgraphs. Finally, *CBD-variables* (identified by the keyword cbdVar) bind to concise bounded descriptions[13].

Another difference is that once an RDF node in an RDF graph has been identified by a query and has been bound to a variable, the very same node can be easily recovered in a subsequent query, since both URI nodes and blank nodes are uniquely named in an RDF graph, whereas an XML Document may very well contain multiple nodes having the same tag name and even the same content. XQuery and Xcerpt 2.0 deal with this problem by introducing node identity for XML elements and attributes, thereby allowing the comparison of variable bindings not only by deep equality, but also by shallow equality [Furo8a]. This distinction is not necessary in RDF processing, since the *value* of a node is already a global (in the case of resources) or local (in the case of blank nodes) identifier.

For the representation of complex values, however, the simplistic data model of RDF graphs as sets of triples is not well-suited. Here, blank nodes are used to group atomic attributes of a node together to form a complex attribute. Often, these complex attributes shall be selected together and collected in a single variable binding. This need has been addressed by the W3C consortium with the introduction of a concept known as *Concise Bounded Descriptions*. XCERPT^{RDF} supports concise bounded descriptions by providing a special kind of variable which does not bind to the value of a node, nor to the subgraph rooted at the node, but to the concise bounded description associated with that node. Table 3 gives an example driven overview of the different types of variables in XCERPT^{RDF} and their binding mechanisms.

Rows 1 and 2 show the simulation of a simple XCERPT^{RDF} variable in subject and object position. Compare the binding of the graph variable

---

[13] http://www.w3.org/Submission/CBD/

Table 3: Query term simulation with variables for nodes, predicates, graphs and concise bounded descriptions.

query term	data term	substitution set	
var X	a{ b → c }	{ { X ↦ a } }	(1)
a{{ b → var O }}	a{ b → c, b → _:X }	{ { O ↦ c }, { O ↦ _:X } }	(2)
a{{ var P → var O }}	a{ b → c, b → e }	{ { P ↦ b, O ↦ c }, { P ↦ b, O ↦ e } }	(3)
graphVar G	a{ b → c }	{ { G ↦ a{ b → c } } }	(4)
graphVar G as g{{ }}	a{ b → c}	{ { } }	(5)
a{{ graphVar G }}	a{ b { a }, c }	{ { G ↦ b{ a { b, c } } } }	(6)
graphVar G as var L	a{ b → c}	{ { G ↦ a{ b → c }, L ↦ a } }	(7)
cbdVar G	_:X{ b → c{ d → e } }	{ { G ↦ _:X{ b → c } } }	(8)
cbdVar G	_:X{ b → _:Y{ d → e } }	{ { G ↦ _:X{ b → _:Y{ d → e } } } }	(9)

G in row 4 with the one of the label variable X in row 1 under simulation with the same data term. Row 3 shows a variable in predicate position, row 5 a graph variable with a restriction, which has the same semantics as in Xcerpt^{XML} (since the label g of the restriction does not appear within the data, the substitution set is empty).

An interesting case is row 6. Since the queried graph d is not a tree, but a graph, the binding for variable G is not a subterm of d, but a subgraph.

Row 7 shows the contemporary use of a graph and label variable, and rows 8 and 9 illustrate the semantics of variables for concise bounded descriptions.

Table 4 shows the syntax of XCERPT^{RDF} query terms as a context free grammar with terminal symbols in single quotes and the usual semantics of the meta-symbols * + ? and |. The nonterminal symbols uriW3C, attvalueW3C and qnameW3C correspond to the syntactic definition of URIs, attribute values and qualified names in the W3C recommendation for XML[BPSM+06]. The non-terminal symbol rpe denotes an XCERPT^{RDF} regular path expression, whose definition is omitted in this contribution for the sake of brevity.

4.2.3 XCERPT^{RDF} Construct Terms and Rules

Consisting of a query part and a construct part, pure XCERPT^{RDF} rules serve to transform RDF data. The query part is used to extract data from an RDF graph into sets of sets of variable bindings, also called substitution sets, and the construct part is used to reassemble these

Table 4: Syntax of XCERPT^{RDF} query terms

term	::=	'desc'? node | 'desc'? node '{{' arc (',' arc)* '}}' | 'desc'? reification
node	::=	blank | uri | literal | qname | variable | graphVar | cbdVar
variable	::=	'var' varname
varname	::=	[A-Z][A-Za-z0-9*]
graphVar	::=	'graphVar' varname | 'graphVar' varname as term
cbdVar	::=	'cbdVar' varname | 'cbdVar' varname as term
arc	::=	uri '→' term | rpe '→' term | container | collection
blank	::=	attvalueW3C
literal	::=	'"' char* '"' | "'" char* "'"
uri	::=	'!' uriW3C
qname	::=	qnameW3C
collection	::=	bag | sequence | alternative
container	::=	'listOf' '{{ }}' | 'listOf' '{{' term (',' term)* '}}'
bag	::=	'bagOf' '{{ }}' | 'bagOf' '{{' term (',' term)* '}}'
sequence	::=	'seqOf' '{{ }}' | 'seqOf' '{{' term (',' term)* '}}'
alternative	::=	'altOf' '{{ }}' | 'altOf' '{{' term (',' term)* '}}'
reification	::=	'<' term '>'

variable bindings within construct patterns, substituting bindings for variables.
Table 5 describes how substitution sets are applied to XCERPT^{RDF} construct terms to yield XCERPT^{RDF} data terms. Apart from the different kinds of variable bindings allowed in XCERPT^{RDF} substitution sets, the algorithm differs from the application of Xcerpt^{XML} substitution sets to Xcerpt^{XML} terms in the following ways:

- In accordance with the most famous RDF query languages such as SPARQL [SP08] and RQL [KMA+04, BK04], URIs are treated as unique identifiers within an RDF graph and do not have any object identity besides the identity given by the URI itself. This convention has as an implication that a substitution set applied to different construct terms may result in semantically equivalent data terms. To see this consider rows 1 and 5 in Table 5. Although the XCERPT^{RDF} construct terms are syntactically different, the data terms resulting from the application of the substitution set are equivalent RDF graphs. As a result, the use of all within construct terms made up of URIs only does not change the semantics of a rule.

- Just as RDFLog [BFLL07, BFL+08a], but unlike SPARQL and other RDF query languages, XCERPT^{RDF} supports arbitrary construction of blank node identifiers. While the majority of RDF query languages does not allow blank node construction at all or only blank nodes depending on all universally quantified variables of a rule (see [BFL+08a] for details), XCERPT^{RDF} and RDFLog support also construction of blank nodes that depend only on some or none of the universally quantified variables of a rule. RDFLog does this by explicit quantifier alternation, XCERPT^{RDF} on the other hand achieves the same goal by using Xcerpt's all grouping construct. To see the difference consider rows 2 and 6 in Table 5. In row 2 the construct contains the free variable var O, whereas in row 6 the construct term does not contain any free variable. Thus in the first case, the substitution set is divided into two substitution sets according to the binding of variable var O, and each of the substitution sets is applied to the construct term. In the second case, however, the substitution set is not divided at all, but applied as a whole to the construct term.

Table 5: Application of substitution sets to XCERPT^{RDF} construct terms

substitution set	construct term	XCERPT^{RDF} result	
{ { O ↦ c }, { O ↦ d } }	a{ b → var O }	a{ b → c } a{ b → d }	(1)
{ { O ↦ c }, { O ↦ d } }	_:X{ b → var O }	_:X$_1${ b → c } _:X$_2${ b → d }	(2)
{ { S ↦ c }, { S ↦ d} }	var S{ b → a }	c{ b → a } d{ b → a }	(3)
{ { S ↦ c }, { S ↦ d} }	var S{ b → _:X }	c{ b → _:X$_1$ } d{ b → _:X$_2$ }	(4)
{ { O ↦ c }, { O ↦ d } }	a{ all b → var O }	a{ b → c, b → d }	(5)
{ { O ↦ c }, { O ↦ d } }	_:X{ all b → var O }	_:X{ b → c, b → d }	(6)
{ { O ↦ c }, { O ↦ d } }	a{ b → var O{ e → f } }	a{ b → c{ e → f } } a{ b → d{ e → f } }	(7)
{ { G ↦ a{ b → c } } }	graphVar G	a{ b → c }	(8)
{ { G ↦ a{ b → c } } }	d{ e → graphVar G }	d{ e → a{ b → c } }	(9)

Special care must be taken that the result of the application of a substitution set to an XCERPT^{RDF} construct term is again an RDF graph. Guaranteeing that pure XCERPT^{RDF} programs convert RDF graphs into valid RDF graphs allows easy composition of Xcerpt programs.

Providing the same input and output format for a language is a feature of many modern query languages and is usually referred to as *answer closedness*. Popular XML query languages in general are only weakly answer closed – which means that they allow for easy authoring of programs that again produce valid XML documents, but that it still *is* possible to generate non-XML data. A notable exception to this rule is Xcerpt^{XML}, which is strongly answer closed in the sense that every outcome of an Xcerpt^{XML} program is an XML fragment. On the other hand, the W3C languages XPath, XQuery and XSLT can also be used to output non-XML content such as PDF, Postscript, or comma separated values.

Definition 13 (Answer Closedness). *A web query language is called answer closed, if the following conditions are fulfilled:*

1. *data in the queried format can be used as queries*
2. *the result of queries is again in the same format as the data*

A web query language is called weakly answer closed, *if condition (2) is possible;* it is called strongly answer closed, *if condition (2) is always enforced.*

The assurance of answer closedness in X<small>CERPT</small>^{RDF} must take the following two thoughts into account:

- *Abidance of RDF triple constraints.* The evaluation of query terms may bind node variables to literals or blank nodes. RDF graphs, however, do not allow literals in subject or predicate position or blank nodes in predicate position.

- *Abidance of RDF graph constraints.* X<small>CERPT</small>^{RDF} supports four different kinds of variables: node variables, predicate variables, graph variables and concise bounded description variables. In general, it is only safe to substitute variables in construct terms by bindings of variables of the same type. Depending on the data, bindings for node, graph and concise bounded description variables may degenerate to plain URIs, and therefore it may be safe to substitute them for predicate or node variables.

With the above two restrictions in mind, there are three different possibilities for implementing answer closedness in X<small>CERPT</small>^{RDF}.

- *Static Checking of Bindings:* Before an X<small>CERPT</small>^{RDF} program is run, it is checked that predicate variables in the construct term are also used as predicate variables in the query term, and the same for graph variables, node variables and CBD variables. To be more precise, the semantics of graph and CBD variables only differ within the query term, and thus a CBD variable binding may be substituted for a graph variable in the construct term. Moreover, the binding of a predicate variable may be substituted for a label variable in the construct term, since predicate variables always bind to URIs. On the other hand, bindings of node variables, may *not* be substituted for predicate variables. While static checking of variable bindings ensures that all terms constructed by X<small>CERPT</small>^{RDF} programs are valid RDF graphs, certain tasks, such as using URIs of nodes of a source graph in predicate position in the target graph, are impossible to achieve with this technique.

- *Dynamic Checking of Variable Bindings:* Dynamic checking of variable bindings is a sensible choice if there is reason to assume that the query author has some knowledge about the data to be queried. It is more flexible than static checking in the sense that a larger number of tasks can be realized, but is less reliable in the sense that runtime errors may occur.

- *Casting of Variable Bindings* unites the best of static checking of variable bindings (i.e. no runtime errors) and dynamic checking of variable bindings (i.e. a higher degree of flexibility). Consider the sources of runtime errors that may occur with dynamic checking of variable bindings – examples for each case are given in Table 6.
  - A literal or blank node bound to a node variable is substituted for a predicate variable in a construct term. Such triples are simply omitted from the resulting RDF graph.
  - A subgraph bound to a CBD or graph variable is substituted for a node variable in a construct term. In this case the subgraph rooted at the occurrence of the node variable in the construct term and the binding of the variable are merged.
  - A subgraph g rooted at a URI u and bound to a graph variable is substituted for a predicate variable in a construct term. The graph g is cast to u.
  - A subgraph g rooted at a blank node b and bound to a graph variable or CBD variable is substituted for a predicate variable. Since blank nodes may not appear in subject positions, the resulting triple is not included in the XCERPT^{RDF} result.
  - A literal lit is substituted for a node variable L appearing in subject position in the construct term. In this case a fresh blank node B is substituted for the variable instead of the literal. If L additionally appears in object position, also the literal itself is substituted for L, but the triples containing lit in subject position are omitted.

Since the last alternative gives an operational semantics to programs which would be either considered invalid under the first approach or would throw runtime errors under the second, XCERPT^{RDF} favors the casting of variable bindings. We acknowledge, however, that the first approach may make more sense for unexperienced users in that it is easier to understand, and that the second approach may uncover errors in the authoring of XCERPT^{RDF} programs, which would pass unnoticed by the third approach.

Table 6: Application of substitution sets to XCERPT^{RDF} construct terms with casting of variable bindings.

substitution set	construct term	XCERPT^{RDF} result
{ { V ↦ _:X } }	a{ var V → b }	
{ { V ↦ _:X } }	a{ var V → b, c → d }	a{ c → d }
{ { V ↦ 'literal1' } }	a{ var V → b, c → d }	a{ c → d }
{ { G ↦ a{ b → c } } }	graphVar G{ d → e }	a{ b → c, d → e }
{ { G ↦ a{ b → c } } }	d{ var G → e }	d{ a → e }
{ { G ↦ _:X{ b → c } } }	d{ var G → e }	_:X{ b → c }
{ { L ↦ 'literal1' } }	a{ b → { var L{ c → d } }, b → 'literal1' }	a{ b → _:X { c → d },

4.3 GLUEING RDF AND XML WITH RULES

Having introduced queries for both XML and RDF data, this section combines both features to realize the truly versatile use case already sketched in Section 4.1. Starting out from the result pages for the terms "LinkedIn Munich" of a popular Web search engine, links to relevant LinkedIn profile pages are extracted by the use of rich XML query patterns with logical variables. In a second step, the profile pages are retrieved and semantic microformat information is exploited to gather reliable information about the users. Finally, in a third step, this information is enriched by semantic information from FOAF profiles in RDF format using the RDF processing capabilities of Xcerpt.

In this use case Xcerpt's capability of handling XML query terms and RDF construct terms in the same rule (and the other way around) comes in particularly handy. As in pure XML querying and in pure RDF querying, the interface between querying and construction is a substitution set. Substitution sets generated by XML query terms differ in the allowed variable types from substitution sets generated by RDF query terms. As a result, there must either be a way to transform XML substitution sets to RDF substitution sets and reversely, or the application of XML substitution sets to RDF construct terms and the application of RDF substitution sets to XML construct terms must be defined. While both ways are feasible, we present here the first alternative, since it is less involved.

4.3.1 Xcerpt^{XML} Query Terms and XCERPT^{RDF} Construct Terms and vice versa in the Same Rule

Note that it is Xcerpt's underlying principle of clear separation of querying and construction that allows for, e.g, an XML query term in a rule body and an RDF construct term in the head of the same rule. The applicability of this design principle remains untouched if further types of query and construct terms are introduced (e.g. for topic maps or queries aimed at specific microformats or at pages of a

Semantic Wiki). The only requirement for these new types of queries and construct terms are the definition of the following four algorithms: (1) a simulation algorithm matching queries with data and returning a substitution set (a set of set of variable bindings),[14] (2) an application algorithm for substitution sets that fills in bindings for logical variables occuring in a construct term[15], (3) a mapping from variable bindings in the new format to variable bindings in the other formats (until now only XML and RDF) and finally (4) a mapping from XML and RDF variable bindings to variable bindings in the new format.

The following list defines informally the mapping of XML bindings to RDF and reversely.

- The XCERPT^{RDF} URI !http://www.example.org/#foo is mapped to the Xcerpt^{XML} qualified name eg:#foo with the namespace prefix eg bound to the namespace http://www.example.org/. We adopt the convention that the XCERPT^{RDF} URI is split into namespace and local name at the last '/', but other methods are also conceivable.

- The XCERPT^{RDF} blank node _:B is mapped to the Xcerpt^{XML} element name _:B.

- The XCERPT^{RDF} literal "some literal" maps to the Xcerpt^{XML} text node "some literal"[16].

- The XCERPT^{RDF} qualified name eg:anna is mapped to the Xcerpt^{XML} qualified name eg:anna. An appropriate namespace binding is added to the Xcerpt^{XML} term. Implementations may choose to expand the qualified name to a URI u, and map u instead.

- The XCERPT^{RDF} term a{ b → c } maps to the Xcerpt^{XML} term a{ b{ c } } in correspondance to past work on querying XML serializations of RDF with Xcerpt [Bol05]. Similarly, the XCERPT^{RDF} term _:X{ a → b{ c → ''another literal'' } } is mapped to the Xcerpt^{XML} term _:X{ a { b { c { ''another literal'' } } } }.

- The XCERPT^{RDF} shorthand notation ex:name{ is [ex:Person -> ex:Name] } is expanded to its corresponding unabbreviated term as introduced in Section 4.2. Then this longer notation is mapped to an Xcerpt^{XML} term as described above.

- The XCERPT^{RDF} reification term a{ believes → _:S{ < b{ c → d } } } is mapped to the Xcerpt^{XML} term a { believes _:S { xcrdf:reification { b { c { d } } } } } with the namespace prefix xcrdf bound to http://www.xcerpt.org/xcrdf.

- The XCERPT^{RDF} term _:X { bagOf { a, b, c } } is mapped to the Xcerpt^{XML} term _:X { xcrdf:bag { a, b, c } }. Expansion to the normalized RDF syntax and applying the standard mapping to Xcerpt^{XML} terms could also be introduced. The choice of the conversion is, however, not of primary importance, as long as all information present in the XCERPT^{RDF} term is preserved. Additional transformation rules can be easily written to change the XML outcome and be provided as an Xcerpt^{XML} module (See [ABB$^+$07] for

---

[14] See Tables 2 and 3 for an informal description of this algorithm for XCERPT^{RDF}
[15] Table 5 gives the relevant ideas for this algorithm in XCERPT^{RDF}
[16] We leave the details of treating typed RDF literals and literals with a language tag as future work.

more about Xcerpt modules). XCERPT^{RDF} sequences, alternatives and lists are treated in the same manner.

- The Xcerpt^{XML} qualified name eg:a is mapped to the XCERPT^{RDF} qualified name eg:a and the binding for the namespace prefix eg is preserved.

- The Xcerpt^{XML} unqualified name a from an Xcerpt term without default namespace is mapped to the XCERPT^{RDF} qualified name xcxml:a with the namespace prefix xcxml bound to the namespace http://www.xcerpt.org/xcxml. Note that the RDF graph data model does not allow for local names other than blank nodes. The unqualified name is not mapped to a blank node to avoid naming conflicts with other resources that may be contained in the resulting RDF Graph.

- The Xcerpt^{XML} unqualified name a from an Xcerpt term with default namespace d is mapped to the XCERPT^{RDF} URI reference da, where da is the concatenation of d and a.

- The Xcerpt^{XML} term eg:a[eg:b, eg:c] is mapped to the XCERPT^{RDF} term eg:a{ xcxml:child → eg:b, xcxml:child → eg:c }, and the binding for the namespace prefix eg is preserved. Note that since RDF graphs are always considered to be unordered, XCERPT^{RDF} does not provide square brackets, and the information about the order is lost in this mapping. Encodings of XML terms as RDF graphs that preserve the order are conceivable.

- The Xcerpt^{XML} term eg:a(id="2"){ eg:b } is converted to the XCERPT^{RDF} term eg:a{ xcxml:child → eg:b }, i.e. XML attributes are not mapped to XCERPT^{RDF} terms. Attribute names and values may, however, also be inserted into an RDF graph by binding them to label variables. Also in this case, a different kind of mapping may be chosen, but it turns out that for the applications considered in this report, this simple mapping suffices.

4.3.2 Transforming LinkedIn embedded Microformat information to DOAC and FOAF

Reconsider the Xcerpt^{XML} query term in Listing 4.4. It extracts bindings for the variables FirstName, LastName and Duration. It is easy to construct RDF data from those variable bindings with an Xcerpt rule featuring the construct term in Listing 4.9.

Listing 4.9: An RDF construct term for aggregation of information collected from XML documents

```
declare namespace doac "http://ramonantonio.net/doac/0.1/"
declare namespace foaf "http://xmlns.com/foaf/0.1/"

_:Person {
  rdf:type → foaf:Person,
  foaf:firstName → var FirstName,
  foaf:surname → var LastName,
  all doac:experience → _:Exp {
    doac:title → "Research Assistant",
    doac:duration → var Duration
  }
```

}

Note the semantics of the all construct in Listing 4.9. The all construct serves to collect a set of variable bindings within a data term to be constructed. The number of data terms generated for construct term c preceded by an all construct depends on the set of free variables inside of c, and the substitution set which is applied to the construct term. A variable v is free within a term t, if it does not occur within the scope of an all construct inside of t. Thus the variable Duration is free within the term doac:duration ..., but not inside of the entire construct term of Listing 4.9. The set of free variables in the term c :=doac:experience → _:Exp { ... } following the all keyword is the unary set {Duration}. The substitution set applied to the construct term is thus separated according to the bindings of the variable Duration only. Then each of the resulting substitution sets is applied to c independently and included as a subterm of the outermost foaf:Person label. Whenever a substitution set is applied to a term with a blank node, a new instantiation of this blank node is created, as showcased in Table 5. This is a major difference to application of substitution sets to terms starting with URIs.

Alternatively, one might want to create a single RDF bag enumerating the working relationships a person has had. This could be achieved by the following XCERPT^{RDF} construct term:

```
_:Person {
  rdf:type → foaf:Person,
  foaf:firstName → var FirstName,
  foaf:surname → var LastName,
  _:Experiences {
    bagof {
      all _:Exp {
        doac:title → var Title,
        doac:duration → var Duration
      }
    }
  }
}
```

Once the microformat information from the LinkedIn page is transformed to the more precise RDF representation at the aid of this rule, it can be combined with RDF data located anywhere on the Web. These FOAF documents can be discovered in a very similar fashion as has been done for the LinkedIn profile pages in Section 4.1.

Since LinkedIn does not provide the hash sums of email-addresses or other globally unique identifiers for persons within their profile pages, combining the extracted RDF information will rely on simple joins over the names of people, which is not particularly reliable – see [Kla07] for an overview of the problems that may occur.

With OpenID [RR06] becoming the de facto standard for distributed authentication and single-sign-on on the Web and with the largest corporations involved in online activities such as Google, Yahoo, Microsoft, etc already joining the bandwagon, it seems likely that also LinkedIn will provide an open identifier within its profiles. Also the extension of the FOAF vocabulary to provide for OpenIDs within FOAF profiles is already discussed. In the presence of this information, the combination of the collected microformat data and other RDF resources can easily and reliably achieved using XCERPT^{RDF}.

5 XCERPT^{RDF} SYNTAX AND SIMULATION

Contents

    5.1 Compound RDF data structures in XCERPT^{RDF} 89
    5.2 A Model Theory for RDF Containers, Collections and Reification   92
        5.2.1 RDFS$^+$ Model Theory and Entailment Rules   92
        5.2.2 RDFCC Model Theory and Entailment Rules   94
        5.2.3 RDFR Model Theory and Entailment Rules   100
    5.3 Abstract Syntax of XCERPT^{RDF} 102
    5.4 XCERPT^{RDF} Declarative Semantics: Term Simulation   109
    5.5 XCERPT^{RDF} Queries, Facts, Rules and Programs   116

XCERPT^{RDF} terms, rules and programs have been informally introduced in Section 4.2. This chapter is split into four sections: Section 5.1 informally introduces the remaining XCERPT^{RDF} querying capabilities for RDF containers, collections and reification. Section 5.2 introduces an extension of the RDFS model theory that formalizes the intuitive semantics of RDF containers, collections and reification. Although these constructs are proposed and described in the RDF primer, to the best of our knowledge no model theory has yet been conceived to formalize their semantics. Section 5.3 introduces the abstract syntax of XCERPT^{RDF}, and shows how XCERPT^{RDF} syntactic sugar notation helps in authoring RDF graphs that are valid under the RDF model theory for containers, collections and reifications. Section 5.4 describes the formal semantics of XCERPT^{RDF} query terms by simulation, and addresses how RDF specificities such as multiple roots within an RDF graph, blank nodes and reifications are handled in graph simulation. Moreover, the relationship between simple RDF entailment and XCERPT^{RDF} term simulation is described. Section 5.5 defines the syntax of pure XCERPT^{RDF} programs, i.e. Xcerpt programs that deal only with RDF data.

5.1 COMPOUND RDF DATA STRUCTURES IN XCERPT^{RDF}

As in any other data description formalism, also in RDF there is a need for describing not only single valued, atomic resources, but groups of resources or complex, structured objects. This need is in conflict with one of the most basic design principles of RDF, namely the one of encoding any information within simple statements made up of atomic subjects, predicates and objects. RDF solves this conflict by a canonical encoding of complex structures (such as sets or lists) in RDF triples, at the cost of sacrificing their "intuitive" semantics. This section introduces the representation of complex data structures in RDF and shows how XCERPT^{RDF} shorthand notation helps to not construct *invalid* complex objects.

Complex data structures in RDF

CONTAINERS AND COLLECTIONS IN RDF AND XCERPT^{RDF}. RDF supplies a predefined vocabulary for RDF Containers and Collections. An RDF container is either a bag, sequence or a set, and is represented by a set of triples involving the predicates rdfs:member, rdf:_1, rdf:_2, rdf:_3, ..., and the classes rdf:Bag, rdf:Seq or rdf:Alt. RDF sequences have the intuitive semantics of being ordered, RDF bags are unordered and may contain the same element more than once, whereas RDF alternatives are also unordered, but should not have duplicate elements. The RDF model theory [Hay04], however, does not enforce this semantics. Therefore, an RDF resource (i) may be typed as an RDF bag and an RDF sequence at the same time, (ii) may contain multiple statements involving the predicate rdf:_i for some integer i, or (iii) may be typed as an RDF alternative, but include the same element more than once, and there would be still valid RDF interpretations for the RDF graph containing this resource.

In XCERPT^{RDF} we (1) provide convenient syntax for containers and collections, and (2) enforce the intuitive semantics of theses concepts. However, the user can vote not to use these syntactic sugar notations. In this way, RDF graphs violating the intuitive semantics of RDF containers and collections, can still be represented.

A shopping cart with the entries eg:milk and eg:coffee represented by an RDF bag is given by the following triples, and the equivalent short hand notation in XCERPT^{RDF}:

```
eg:cart123 rdf:type rdf:Bag .
eg:cart123 rdf:_1 eg:milk .
eg:cart123 rdf:_2 eg:milk .
eg:cart123 rdf:_3 eg:coffee .
```

```
eg:cart123{ bagOf{ eg:milk, eg:milk, eg:coffee } }
```

RDF sets and sequences are written in the same way with the keywords seqOf and setOf. XCERPT^{RDF} not only provides shorthand notations for *representing* RDF graphs including containers, but also for *querying* such graphs.

eg:cart123{ bagOf{{ var Item }} } is a query that binds each item in the shopping cart to the variable Item. The query matches with the data above and yields the bindings eg:milk, and eg:coffee. Substituting double curly braces by single ones in the query would result in a query that only matches with RDF bags containing a single item.

RDF Containers may only be used to state that some resource r_m is member of some other resource r_c, but cannot be used to state that there are no *other* members r_o of r_c.

In contrast, RDF collections are used to model data that is completely specified, i.e. closed, and are written as RDF statements involving the vocabulary rdf:List, rdf:first and rdf:rest. The XCERPT^{RDF} term in Listing 5.1 corresponds to Fig. 16 of [MM04] and asserts that Amy, Mohamed and Johann are the only students of the course 6.001.

Again, the RDF model theory does not enforce the intuitive semantics of closedness of RDF collections. An RDF graph may contain a node that is subject of multiple statements with the predicate rdf:first or rdf:rest, and a container may also be unclosed. A model theory that formalizes the intuitive semantic extensions brought to RDF by containers and collections has, to the best of our knowledge, not yet been specified (see Section 5.2 for a proposal).

Listing 5.1: Shorthand notation for RDF lists in Xcerpt numbers

```
eg:courses/6.001 {
  eg:students/vocab/#students{
    listOf [
      eg:students/Amy,
      eg:students/Mohamed,
      eg:students/Johann ] } }
```

Listing 5.2: Finding all Lists with eg:Mohamed

```
desc var List as listOf[[ eg:students/Mohamed ]]
```

In accordance with the intuitive semantics of RDF containers and collections, XCERPT^{RDF} only allows one of the keywords bagOf, setOf, seqOf and listOf as a child of a term. Moreover, if one of these keywords is used to describe a resource, there must not be any other statements describing the same resource and involving the vocabulary rdf:Bag, rdf:Set, rdf:Seq, rdf:List, rdf:_1, rdf:_2, etc. Hence the term a{ bagOf { b }, rdf:type→ c} is *not* a valid XCERPT^{RDF} term. As a result of this convention, any RDF graph that can be represented as an XCERPT^{RDF} term making use only of the syntactic sugar key words for representing RDF containers and collections, is guaranteed to respect the intuitive semantics. Nevertheless, there is still the possibility of representing arbitrary RDF graphs by writing the RDF triples that make up a container or a collection directly as an XCERPT^{RDF} term, thereby doing without the keywords. Listing 5.2 shows an XCERPT^{RDF} query that matches with all RDF graphs containing an RDF list with the entry eg:students/Mohamed.

REPRESENTATION AND QUERYING OF REIFIED TRIPLES Reification is an RDF mechanism to encode information about statements, in other words to make RDF *meta statements*. For this purpose, RDF provides a reification vocabulary consisting of the RDF predicates rdf:subject, rdf:predicate and rdf:object and the RDF resource rdf:Statement. The XCERPT^{RDF} term in Listing 5.3 states that bob believes that anna likes him. Listing 5.4 gives the corresponding shorthand notation. The query below selects all reified statements with the predicate eg:likes.

Listing 5.3: RDF reification

```
eg:bob{ eg:believes→ _:St{
  rdf:type→ rdf:Statement,
  rdf:subject→ eg:anna,
  rdf:predicate→ eg:likes,
  rdf:object→ eg:bob
}
```

Listing 5.4: Reification shorthand

```
eg:bob{ eg:believes→ _:St{ <eg:anna{ eg:likes→ eg:bob }> } }
```

```
desc var Statement {{ < var _ {{ eg:likes→ var _ }} }}
```

Just as with the RDF container and collection vocabulary, the RDF model theory does not associate any formal semantics with the reification vocabulary. The intuitive semantics suggests that there must not be two distinct statements with the predicate rdf:subject, rdf:predicate, or rdf:object originating from the same node of an RDF graph. Secondly, if a node is subject of a statement with one of these three properties, it must also be subject of statements with the other two properties and be typed as an rdf:Statement. Third, all resources appearing as the object of a statement with predicate predicate must be of type rdf:Property. While RDF graphs that do not agree with these conventions are perfectly valid under the RDF model theory, they cannot be represented by XCERPT^{RDF} terms that use the XCERPT^{RDF} shorthand syntax for reification. In other words, every XCERPT^{RDF} term that only uses the shorthand syntax for asserting reified statements agrees with the intuitive semantics of RDF reification. Still, arbitrary RDF graphs can be encoded in XCERPT^{RDF} making use of the unabbreviated syntax.

5.2 A MODEL THEORY FOR RDF CONTAINERS, COLLECTIONS AND REIFICATION

In this section we introduce two extensions of the RDFS model theory; RDFCC for RDF containers and collections, and RDFR for RDF reification. While RDF containers, collections and reification are introduced in the well known RDF Primer [MM04], to the best of our knowledge, no model theoretic nor any other formal semantics has been specified for these RDF vocabularies. Interpretations valid under the RDFCC model theory respect the intuitive semantics of RDF containers and collections, interpretations valid under the RDFR model theory respect the intuitive semantics of RDF reification. Both extensions are orthogonal to each other, in the sense that interpretations that are valid under both RDFCC and RDFR respect the intuitive semantics for both containers and collections on the one hand and RDF reification on the other. Moreover, RDFCC and RDFR are orthogonal to the RDFS extension for data types. In Section 5.3 we show that all XCERPT^{RDF} data terms respect the RDFCC and RDFR model theory, provided that the XCERPT^{RDF} shorthand notation for RDF containers, collections and reification is used instead of direct usage of the RDF container, collection and reification vocabulary.

5.2.1 RDFS$^+$ Model Theory and Entailment Rules

The RDFS entailment rules have been shown to be incomplete in [tero5b] for the following reason: Given two RDF properties p_1 and p_2 with p_1 subproperty of p_2, one can derive that for a triple (a, p_1, b) also the triple (a, p_2, b) must hold (RDFS entailment rule rdfs7). Moreover, given a property p with domain u, and an RDF triple (v, p, w), the triple (v, type, u) is entailed (RDFS entailment rule rdfs2). Now consider the following RDF graph:

$$G = \{(\text{friend}, \text{subPropertyOf}, \_\!:\!\text{Knows}), \qquad (5.1)$$
$$(\_\!:\!\text{Knows}, \text{domain}, \text{Person}),$$
$$(\text{john}, \text{friend}, \text{chuck})\}$$

The graph G in Equation 5.1 RDFS-entails the triple (john, type, Person), but this triple cannot be derived by the entailment rules rdfs2 and rdfs7, since it would require an intermediate triple with a blank node in predicate position, which is forbidden in RDF. As a solution

5.2 A MODEL THEORY FOR RDF CONTAINERS, COLLECTIONS AND REIFICATION

[tero5b] proposes the notion of *generalized RDF graphs*, which are RDF graphs that allow blank nodes in predicate position.

In this contribution, we take a different approach. We argue that the RDFS semantics is unintuitive in one respect: It does not transfer the domain and range specifications from super-properties to subproperties. To see this, consider the RDF graph H in Equation 5.2. It is the same as G except that for the blank node _:Knows, we use a URI knows, serving both as a resource and a predicate name. While it is clear that H RDFS-entails the triples (john, knows, chuck) and (john, type, Person), does H also RDFS-entail the triple (friend, domain, Person)?

$$H = \{(friend, subPropertyOf, knows), \qquad (5.2)$$
$$(knows, domain, Person),$$
$$(john, friend, chuck)\}$$

According to the RDFS model theory, it does not. However, it is intuitive that the domain of a subproperty p_1 is a subclass of the domain of the corresponding superproperty p_2, since the RDFS model theory requires that $IEXT(I(p_1)) \subseteq IEXT(I(p_2))$. Moreover, altering the RDFS model theory such that domain and range specifications are inherited from superproperties to subproperties, results in no additional entailments other than just this inheritance. To see this, consider the graph RDFS(H) which is the closure of H under the RDFS entailment rules:[1]

$$RDFS(H) = \{(friend, subPropertyOf, knows),$$
$$(knows, domain, Person),$$
$$(john, friend, chuck),$$
$$(john, knows, chuck),$$
$$(john, type, Person)\}$$

Adding the triple (friend, domain, Person) would once again allow the derivation of (john, type, Person), but no other additional triples. This is easy to see, since domain and range appear as premises only in the RDFS entailment rules rdfs2 and rdfs3.[2]

We thus propose to add to the Definition of RDFS interpretations the semantic condition in 14 and to the RDFS entailment rule Equations 5.3 and 5.4.

Definition 14. *An RDFS$^+$ interpretation is an RDFS interpretation with the following additional semantic conditions:*[3]

- *If* $(p_1, p_2) \in IEXT(I(subPropertyOf))$ *and* $(p_2, C) \in IEXT(I(domain))$ *then* $(p_1, C) \in IEXT(I(domain))$.

- *If* $(p_1, p_2) \in IEXT(I(subPropertyOf))$ *and* $(p_2, C) \in IEXT(I(range))$ *then* $(p_1, C) \in IEXT(I(range))$.

---
[1] We omit blank nodes introduced by the RDF entailment rules.
[2] Obviously, this reasoning is based on the correctness and completeness of the RDFS entailment rules.
[3] Namespace prefixes are omitted for the sake of brevity.

Analogously to the other RDF entailment relationships, we say that an RDF graph H RDFS$^+$-entails an RDF graph G, iff all RDFS$^+$ interpretations of H are also RDFS$^+$ interpretations of G.

$$\frac{(p_1, \text{subPropertyOf}, p_2), (p_2, \text{domain}, C)}{(p_1, \text{domain}, C)} \quad (5.3)$$

$$\frac{(p_1, \text{subPropertyOf}, p_2), (p_2, \text{range}, C)}{(p_1, \text{range}, C)} \quad (5.4)$$

We denote the union of the set of RDFS entailment rules from [Hay04] and Equations 5.3 and 5.4 as the set of RDFS$^{(+)}$ entailment rules.

Theorem 1 (Completeness and Complexity of the RDFS$^+$ entailment).

Given two RDF graphs H and G, H RDFS$^+$-entails G, if and only if an instance of G is in the RDFS$^{(+)}$ closure of H. RDFS$^+$ entailment is NP-complete in general, but in P if H is ground.

Proof. Theorem 1 is based on the completeness of the RDFS entailment rules from [Hay04] apart from the exception identified by [tero5b] for blank nodes in predicate position. To see that the RDFS$^+$ extension eliminates the problem of intermediate triples with blank nodes in predicate position, note that the RDFS entailment rule rdfs7 is the only one which may derive such invalid triples. Moreover, take notice that the RDFS$^{(+)}$ closure of the graph G in Equation 5.1 contains the triple (john, type, Person).

NP-hardness of RDFS$^+$ entailment is a direct consequence of NP-hardness of RDFS entailment [tero5b]. RDFS$^+$ entailment is in NP, since the RDFS$^{(+)}$ closure RDFS$^{(+)}$(H) of H can be computed in polynomial time, if the axiomatic triples for the _i predicates are restricted to the ones occurring in H. Entailment can then be checked by guessing the right assignment ϕ of URIs in H to blank nodes of the entailed graph G, and testing the subset relationship $\phi(G) \subseteq \text{RDFS}^{(+)}(H)$ in linear time. For ground graphs, ϕ need not be guessed, because it is the empty mapping. □

5.2.2 RDFCC Model Theory and Entailment Rules

In this section, we introduce the RDFCC extension of RDFS, i.e. the formalization of the intuitive semantics of RDF containers and collections as specified in [MM04], [Hay04] and [McB04]. Moreover we give a sound and complete set of entailment rules as a purely syntactical characterization of RDFCC entailment.

The RDF container vocabulary consisting of the names Bag, Seq, Alt, List, first, rest, nil, _1, _2, ... must be used with care in order to respect its intuitive semantics:

Definition 15 (RDFCC interpretation). *An RDFCC interpretation is an RDFS interpretation (see Definition 9) which satisifes the following conditions:*

1. $(x, y) \in \text{IEXT}(\_i), i \in \mathbb{N} \Rightarrow x \in \text{ICEXT}(Container)$[4]

---

[4] This semantic condition is stronger than the RDFS axiomatic triples stating that the domains and ranges of the numbered container membership properties (NCMPs for short) _1, _2, etc. are simply Resource.

2. $(x,y) \in IEXT(member) \Rightarrow x \in ICEXT(Container)$

3. $(x,y), (x,z) \in IEXT(\_i), i \in \mathbb{N}, x \in ICEXT(Seq) \Rightarrow y = z.$[5]

4. $(x,y) \in IEXT(first) \cup IEXT(rest) \Rightarrow x \in ICEXT(List).$[6]

5. $(x,y), (x,z) \in IEXT(first) \Rightarrow y = z.$

6. $(x,y), (x,z) \in IEXT(rest) \Rightarrow y = z.$

7. $x \in ICEXT(List) \Rightarrow x = I(nil) \vee$
   $(\exists y, z \in IR . (x,y) \in IEXT(first) \wedge (x,z) \in IEXT(rest)).$

8. $(x,y) \in IEXT(\_i), i \in \mathbb{N} \Rightarrow \exists y_1, \ldots y_{i-1} \in IR . (x, y_j) \in IEXT(\_j)$
   $\forall 1 \leq j \leq i.$

9. *for any bijective mapping* $\pi : \{1, \ldots, n\} \rightarrow \{1, \ldots, n\}$ *holds:*
   $(x, y_1) \in IEXT(\_1), \ldots, (x, y_n) \in IEXT(\_n), x \in ICEXT(Alt) \Rightarrow$
   $(x, y_{\pi(1)}) \in IEXT(\_1), \ldots, (x, y_{\pi(n)}) \in IEXT(\_n)$

10. *The class extensions of bags, lists, sequences and alternatives are disjunct:* $C, D \in \{Bag, Seq, Alt, List\} \wedge C \neq D \Rightarrow$
    $ICEXT(C) \cap ICEXT(D) = \emptyset$

Conditions 7 and 8 of Definition 15 possibly require the existence of certain elements of the domain. Care must be taken to ensure that these conditions do not cause an infinite number of derivations in conjunction with other RDF statements, such as RDFS statements. Condition 7 is of disjunctive nature, and would only require the existence of new elements in the domain, if $x \neq I(nil)$. However, in RDF there is no way of asserting that a resource is distinct from another resource. Thus Condition 7 is harmless. Condition 8 requires the existence of a constant number of additional elements of the domain. But the model theory does not require that any of these elements are in $\pi_1(IEXT(\_l))$ with π_1 denoting the projection of a relation on the first element, and l a natural number. If it did, an infinite number of triples could be derived. Hence also Condition 7 is harmless.

RDF provides both the unnumbered container membership property (short UCMP) member and the numbered container membership properties _1, _2, ... (NCMPs). Since the intuitive semantics of alternatives is independent of the order of its elements, the member property suggests itself for their specification. However, RDF bags and alternatives are mostly specified using numbered container membership properties, as in the RDF Primer. Condition 9 above ensures that an RDF alternative entails all reorderings of its elements, as Example 10 illustrates.[7]

Example 10 (Semantics of NCMPs in RDF alternatives and sequences).

Condition 9 states that an RDF alternative RDFCC-entails any reordering of the alternative, such that the RDF graphs in Equations 5.5 and 5.6 entail each other.

---

[5] This semantic condition is equivalent to stating that the numbered container membership properties are all functional properties (owl:FunctionalProperty in OWL).
[6] This semantic condition is in line with the RDFS axiomatic triples stating that the domain of first and rest is List.
[7] RDF bags are discussed later on in this section.

$$\{(eg{:}alt, type, Alt), (eg{:}alt, \_1, eg{:}a), (eg{:}alt, \_2, eg{:}b)\} \qquad (5.5)$$
$$\{(eg{:}alt, type, Alt), (eg{:}alt, \_1, eg{:}b), (eg{:}alt, \_2, eg{:}a)\} \qquad (5.6)$$

There is no equivalent semantic condition for RDF sequences, since for sequences, the order is relevant, and thus two sequences with the same members but different order must be interpreted as two different elements in IR. Thus the RDF graph in Equation 5.7 does not RDFCC-entail the RDF graph in Equation 5.8 nor the other way around. This is reflected in the RDFCC model theory in that there are RDFCC interpretations for 5.7 and 5.8 which are not RDFCC interpretations for 5.8 and 5.7, respectively.

$$\{(eg{:}alt, type, Seq), (eg{:}alt, \_1, eg{:}a), (eg{:}alt, \_2, eg{:}b)\} \qquad (5.7)$$
$$\{(eg{:}alt, type, Seq), (eg{:}alt, \_1, eg{:}b), (eg{:}alt, \_2, eg{:}a)\} \qquad (5.8)$$

Example 11 (Openness/Closedness of RDF Containers/Collections). The RDFCC model theory formalizes the intuitive notion of openness of RDF containers and closedness of RDF collections given in [MM04]. To see this, consider the RDF graphs H_1, H_2, G_1 and G_2 below. While the graphs H_1 and H_2 are always compatible, G_1 and G_2 are only compatible under the assumption that eg:a denotes the same resource as eg:b. Therefore the membership of eg:x is fixed, once it is given an first and a rest predicate.

$$H_1 = \{(eg{:}x, type, Alt), (eg{:}x, member, eg{:}a)\}$$
$$H_2 = \{(eg{:}x, member, eg{:}b), (eg{:}x, member, eg{:}c)\}$$
$$G_1 = \{(eg{:}x, type, List), (eg{:}x, first, eg{:}a)\}$$
$$G_2 = \{(eg{:}x, first, eg{:}b), (eg{:}x, rest, nil)\}$$

The specification of RDF bags is problematic with the currently available RDF vocabulary. On the one hand, RDF bags are unordered like RDF alternatives, and thus an RDF bag should entail any reordering of its elements. On the other hand, multiple occurrences of the same element within a bag *do* matter – the bag (or multi-set) $\{a, a\}$ is different from the bag $\{a\}$. Entailment of all reorderings would thus loose the information about the cardinality of elements in a bag.

Specificiation of RDF bags with the UCMP `member` does not solve the problem either, since the model theory is set-based. A clean solution to this dilemma would be the introduction of URIs `card_1`, `card_2` ..., which are used to specify the cardinality of an element within an RDF bag.

Definition 16 gives a formalization of the intuitive semantics of RDF bags, if the cardinality of elements within a bag are specified via the predicates `card_1`, `card_2`.

Definition 16 (Formalization of RDF bags). *An RDFCC interpretation is an RDFCCBag interpretation, if the following additional semantic conditions hold:*

1. *if $(x, y) \in \text{IEXT}(card\_i)$ for some natural number $i > 0$, then $x \in \text{ICEXT}(Bag)$.*

2. *if $(x, y) \in \text{IEXT}(card\_i)$ and $(x, y) \in \text{IEXT}(card\_j)$ for two natural numbers $i, j > 0$ then $i = j$.*

Condition 1 in Definition 16 ensures that the cardinality properties are only used for the specification of RDF bags. Condition 2 ensures that the cardinality of an element within an RDF bag is uniquely determined. Since this formalization of RDF bags introduces new vocabulary and requires a redefinition of the merge of an RDF graph, it is not part of the RDFCC model theory.

With the RDFCC model theory requiring the disjointness of the class extensions of RDF bags, sequences, alternatives and lists, there are RDF graphs that have no interpretation under the RDFCC semantics. One such graph is $\{(a, type, Bag), (a, type, Alt)\}$. We call this situation an *RDFCC clash*. In the RDFS extension for datatypes, similar cases can occur: The graph

$$\{(\_:x, type, xsd:string), (\_:x, type, xsd:decimal)\}$$

has no interpretation under the datatype extension of RDFS. This situation is referred to as a *datatype clash*.

RDFCC entailment is analogous to RDF simple entailment, RDF entailment and RDFS entailment: We say that an RDF graph G_1 entails an RDF graph G_2 under the RDFCC semantics (written $G_1 \models_{RDFCC} G_2$), iff all RDFCC interpretations of G_1 are also RDFCC interpretations of G_2.

The model theoretic characterization of RDFCC implies the following triples[8] and *syntactic* entailment rules, which are valid in the sense of Definition 10.[9]

$$(\_i, domain, Container) \quad \forall i \in \mathbb{N} \tag{5.9}$$

$$(member, domain, Container) \tag{5.10}$$

$$(first, domain, Container) \tag{5.11}$$

$$(rest, domain, Container) \tag{5.12}$$

$$\frac{(a, type, List), a \neq nil}{(a, first, \_:X), (a, rest, \_:Y)} \tag{5.13}$$

$$\frac{(a, \_i, b)}{(a, \_j, \_:Z\_j) \quad \forall 1 \leqslant j < i} \tag{5.14}$$

$$\frac{(a, \_i, b)}{(a, member, b)} \quad \forall i \in \mathbb{N} \tag{5.15}$$

$$\frac{(a, \_i, b), (a, type, Alt)}{(a, \_j, b)} \quad \forall 1 \leqslant j \leqslant i \tag{5.16}$$

Note that in Equation 5.13 we assume the unique name property for the URI nil. While in general, the unique name assumption is insensible for a distributed environment like the Web, in this particular case we can argue that anybody who uses (and thus knows) the URI List should also know (and thus use) the URI nil for referencing the empty RDF list.

For an RDF graph G, RDFCC(G) is the closure of G under the RDFCC and the RDF and RDFS entailment rules. Unfortunately, the RDFCC entailment rules are not complete in the sense that they allow to derive all graphs G′ RDFCC-entailed by an RDF Graph G. In particular, $G_1 \models_{RDFCC} G_2 \Leftrightarrow RDFCC(G_1) \models_{RDFS} RDFCC(G_2)$ is *not* true for arbitrary RDF graphs G_1 and G_2 as Example 12 shows.

---
[8] triples can obviously be considered as entailment rules with an empty condition
[9] $\_:X, \_:Y, \_:Z\_1, \ldots$ denote fresh blank node identifiers.

Example 12 (Incompleteness of the RDFCC entailment rules). *Consider the RDF graphs g_1 and g_2 below. Clearly g_1 RDFCC-entails g_2, but g_2 is not in the RDFCC closure of g_1. The missing entailment rules are borrowed from OWL, and given in Definition 17.*

$$g_1 = \{(eg{:}a, \_1, eg{:}b), (eg{:}a, \_1, eg{:}c), (eg{:}c, type, foaf{:}Person)\}$$
$$g_2 = \{(eg{:}b, type, foaf{:}Person)\}$$

To complete the RDFCC entailment rules, the `owl:functionalProperty` and `owl:sameAs` properties are necessary for the formulation of entailment rules reflecting Condition 3 of Definition 15. These additional entailment rules are given together with the RDFCC axiomatic triples $\mathcal{A}^{CC}$ in Definition 17.

Definition 17 (RDFCC$^{(+)}$ closure). *The set $\mathcal{A}^{CC}$ is the following set of RDFCC axiomatic triples:*

- $(\_1, type, owl{:}functionalProperty)$
- $(\_2, type, owl{:}functionalProperty)$
- ...,
- $(first, type, owl{:}functionalProperty)$
- $(rest, type, owl{:}functionalProperty)$
- $(owl{:}sameAs, type, owl{:}symmetricProperty)$

The RDFCC$^+$ *entailment rules are as follows:*

$$\frac{(p, type, owl{:}functionalProperty), (a, p, b), (a, p, c)}{(a, owl{:}sameAs, c)} \quad (5.17)$$

$$\frac{(a, owl{:}sameAs, b), (a, pred, obj)}{(b, pred, obj)} \quad (5.18)$$

$$\frac{(a, owl{:}sameAs, b), (subj, a, obj)}{(subj, b, obj)} \quad (5.19)$$

$$\frac{(a, owl{:}sameAs, b), (subj, pred, a)}{(subj, pred, b)} \quad (5.20)$$

$$\frac{(p, type, owl{:}symmetricProperty), (a, p, b)}{(b, p, a)} \quad (5.21)$$

With RDFCC$^{(+)}$ *we refer to the union of the RDFCC entailment rules and the RDFCC$^+$ entailment rules. Given an RDF graph G, RDFCC$^{(+)}$(G) denotes the closure of $G \cup \mathcal{A}^{CC} \cup \mathcal{A}^{RDFS}$ under the RDFCC$^{(+)}$ and RDF and RDFS entailment rules.*

Theorem 2 (Soundness and Completeness of RDFCC$^{(+)}$). *Given two RDF graphs G_1 and G_2 which are free of RDFCC clashes, $(G_1 \cup \mathcal{A}^{CC}) \models_{RDFCC} (G_2 \cup \mathcal{A}^{CC})$ iff RDFCC$^{(+)}$(G$_1$) $\models_{RDFS}$ RDFCC$^{(+)}$(G$_1$).*

The correctness of Theorem 2 can be seen by the following assignment of entailment rules to the semantic conditions in Definition 15.

- Conditions 1 and 2 are reflected by entailment rules 5.9 and 5.10, respectively.

- Condition 3 is reflected by the RDFCC$^+$ entailment rules 5.17, 5.18, 5.19 and 5.20 together with the axiomatic triples (_i, type, owl:functionalProperty) for $i \in \mathbb{N}, i > 0$.

- Condition 4 is reflected by the rules 5.11 and 5.12.

- Conditions 5 and 6 are reflected by the RDFCC$^+$ rules 5.17, 5.18, 5.19 and 5.20, together with the axiomatic triples (first, type, owl:functionalProperty) and (rest, type, owl:functionalProperty), respectively.

- Condition 7 is reflected by rule 5.13.

- Condition 8 is reflected by rule 5.14.

- Condition 9 is reflected by rule 5.16.

- Condition 10 is ensured by the assumption that the graphs are free of RDFCC clashes.

Lemma 9 (Interpolation Lemma for RDFCC). *Given two RDF graphs H and G free of RDFCC clashes, $H \cup \mathcal{A}^{CC} \models_{RDFCC} G \cup \mathcal{A}^{CC}$, iff an instance of G is a subset of the RDFCC$^{(+)}$ closure of H.*

Lemma 9 is a direct consequence of the RDFS entailment lemma and Theorem 2. It gives rise to the following complexity results about RDFCC entailment:

Theorem 3 (Complexity of RDFCC entailment). *Given two RDF graphs H and G, deciding $H \models_{RDFCC} G$ is NP-complete, and in P if G is ground.*

Proof. NP-hardness of RDFCC entailment is inherited from simple entailment [tero5b], whose NP-hardness has been shown by a reduction from the Clique problem. That proof does not make use of any vocabulary that is further constrained in the RDFCC model theory.

Polynomial time RDFCC entailment for ground target graphs would be immediate if the RDFCC closure of an RDF graph were of polynomial size. Unfortunately, this is not the case because for the following three reasons: (i) Both the set of RDFS axiomatic triples, and the set of RDFCC axiomatic triples are infinite. (ii) Rule 5.14 adds an apriori unknown number of triples to the closure, and (iii) Rule 5.16 considers an exponential number of permutations. These issues are solved as follows: (a) Only those RDFS and RDFCC axiomatic triples for the predicates _i are considered in the computation of the closure that are actually relevant for the graph – i.e. the predicate must occur somewhere in the graph. (b) When syntactically deciding entailment, Rule 9 need not be applied for the computation of the closure. Instead a simple integer comparison can check if for a triple $(a, \_i, b)$ in the entailed graph, there is some triple $(a, \_j, b)$ with $i < j$ in the entailing graph. (c) We replace all numbered container membership properties (NCMP) used for RDF alternatives with the unnumbered container membership property (UCMP) member. Moreover, we include only the RDFS axiomatic triples for those NCMPs which are used in the entailing graph, as detailed in [tero5b]. With these three restrictions, the size of RDFCC closure of an RDF graph G is polynomial in G. Since for ground target graphs, checking entailment reduces to checking the subset relationship, this implies the second part of Theorem 3.

As for RDFS$^{(+)}$ entailment, RDFCC entailment for non-ground graphs is in NP, since we may guess a mapping ϕ from the blank nodes in the entailed graph G to the vocabulary of the entailing graph H, and subsequently check that $\phi(G) \subseteq \text{RDFCC}^{(+)}(H)$, where $\text{RDFCC}^{(+)}(H)$ is computed with restrictions (a), (b) and (c) above.

□

5.2.3 RDFR Model Theory and Entailment Rules

In this section we introduce the RDFR extension of RDFS, i.e. the formalization of the intuitive semantics of RDF reification. We distinguish a *cautious reification semantics* that allows different occurrences of the same reified statement, and a *brave reification semantics*, that assumes that the identity of a reified statement is given only by the values of its subject, predicate and object properties. As for RDFCC, we give a sound and complete set of entailment rules for the syntactical characterization of RDFR entailment, and we show that RDFR entailment is NP complete for arbitrary graphs, and in P if the target graph is ground.

Definition 18 gives a formal meaning to the RDF reification vocabulary Statement, subject, predicate and object.

Definition 18 (Cautious RDFR interpretations). *An RDFR interpretation is an RDFS interpretation satisfying the following conditions and the axiomatic triples in Definition 19.*

1. *If* $(x, y), (x, z) \in \text{IEXT}(p)$ *for* $p \in \{\text{subject}, \text{predicate}, \text{object}\}$ *then* $x = z$. *In other words,* subject, predicate, *and* object *are functional properties.*

2. *If* $(x, y) \in \text{IEXT}(p)$ *for* $p \in \{\text{subject}, \text{predicate}, \text{object}\}$ *then* $x \in \text{ICEXT}(Statement)$.

3. *If* $x \in \text{ICEXT}(Statement)$ *then* $\exists s, p, o \in \text{IR} . (x, s) \in \text{IEXT}(subject)$, $(x, p) \in \text{IEXT}(predicate)$ *and* $(x, o) \in \text{IEXT}(object)$.[10]

Definition 19 (RDFR axiomatic triples). *The RDFR axiomatic triples* $\mathcal{A}^{\text{RDFR}}$ *are the following:*

1. $(subject, tpe, owl{:}functionalProperty)$

2. $(predicate, tpe, owl{:}functionalProperty)$

3. $(object, tpe, owl{:}functionalProperty)$

4. $(subject, domain, Statement)$

5. $(predicate, domain, Statement)$

6. $(object, domain, Statement)$

7. $(owl{:}sameAs, type, owl{:}symmetricProperty)$

Example 13 (Infinite derivations). *Consider the RDF graph G:*

$$G = \{(\_{:}X, type, Statement), (object, range, Statement)\}$$

---

[10] This semantic condition is stronger than the RDFS axiomatic triples stating that the domains of subject, predicate, and object are Statement. Together with these axiomatic triples, this condition ensures that any resource with an subject has also an predicate and object (and vice versa).

Since $\_{:}X$ is typed as an RDF statement, the RDFR model theory requires the existence of some resource that is the object of the statement. Hence G entails a triple $(\_{:}X, object, \_{:}Y)$ for some blank node $\_{:}Y$. The RDFS model theory, on the other hand, requires that $\_{:}Y$ is itself a Statement, since G includes the triple (object, range, Statement). Hence G entails the triples $(\_{:}Y, type, Statement)$, $(\_{:}Y, object, \_{:}Z)$, $(\_{:}Z, type, Statement)$, etc.[11] To avoid such infinite derivations, the notion of RDFR clashes is introduced.

Definition 20 (RDFR clash). *An RDF graph containing any of the triples*

$$(rdfs{:}subject, rdfs{:}range, rdfs{:}Statement)$$
$$(rdfs{:}predicate, rdfs{:}range, rdfs{:}Statement)$$
$$(rdfs{:}object, rdfs{:}range, rdfs{:}Statement)$$

is said to contain an **RDFR** *clash.*

Definition 21 (Brave RDFR interpretations). *A cautious RDFR interpretation is a brave RDFR interpretation, iff it additionally satisifies the following condition:*

- *if* $(x, s) \in IEXT(I(subject))$ *and* $(y, s) \in IEXT(I(subject))$ *and* $(x, p) \in IEXT(I(predicate))$ *and* $(y, p) \in IEXT(I(predicate))$ *and* $(x, o) \in IEXT(I(object))$ *and* $(y, o) \in IEXT(I(object))$ *then* $x = y$.

Cautious and brave RDFR entailment are defined analogously to RDFS entailment.

Definition 22 (RDFR Entailment Rules). *The* RDFR *entailment rules include the RDFCC entailment rules 5.17, 5.18, 5.19 and 5.20. Rule 5.22 makes the set of RDFR entailment rules complete:* [12]

$$\frac{(a, type, Statement)}{(a, subject, \_{:}S), (a, predicate, \_{:}P), (a, object, \_{:}O)} \quad (5.22)$$

The RDFR *closure* RDFR(G) *of an RDF graph* G *is the closure of* $(G \cup \mathcal{A}^{RDFR})$ *under the RDFR and the RDF/S entailment rules.*

Theorem 4 (Soundness, Completeness and Complexity of RDFR). *Given two RDF graphs* H *and* G, $H \models_{RDFR} G$ *iff* $RDFR(H) \models_{RDFS} RDFR(G)$. *RDFR entailment is NP-complete for arbitrary graphs and in P, if the target graph is ground.*

The validity of the RDFR entailment rules is substantiated by the following association of entailment rules and axiomatic triples to the semantic conditions of RDFR interpretations:

- Axioms 1, 2 and 3 together with the entailment rules 5.17, 5.18, 5.19 and 5.20 are valid due to Condition 1 in Definition 18.

- Axioms 4, 5 and 6 are valid due to Condition 2 of RDFR interpretations.

- Entailment rule 5.22 is valid due to Condition 3 in Definition 18.

---

[11] Since distinct blank node identifiers are not required to be distinct, G has both an infinite number of finite models and an infinite model.
[12] $\_{:}S$, $\_{:}P$ and $\_{:}O$ are fresh blank node identifiers.

The RDFR entailment rules are complete, since the semantic conditions of Definition 18 are orthogonal to each other, and because the semantic conditions on the interpretations are spelt out by the entailment rules according to the association given above.

The complexity results are proven in the same way as for RDFS$^{(+)}$.

5.3 ABSTRACT SYNTAX OF XCERPT^{RDF}

Definition 23 (XCERPT^{RDF} Variable). *An XCERPT^{RDF} variable is either a graph variable, an arc variable, a node variable, a predicate variable, or a concise bounded description variable. Formally, an XCERPT^{RDF} variable V has a name n and an associated type $t(V) \in \{\mathsf{graph, arc, node, predicate, CBD}\}$.*

Definition 24 (XCERPT^{RDF} Term). *The set $\mathcal{T}^{RDF}$ of XCERPT^{RDF} terms is recursively defined as follows:*

- *The set of atomic XCERPT^{RDF} terms is the union of the set of URIs, qualified names, RDF literals, RDF blank nodes and XCERPT^{RDF} variables minus the set of XCERPT^{RDF} predicate and arc variables.*

- *An XCERPT^{RDF} predicate is either a URI, a qualified name or an XCERPT^{RDF} predicate variable.*

- *If p is an XCERPT^{RDF} predicate and t is an XCERPT^{RDF} term, then the pair (p, t) is an XCERPT^{RDF} arc. When serialized, an XCERPT^{RDF} arc (p, t) is written $p \to t$. Also an XCERPT^{RDF} arc variable is an XCERPT^{RDF} arc.*

- *If $t_1, \ldots, t_n$ with $n \geqslant 0$ are XCERPT^{RDF} terms, then $\mathsf{listOf}\{t_1, \ldots, t_n\}$, $\mathsf{listOf}\{\{t_1, \ldots, t_n\}\}$, $\mathsf{listOf}[t_1, \ldots, t_n]$, $\mathsf{listOf}[[t_1, \ldots, t_n]]$, $\mathsf{bagOf}\{t_1, \ldots, t_n\}$, $\mathsf{bagOf}\{\{t_1, \ldots, t_n\}\}$, $\mathsf{seqOf}\{\{t_1, \ldots, t_n\}\}$, $\mathsf{seqOf}[t_1, \ldots, t_n]$, $\mathsf{seqOf}[[t_1, \ldots, t_n]]$, $\mathsf{altOf}\{t_1, \ldots, t_n\}$, and $\mathsf{altOf}\{\{t_1, \ldots, t_n\}\}$ are XCERPT^{RDF} lists, bags, sequences and alternatives, respectively. The set of XCERPT^{RDF} containers is the union of the sets of XCERPT^{RDF} bags, sequences and alternatives. In agreement with common RDF nomenclature, an XCERPT^{RDF} list is also called an XCERPT^{RDF} collection.*

- *If sub is a blank node or URIs, pred is a URI, and obj a blank node, URI or RDF literal, then $< \mathsf{subj\{pred} \to \mathsf{obj}\} >$ is an XCERPT^{RDF} reified statement.*

- *If p is in the set RPL of conditional RDF path expressions, and t is an XCERPT^{RDF} term, then the pair (p, t) is an XCERPT^{RDF} arc.*

- *An XCERPT^{RDF} subject term is either a node variable, a URI, a qualified name or a blank node.*

- *Let $a_1, \ldots, a_n$ with $n \geqslant 0$ be XCERPT^{RDF} arcs, containers, collections, or reified statements, with at most one of the a_i a container or collection, at most one of the a_i a reified statement, and s an XCERPT^{RDF} subject term. Then $s\{a_1, \ldots, a_n\}$ and $s\{\{a_1, \ldots, a_n\}\}$ are compound XCERPT^{RDF} terms.*

- *If t is an XCERPT^{RDF} term, then $\mathsf{without}\ t$, $\mathsf{desc}\ t$, and $\mathsf{optional}\ t$ are negated, descendant and optional XCERPT^{RDF} terms, respectively. desc, without and optional are called term modifiers. An XCERPT^{RDF} term beginning with a term modifier is a modified XCERPT^{RDF} term. Modified terms must satisfy the following conditions:*

- *The modifiers* optional *and* without *cannot be applied to the same term – i.e.* optional without t *and* without optional t *are invalid* XCERPT^{RDF} *terms. They may, however, occur in the same term at different levels, as in the term* optional a{{ b → without c }}.
- *If the modifiers* optional *and* desc *are applied to the same term, then the* optional *modifier must precede the* desc *modifier.*
- *Similarly, the* without *modifier must precede the* desc *modifier when applied to the same* XCERPT^{RDF} *term.*

- *If* a *is an* XCERPT^{RDF} *arc, and* $v_1, \ldots, v_n$ *are* XCERPT^{RDF} *variables, then* all a *and* all a group by { $v_1, \ldots, v_n$ } *are also* XCERPT^{RDF} *arcs. Arcs of the form* all all a *are not allowed. As in Xcerpt*^{XML}, all *is called a* grouping construct. all *in combination with* group-by *is called an* explicit grouping construct.

- *If* a *is an* XCERPT^{RDF} *arc, container, collection or reified statement, then* without a, optional a *and* desc a *are* XCERPT^{RDF} *arcs. Not all combinations of the term modifiers* without, optional *and* desc *can b applied to the same the same construct* a. *Instead, the same conditions apply as for the application of term modifiers to* XCERPT^{RDF} *terms.*

Atomic and compound XCERPT^{RDF} terms are simply named XCERPT^{RDF} terms in the following. XCERPT^{RDF} arcs and predicates are not considered as XCERPT^{RDF} terms since they cannot occur by themselves, but are mere building blocks. The keywords listOf, bagOf, seqOf and altOf are XCERPT^{RDF} *arc constructors*, and are used to represent RDF containers and collections within XCERPT^{RDF} data terms and to query RDF containers and collections when used within XCERPT^{RDF} query terms. An XCERPT^{RDF} term is called ground, if it does not contain any variables or blank node identifiers.

XCERPT^{RDF} *arc constructors, ground* XCERPT^{RDF} *terms*

Example 14. *Consider the following* XCERPT^{RDF} *term* t:

  _:X { listOf[a, b, c], < a{ b → c} > }

It states that there is some resource x *represented by the blank node* _ : X, *that is both an RDF collection, and a reified statement. Since the RDFCC and RDFR model theories are independent of each other, and do not, in particular, demand that the RDFS classes* rdfs:Statement *and* rdf:List *are disjunct,* t *has an RDFR interpretation that is also an RDFCC interpretation. The collection in* t *happens to have the subject, predicate and object of the statement as elements. Also this is no problem under the RDFR and RDFCC semantics.*

Let t be an XCERPT^{RDF} term, a = (p, t') an XCERPT^{RDF} arc, and c an XCERPT^{RDF} container or collection. subj(t) denotes the subject of t, arcs(t) the arcs nested in t and cc(t) the containers or collection nested in t – if present. An arc or term is called *negative (optional)*, if it is preceded by the keyword without (optional). An arc or term that is neither negative nor optional is *positive*. arcs$^+$(t), arcs$^-$(t), and arcs$^?$ denote the positive, negative and optional arcs nested in t, respectively. pred(a) denotes the predicate p of a and obj(a) the object term t' of a. terms(c) denotes all subterms of c. terms$^+$(c), terms$^-$(c) and terms$^?$(t) denotes the positive, negative and optional subterms of c, respectively. For some syntactic XCERPT^{RDF} element e, blanks(e), uris(e) and vars(e) denotes the set of blank node identifiers, URIs, and variables in e, respectively.

Notation for XCERPT^{RDF} *term access*

Definition 25 (XCERPT^{RDF} data term). *An XCERPT^{RDF} data term is a compound XCERPT^{RDF} term that does not contain any term modifiers, double braces, conditional RDF path expressions, variables or grouping constructs. Moreover curly braces do not appear in combination with the* seqOf *and* listOf *keywords. We denote the set of all XCERPT^{RDF} data terms by* $\mathcal{T}_D^{RDF}$.

A NOTE ON NODE IDENTITY IN RDF GRAPHS AND XML TREES.
Xcerpt has originally been invented for querying XML, and semi-structured data in general. In semi-structured data, nodes carry labels which are distinct from their identities. In RDF graphs, on the other hand, the identity of a node is given by its URI, which is, at the same time, its label. While the same XML or HTML tag appears within an XML document at different locations, RDF graphs contain a given URI only once (though often multiple times in RDF graph serializations). For referencing the same XML element twice in a document, the ID/IDREF [BPSM+06] mechanism for intra-document referencing and XLink [OMD01] for inter-document referencing have been invented. There is no need for intra-graph or inter-graph linking between nodes of RDF graphs. Nevertheless, the serialization of a two dimensional structure such as RDF graphs in a one-dimensional sequence of characters requires some referencing mechanism, and thus URIs and blank node identifiers are allowed to appear multiple times within an XCERPT^{RDF} data term. For the sake of readability, and for the sake of compatibility with Xcerpt^{XML}, we adopt the convention that XCERPT^{RDF} data terms have only one defining occurrence of URIs (the first one in subject or object position), and all subsequent occurrences must be referencing only. A defining occurrence of a URI may have subterms, referencing ones must not. Thus, the term a{p → a} is allowed, but the term a{b → a{c → d}} is not. The second term is equivalent to its normal form a{b → a, c → d}. In the following, we will assume all XCERPT^{RDF} data terms to be in normal form.

Normal form for XCERPT^{RDF} data terms

Definition 26 (Mapping from XCERPT^{RDF} data terms to RDF graphs). *Let* d *be an* XCERPT^{RDF} *data term. The RDF graph* ρ(d) *corresponding to* d *is given by the mutually recursive mappings* ρ, α, γ, $γ_{alt}$, $γ_{bag}$, $γ_{seq}$, $γ_{list}$:

- $ρ(d) = \bigcup_{a \in arcs(d)} α(subj(d), a) \cup γ(subj(d), cont(d))$

- $α(s, a) = \{(s, pred(a), subj(obj(a)))\} \cup ρ(obj(a))$

- *The mappping* γ *serves the translation of* XCERPT^{RDF} *containers and reifications:*

$$γ(s, d) = \begin{cases} γ_{alt}(s, d) & \textit{if d is an XCERPT}^{RDF} \textit{ alternative} \\ γ_{bag}(s, d) & \textit{if d is an XCERPT}^{RDF} \textit{ bag} \\ γ_{seq}(s, d) & \textit{if d is an XCERPT}^{RDF} \textit{ sequence} \\ γ_{list}(s, d) & \textit{if d is an XCERPT}^{RDF} \textit{ list} \\ γ_{reif}(s, d) & \textit{if d is an XCERPT}^{RDF} \textit{ reification} \end{cases}$$

- $γ_{alt}(s, d) = \{(s, \textit{rdf:type}, \textit{rdf:Alt})\} \cup \bigcup_{1 \leqslant i \leqslant n} \{(s, \textit{rdfs:member}, t_i)\}$ *with* terms(d) $= t_1, \ldots t_n$.

- $\gamma_{bag}(s, d) = \{(s, \textit{rdf:type}, \textit{rdf:Bag})\} \cup \bigcup_{1 \leqslant i \leqslant n}\{(s, \textit{rdfs:member}, t_i)\}$
  with $\text{terms}(d) = t_1, \ldots t_n$.

- $\gamma_{seq}(s, d) = \{(s, \textit{rdf:type}, \textit{rdf:Seq})\} \cup \bigcup_{1 \leqslant i \leqslant n}\{(s, \text{rdf} : \_i, t_i)\}$
  with $\text{terms}(d) = t_1, \ldots t_n$.

- $\gamma_{list}(s, d) = \{(s, \textit{rdf:type}, \textit{rdf:List}), (s, \textit{rdf:first}, t_1), (s, \textit{rdf:rest}, b_1)\} \cup$
  $\bigcup_{2 \leqslant i \leqslant n}\{(b_{i-1}, \textit{rdf:rest}, b_i), (b_{i-1}, \textit{rdf:first}, t_i)\}$
  with $\text{terms}(d) = t_1, \ldots t_n$, and $b_1, \ldots b_{n-1}$ fresh blank node identifiers.

- $\gamma_{reif}(s, d) = \{ (s, \textit{rdf:type}, \textit{rdfs:Statement}), (s, \textit{rdf:subject}, s),$
  $(s, \textit{rdf:predicate}, p), (s, \textit{rdf:object}, o) \}$ where $d = < s\{p \rightarrow o\} >$.

Example 15 (Representation of RDF graphs as data terms). *While any XCERPT^{RDF} data term can be converted into an RDF graph, the inverse is not true, simply because RDF graphs may be disconnected or have multiple roots. Consider the RDF graphs $G_1 = (a, b, c), (d, e, f)$ and $G_2 = (a, b, c), (d, e, c)$. Neither G_1 nor G_2 can be encoded as an XCERPT^{RDF} data term, but only as sets of XCERPT^{RDF} data terms. For this simple reason, XCERPT^{RDF} term simulation in Section 5.4 is not defined on pairs of query terms and data terms, but on pairs consisting of a query term and a set of XCERPT^{RDF} data terms.*

Definition 27 (XCERPT^{RDF} named graphs). *An XCERPT^{RDF} named graph $\mathcal{N}$ is a tuple $(u, \mathcal{D})$ where u is a URI, and $\mathcal{D}$ is a set of XCERPT^{RDF} data terms. The URI u is assumed to be unique. The RDF graph corresponding $\mathcal{N}$ is given by $\bigcup_{d \in \mathcal{D}}(\rho(d))$. To avoid ambiguity we adopt the same restrictions concerning defining and consuming occurrences for URIs and blank nodes as for XCERPT^{RDF} data terms: For each URI u and blank node b in $\mathcal{N}$ there must exactly one defining occurrence, which is at the same time the first occurrence.*

XCERPT^{RDF} named graphs correspond to named graphs as described in [PFH06] and [CBHS05b]. XCERPT^{RDF} named graphs can be thought of as XCERPT^{RDF} data terms with a virtual root note given by its URI u. All data terms $d \in \mathcal{D}$ of the named XCERPT^{RDF} graph must then be directly nested within u. In this way ground XCERPT^{RDF} simulation could be defined between XCERPT^{RDF} query terms and XCERPT^{RDF} named graphs. In [CBHS05b] named graphs are used to track provenance information of RDF triples in order to better estimate the reliability of information. In [PFH06] named graphs are introduced to justify and promote the concept of *scoped negation as failure*. With named graphs at hand, reasoning about provenance information is possible in Xcerpt, and scoped negation allows the formulation of otherwise not expressible queries.

Atomic XCERPT^{RDF} terms are not considered as XCERPT^{RDF} data terms, since all XCERPT^{RDF} data terms must correspond to RDF graphs. A single URI, literal or blank node is, however, not a valid RDF graph (see Definition 43). Example 16 illustrates the transformation of an XCERPT^{RDF} data term into an RDF graph:

Example 16 (Transformation of an XCERPT^{RDF} data term into an RDF graph). *Consider the XCERPT^{RDF} data term d in Listing 5.5. It corresponds to the RDF graph G in Equation 5.23.*

Listing 5.5: An XCERPT^{RDF} data term.

```
eg:bob{
```

```
eg:believes → eg:l{
  rdf:type → rdf:List,
  rdf:first → _:X {
    <xsd:integer{ rdfs:label → "Integer" }> },
  rdf:rest → _:B1 {
    rdf:first → _:Y {
      <xsd:string{ rdfs:label → "String"}>,
      rdf:rest → rdf:nil
    }
  }
}
```

$$G = \{(eg{:}bob, eg{:}believes, eg{:}l), (eg{:}l, rdf{:}type, rdf{:}List) \quad (5.23)$$
$$(eg{:}l, rdf{:}first, \_{:}X), (eg{:}l, rdf{:}rest, \_{:}B1),$$
$$(\_{:}B1, rdf{:}first, \_{:}Y), (\_{:}B1, rdf{:}rest, rdf{:}nil),$$
$$(\_{:}X, rdf{:}subject, xsd{:}integer), (\_{:}X, rdf{:}predicate, rdfs{:}label),$$
$$(\_{:}X, rdf{:}object, "Integer"), (\_{:}X, rdf{:}type, rdfs{:}Statement)$$
$$(\_{:}Y, rdf{:}subject, xsd{:}string), (\_{:}Y, rdf{:}predicate, rdfs{:}label),$$
$$(\_{:}Y, rdf{:}object, "String"), (\_{:}Y, rdf{:}type, rdfs{:}Statement)\}$$

Theorem 5 (Satisfiability of XCERPT^{RDF} data terms). *XCERPT^{RDF} data terms using solely the shorthand notation for construction of RDF containers and collections are satisfiable under the RDFCC semantics. XCERPT^{RDF} data terms using solely the shorthand notation for construction of RDF reified statements are satisfiable under the RDFR semantics. XCERPT^{RDF} data terms using solely the shorthand notation for construction of RDF conainters, collections* and *reified statements have a valid RDFS interpretation that is both an RDFCC interpretation* and *an RDFR interpretation.*

As data terms, construct terms are used to construct RDF graphs, and must therefore also be compound:

Definition 28 (XCERPT^{RDF} construct term). *An XCERPT^{RDF} construct term is a compound XCERPT^{RDF} term that does not contain any term modifiers, double braces, or conditional RDF path expressions. Ground construct terms must not include any grouping constructs.*[13] *We denote the set of all XCERPT^{RDF} construct terms by* $\mathcal{T}_C^{RDF}$.

Definition 29 (XCERPT^{RDF} query term). *An XCERPT^{RDF} query term is an XCERPT^{RDF} term without grouping constructs. We denote the set of all XCERPT^{RDF} query terms by* $\mathcal{T}_Q^{RDF}$.

While all data terms can be translated to RDF grpahs, query terms do not correspond to RDF graphs, but specify that (i) some triples are mandatory – must be present in the queried graph –, (ii) some triples are negated – i.e. must not be present –, and (iii) some triples are optional – i.e. may or may not be present in the queried graph and may yield additional variable bindings. Indeed, the semantics of a query term q involving the constructs double curly braces ({{ and }}), atomic

---

[13] One could just as well allow ground construct terms with grouping constructs, but their semantics would be equivalent to their versions without grouping constructs (see Definition 37). To avoid redundancy and confusion, grouping constructs in ground construct terms are disallowed.

negation (without over a single triple, a without spanning more than one triple is referred to as *compound negation*), optional, reification, and atomic variables only, can be precisely encoded in three *sets* of *independent* triples $\rho^m(q)$, $\rho^n(q)$ and $\rho^o(q)$ denoting the mandatory, negated and optional statements, respectively. Moreover, this fragment correponds roughly to SPARQL query patterns without filter clauses, and allows the translation of SPARQL query patterns to XCERPT^{RDF} and vice versa. Unfortunately, the other constructs – single curly braces, listOf, seqOf, bagOf, altOf, variables for concise bounded descriptions, arcs and graphs, and compound negation cannot be encoded in these three sets of triples. We denote the set of XCERPT^{RDF} query terms not making use of constructors for containers and collections, with atomic negation, and double curly braces only, as the set $\mathcal{T}_Q^{\{\{\{\}\}\},\neg a,?}$. The semantics of abritrary XCERPT^{RDF} query terms is more involved, and cannot be translated to these three sets of triples. When translated to some extension of conjunctive queries or some fragment of first order logic, the required formalism must provide disjunction, negation and existential quantification over *sets of triples*. The precise semantics of arbitrary XCERPT^{RDF} query terms is given in the following section by (ground) XCERPT^{RDF} term simulation.

Example 17 (Transformation of an XCERPT^{RDF} query term to triple sets). *Consider the* XCERPT^{RDF} *query term* q *in Listing 5.6*

Listing 5.6: An XCERPT^{RDF} query term with atomic negation and optional parts.

```
eg:bob{{
  eg:believes → var List {{
    rdf:type → rdf:List,
    rdf:first → var First {{
      <xsd:integer{{ rdfs:label → "Integer" }}> }},
    optional rdf:rest → var Second {{
      rdf:first → _:Y {{
        <xsd:string{{ rdfs:label → "String"}}>,
        rdf:rest → rdf:nil
      }}
    }}
  }}
  without foaf:knows → eg:anna
}}
```

Note that there is no possibility of expressing the same XCERPT^{RDF} *query only with the shorthand notation for RDF containers, collections and reification. In fact,* q *may return non-empty substitution sets even on RDF graphs that do* not *respect the RDFR and RDFCC intuitive semantics. On the other hand,* XCERPT^{RDF} *query terms making use of the shorthand notation only, will return the empty substitution set (i.e. false), on graphs that have not RD-FCC or RDFR interpretation. The RDF container and reification vocabulary in Listing 5.5 is used just as any other URI without a predefined semantics. The sets of mandatory, optional, and negated triples corresponding to* q *are as follows:*

$\rho^m(q)$ = {(eg:bob, eg:believes, var List), (var List, rdf:type, rdf:List),
(var List, rdf:first, var First),
(var First, rdf:type, rdfs:Statement),
(var First, rdf:subject, xsd:integer),
(var First, rdf:predicate, rdfs:label),
(var First, rdf:object, "Integer")}

$\rho^n(q)$ = {(eg:bob, foaf:knows, eg:anna)}

$\rho^o(q)$ = {(var List, rdf:rest, var Second), (var Second, rdf:first, _:Y),
(_:Y, rdf:type, rdfs:Statement), (_:Y, rdf:subject, xsd:string),
(_:Y, rdf:predicate, rdfs:label), (_:Y, rdf:subject, "String"),
(var Second, rdf:rest, rdf:nil), }

The remaining constructs listOf, bagOf, altOf, seqOf, compound negation, variables for arcs, concise bounded descriptions and graphs cannot be encoded in $\rho^m(q)$, $\rho^n(q)$ and $\rho^o(q)$ for the following reasons:

- listOf{a, b} *is (almost) equivalent to the following union of conjunctive queries. However, it cannot be expressed as a single conjunctive query, since there are two possibilities for encoding an RDF list with two elements. Both these possibilities must be reflected in the query. Still, since SPARQL allows unions of graph patterns, it could be encoded in SPARQL. Note that the triple-encoding of* listOf{a, b} *will still match with graphs invalid under the RDFCC semantics, while the original query* listOf{a, b} *does not. For the precise semantics see Definition 32. This precise semantics cannot be encoded as a SPARQL query.*

$$\exists l, b_1. \quad (\quad (l, rdf:type, rdf:list), (l, rdf:first, a),$$
$$(l, rdf:rest, b_1), (b_1, rdf:type, rdf:list),$$
$$(b_1, rdf:first, b), (b_1, rdf:rest, rdf:nil))$$
$$\lor (\quad (l, rdf:type, rdf:list), (l, rdf:first, b),$$
$$(l, rdf:rest, b_1), (b_1, rdf:type, rdf:list),$$
$$(b_1, rdf:first, a), (b_1, rdf:rest, rdf:nil))$$

- *Still more complicated is the query* listOf{{a, b}}, *it allows for an arbitrary number of elements in the list to be queried, as long as the two elements* a *and* b *are contained. Translation to a conjunctive query or a SPARQL graph pattern would require an infinite disjunction of triples. We do not even attempt the translation but refer to Definition 32.*

- *When translating the remaining constructors* bagOf, altOf, seqOf, *one experiences essentially the same difficulties as with* listOf. *Again, the precise semantics of these constructs (Definition 32) cannot be expressed as finite conjunctive queries or SPARQL query patterns.*

- *Compound negation such as* a{{b → c, without d → {{e → f}} }} *could be expressed as the following conjunctive query with negation:*

$$(a, b, c) \land \neg((a, d, e) \land (d, e, f))$$

Note that the negation spans two triples. A graph including only one of the triples would still match the query. In SPARQL, this query would have to be encoded using multiple optional graph patterns and multiple filter-clauses with the unbound operator, such that the query would become quite involved.

- XCERPT^{RDF} treats variables for arcs, concise bounded descriptions and graphs differently from atomic variables, in that arc variables may only appear within predicate position, and concise bounded description variables and graph variables only in subject or object position. Moreover, the bindings for these variables are not single URIs, Literals or blank nodes, but entire subgraphs of the queried graph. Obviously this binding mechanism cannot be encoded in a conjunctive query language that is missing these types of variables nor within SPARQL. An extension of SPARQL in this direction seems to be, however, straightforward and feasible.

In contrast to XCERPT^{RDF} data and construct terms, XCERPT^{RDF} query terms include atomic XCERPT^{RDF} terms. A query term consisting of the single URI u (a qualified name q) simply returns true on all RDF graphs which contain u (the expansion of q) in subject or object position. Since XCERPT^{RDF} adopts the same view as SPARQL of blank nodes in queries – i.e. the one of an undistinguished variable – a query term consisting of a single blank node b returns true on all but the empty RDF graph. In contrast, a query term consisting of a single node variable v_n evaluated over an RDF graph G yields the substitution set mapping v_n to each of the nodes of G. The semantics of these atomic XCERPT^{RDF} query terms and of compound XCERPT^{RDF} query terms is formalized in the following section by graph simulation in a similar way as the semantics of Xcerpt^{XML} terms.

5.4 XCERPT^{RDF} DECLARATIVE SEMANTICS: TERM SIMULATION

The declarative semantics of Xcerpt programs is based on the notion of ground term simulation. In [Scho4a] ground term simulation is defined on $\mathcal{T}^Q \times \mathcal{T}^Q$, i.e. on *pairs of ground query terms*. This is more than is needed for the specification of the fixpoint semantics of stratified Xcerpt programs and also for the well-founded-semantics introduced in this work (Section 7), which extends the semantics to non-stratified programs. Instead, ground simulation as a function on $\mathcal{T}^Q \times \mathcal{T}^D$, i.e. between query terms and *data terms* is sufficient. Note, however, that term simulation between query terms is helpful for showing that the subsumption relationship between Xcerpt query terms is decidable (see Section 8). In order to extend the semantics from Xcerpt^{XML} programs to XCERPT^{RDF} programs, ground term simulation must be specified for XCERPT^{RDF} terms. To not carry out any superfluous work, XCERPT^{RDF} ground term simulation is indeed specified only between pairs of ground query terms and *data terms*.

Signature of Xcerpt term simulation

Ground XCERPT^{RDF} simulation (Definition 30) is defined in a similar way as ground Xcerpt^{XML} simulation. Due to the problem of multiple roots in RDF graphs (see Example 15), term simulation in XCERPT^{RDF} cannot be specified on $\mathcal{T}_Q \times \mathcal{T}_D$, but must be specified on pairs of query terms and *sets of data terms* – i.e on $\mathcal{T}_Q \times \mathcal{P}(\mathcal{T}_D)$.

Moreover, special attention must be payed to the simulation of arcs (Definition 31), containers and collections (Definition 32) and of reified statements (Definition 33).

Finally, blank nodes within XCERPT^{RDF} terms must be treated as existentially quantified variables, and thus occupy a special role in XCERPT^{RDF} term simulation. On the one hand, extending simulation from ground XCERPT^{RDF} terms (without blank nodes) to XCERPT^{RDF} terms that contain blank nodes, but no variables, can be handled in the same way as extending ground XCERPT^{RDF} term simulation to arbitrary XCERPT^{RDF} term simulation (i.e. also to terms with variables). This observation suggests to handle blank nodes in the very same way as XCERPT^{RDF} variables. On the other hand, blank nodes (but not variables) may appear within the results of XCERPT^{RDF} programs (i.e. within RDF graphs), or within intermediate results of an XCERPT^{RDF} program. Thus, RDF graphs containing blank nodes must be seen as part of the Herbrand Universe in the specification of the declarative semantics. Ground query term simulation for graphs without blank nodes would thus be insufficient for the specification of the stratified fixpoint procedure and the well-founded semantics.

Treatment of blank nodes in term simulation

The definition of ground term simulation in XCERPT^{RDF} is split into several parts. Defintions 30, 31, 32 and 33 are mutually dependant and define the *ground* simulation of terms, arcs, containers and collections, and reifications, respectively.

Definition 30 (Ground XCERPT^{RDF} term simulation). *Let t_1 be some ground XCERPT^{RDF} query term, and $\mathcal{D}$ some set of XCERPT^{RDF} data terms. t_1 simulates into $\mathcal{D}$ (short $t_1 \preceq \mathcal{D}$) iff one the following conditions hold:*

- t_1 *is some URI or RDF Literal, and t_1 occurs in the RDF graph $\bigcup_{d \in \mathcal{D}} (\rho(d))$ corresponding to $\mathcal{D}$ (see Definition 26).*

- t_1 *is of the form $l_1\{t_1^1, \ldots t_1^n\}$ and some data term $d \in \mathcal{D}$ contains some subterm t_2 of the form $l_2\{t_2^1, \ldots t_2^m\}$ with $l_1 = l_2$ and $t_1^i \preceq \pi(t_1^i)$ for some total, surjective mapping $\pi: \text{arcs}(t_1) \to \text{arcs}(t_2)$.*[14][15]

- t_1 *is of the form $l_1\{\{t_1^1, \ldots t_1^n\}\}$ (note the double braces) and some data term $d \in \mathcal{D}$ contains some subterm t_2 of the form $l_2\{t_2^1, \ldots t_2^m\}$ satisfying $l_1 = l_2$ and $t_1^i \preceq \pi(t_1^i)$ for some total mapping $\pi: \text{arcs}^+(t_1) \to \text{arcs}(t_2)$ (since t_2 is a data term, there are no negated arcs within t_2). Furthermore there is no pair $(t_1^i, t_2^j) \in \text{arcs}^-(t_1) \times (\text{arcs}(t_2) \setminus \text{img}(\pi))$ such that $t_1^i \preceq t_2^j$. Finally, if there is some (negated) container, collection or reification c_1 nested in t_1, then there is some (is no) container, collection or reification c_2 in t_2 with $t_1 \preceq t_2$.*

Definition 31 (Ground simulation of XCERPT^{RDF} arcs). *Let $a_1 = p_1 \to t_1$ and $a_2 = p_2 \to t_2$ be two ground XCERPT^{RDF} arcs. a_1 simulates into a_2 iff $p_1 \preceq p_2$ and $\text{ref}(t_1) \preceq \text{ref}(t_2)$.*[16]

---

14 Note that there will be at most one subterm t_2 satisfying the above conditions, since for any URI or blank node, there is only one defining occurrence within an XCERPT^{RDF} graph.
15 We assume there are no negative arcs or containers within a term with single braces. If there are, they can simply be ignored.
16 The function ref is for reference resolution: if t_1 is a referencing occurrence of a URI, then $\text{ref}(t_1)$ yields the referenced term. Otherwise, $\text{ref}(t_1) = t_1$. Note that reference resolution is not needed for arcs in Definition 30, since the same URI may appear multiple times as a predicate in an RDF graph.

Definition 32 (Ground simulation of containers and collections). *Let c_1 and c_2 be two XCERPT^{RDF} containers. c_1 simulates into c_2 iff one of the following conditions hold.*

1. $c_1 = \text{bagOf}\{t_1^1, \ldots, t_1^n\}$ and $c_2 = \text{bagOf}\{t_2^1, \ldots, t_2^m\}$ are XCERPT^{RDF} bags, and the term $t_1 := s\{p \to t_1^1, \ldots, p \to t_1^n\}$ simulates into the term $t_2 := s\{p \to t_2^1, \ldots, p \to t_2^m\}$ for two fresh URIs s and p.

2. $c_1 = \text{bagOf}\{\{t_1^1, \ldots, t_1^n\}\}$ and $c_2 = \text{bagOf}\{t_2^1, \ldots, t_2^m\}$ (note the double braces) are XCERPT^{RDF} bags, and the term $t_1 := s\{\{p \to t_1^1, \ldots, p \to t_1^n\}\}$ simulates into the term $t_2 := s\{p \to t_2^1, \ldots, p \to t_2^m\}$ for two fresh URIs s and p.

3. c_1 and c_2 are XCERPT^{RDF} alternatives, and the same conditions hold as for XCERPT^{RDF} bags.

4. $c_1 = \text{listOf}[t_1^1, \ldots, t_1^n]$ and $c_2 = \text{listOf}[t_2^1, \ldots, t_2^n]$ are XCERPT^{RDF} lists, and the same conditions as for case 1 are fulfilled.

5. $c_1 = \text{listOf}[\{t_1^1, \ldots, t_1^n\}]$ and $c_2 = \text{listOf}[t_2^1, \ldots, t_2^m]$ are XCERPT^{RDF} lists, and the same conditions as for case 2 are fulfilled.

6. $c_1 = \text{listOf}[t_1^1, \ldots, t_1^n]$ and $c_2 = \text{listOf}[t_2^1, \ldots, t_2^n]$ are XCERPT^{RDF} lists, and $\text{ref}(t_1^i) \preceq \text{ref}(t_i^2)^{16}$ $\forall 1 \leq i \leq n$.

7. $c_1 = \text{listOf}[[t_1^1, \ldots, t_1^n]]$ and $c_2 = \text{listOf}[t_2^1, \ldots, t_2^m]$ are XCERPT^{RDF} lists, and there is some monotone and injective mapping $\pi : \text{terms}^+(c_1) \to \text{terms}^+(c_2)$ with $\text{ref}(c_i) \preceq \text{ref}(\pi(c_i))$ $\forall t_i \in \text{terms}^+(c_1)$. Furthermore, π is not extensible to any monotone mapping $\pi' : \text{terms}^+(c_1) \cup \{t_1^i\} \to \text{terms}^+(c_2)$ for some $t_1^i \in \text{terms}^-(c_1)$ such that $\text{ref}(\text{pos}(t_1^i)) \preceq \text{ref}(\pi'(t_1^i))^{16}$ and $\pi'(t_1^i) \in (\text{terms}^+(c_2) \setminus \text{img}(\pi))$.

8. c_1 and c_2 are two XCERPT^{RDF} sequences, and the same conditions as for XCERPT^{RDF} lists are fulfilled.

Example 18. *Consider the following examples for ground simulation of containers and collections.*

- listOf[[a, c]] *and* listOf{a, c, d, b} *simulate into* listOf[a, b, c, d], *but* listOf[a,c], seqOf[[a,c]], bagOf{{a,c}}, *and* altOf{{a,c}} *do not.*

- *for* q_1, q_2 *in* {listOf[], seqOf[], bagOf{}, altOf{}} *holds* $q_1 \preceq q_2 \Leftrightarrow q_1 = q_2$.

Definition 33 (Ground simulation of XCERPT^{RDF} reifications). *Let $r_1 = st_1 < \text{subj}_1\{\text{pred}_1 \to \text{obj}_1\} >$ and $r_2 = st_2 < \text{subj}_2\{\text{pred}_2 \to \text{obj}_2\} >$ be two XCERPT^{RDF} reifications. r_1 simulates into r_2 iff $st_1 \preceq st_2$, $\text{subj}_1 \preceq \text{subj}_2$, $\text{pred}(r_1) \preceq \text{pred}(r_2)$, and $\text{obj}(r_1) \preceq \text{obj}(r_2)$.*

Example 19 (On sibling injectivity in XCERPT^{RDF}). *In Xcerpt^{XML} and XCERPT^{RDF}, the simulation relationship between two terms must be injective on the siblings of the query term, which means that the term $q = \text{var Element}\{\{b, b\}\}$ does not simulate in the term $d = a\{b\}$ (See Chapter 7 for the precise definition of Xcerpt^{XML} term simulation). In this way, one can find all XML elements that contain more than one subterm of a given name, or more than one arbitrary subterm (e.g. with the query term var Element{{var First, var Second}}). Since URIs are unique within an RDF graph (in contrast to XML labels, which are not unique within an XML document), and since RDF graphs are sets (not multi-sets) of RDF triples this observation is not true for XCERPT^{RDF} querying: An XCERPT^{RDF} term such as $q' = a\{\{b \to c, b \to c\}\}$ is simply unsatisfiable.*

Example 20 (Ground simulation and multiple URI occurrences). *Consider the XCERPT^{RDF} query term $q = a\{b \to a\{c \to d\}\}$ and the XCERPT^{RDF} data term $d = a\{b \to a, c \to d\}$. Does q simulate into d? On the one hand, a bijective mapping is impossible since there is only one arc explicitly nested in q, and d contains two arcs. On the other hand, the node a in q does have two distinct arcs, specified at different places. To avoid confusions of this kind, we adopt the same kind of normal forms for XCERPT^{RDF} query terms as for XCERPT^{RDF} data terms: For a given URI u, its first occurrence in subject or object position within a term is defining (may have subterms), and all subsequent occurrences are referring only (must not have subterms). The normal form for q is d and obviously, d simulates into itself. Note that occurrences of URIs in predicate position are never defining. Occurrences of URIs in predicate position correspond to edges in an RDF graph.*

Normal form for XCERPT^{RDF} query terms

Example 21 (The necessity for reference resolution). *Consider the query term $q = a\{\{b \to c\{\{b \to a\}\}\}\}$ and the data term $d = c\{b \to a\{b \to c\}\}$. From Definition 30 an algorithm for deciding term simulation can be almost immediately derived, which works as follows on q and d (multiple occurrences of the same name in q and d are distinguished by indices):*

$$a_1\{\{b \to c\{\{b \to a_2\}\}\}\} \preceq c_1\{b \to a\{b_2 \to c_2\}\} \tag{5.24}$$

$$a_1\{\{b \to c\{\{b \to a_2\}\}\}\} \preceq a\{b_2 \to c_2\} \tag{5.25}$$

$$b \to c\{\{b \to a_2\}\} \preceq b_2 \to c_2 \tag{5.26}$$

$$c\{\{b \to a_2\}\} \preceq \mathsf{ref}(c_2) \tag{5.27}$$

$$c\{\{b \to a_2\}\} \preceq \mathsf{ref}(c_2) \tag{5.28}$$

$$c\{\{b \to a_2\}\} \preceq c\{b \to a\{b \to c\}\} \tag{5.29}$$

$$b \to a_2 \preceq b \to a\{b \to c\} \tag{5.30}$$

$$a_2 \preceq a\{b \to c\} \tag{5.31}$$

$$\top \tag{5.32}$$

Ground term simulation is an assymmetric relation between the set of ground XCERPT^{RDF} query terms and ground XCERPT^{RDF} data terms. As described above, ground term simulation does not suffice for the specification of the declarative semantics of XCERPT^{RDF} programs, because ground RDF graphs and ground XCERPT^{RDF} terms do not contain blank nodes, but ordinary RDF graphs generally do. But how are blank nodes supposed to be treated in term simulation? Consider the XCERPT^{RDF} data term $d = \_:C\{\ eg:hasfather\ \_:F\ \}$, stating that two persons c, f (or some other type of creature) exist, such that c is child of f. Given the queries $q_1 = \_:Z$ and $q_2 = eg:bob$, are q_1 and q_2 supposed to simulate into d? Note that while q_1 and q_2 are not valid data or construct terms, they are valid XCERPT^{RDF} query terms. This is a major difference to SPARQL, where the smallest query possible is a single triple. We consider q_1 as the question if there exists something in the universe. Thus any RDF interpretation (see Definition 8) with at least one element in IR would satisfy q_1. q_2, on the other hand, is interpreted as the question if the graph G that is queried contains some information about the resource denoted by $eg:bob$, i.e. if for a valid interpretation $I = (IR, IP, IEXT, LV, IS, IL, LV)$ of G $I(eg:bob)$ is in IR. Obviously, this is the case if and only if the URI $eg:bob$ occurs within G. Thus we adopt the view that q_1 simulates into d, but q_2 does not. With the same reasoning we come to the conclusion that $\_:A\{\ b \to c\}$ simulates into $a\{\ b \to c\ \}$, but not the other way around.

Figure 1: Example terms for the illustration of blank node simulation.

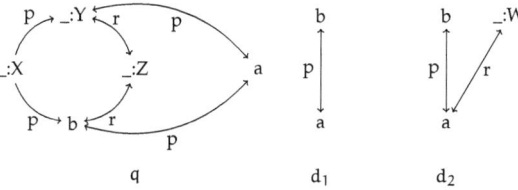

Definition 34 (Term simulation with blank nodes). *Let q be an XCERPT^{RDF} query term without variables, but possibly with blank nodes. Let $\mathcal{D}$ be some set of XCERPT^{RDF} data terms possibly containing blank nodes. q simulates into D iff there is some mapping μ : $\text{blank}(q) \to \text{blank}(\mathcal{D}) \cup \text{uris}(\mathcal{D})$ such that for all mappings τ : $\text{blank}(\mathcal{D}) \to \{u_1, \ldots, u_n\}$ with $u_1, \ldots, u_n$ fresh URIs, $\tau(\mu(q))$ simulates into $\tau(\mathcal{D})$.* [17]

Example 22 (Term simulation with blank nodes). Let q :=

```
_:X{{
  p → _:Y{{
    p → a{{ p → _:Y, p → b }},
    r → _:Z
  }},
  p → b {{ r → _:Z, p → a }}
}}
```

, $d_1 := b\{ p \to a \{ p \to b \} \}$ and $d_2 := b\{ p \to a \{ p \to b, r \to \_:W\{ r \to a \} \} \}$ as illustrated in Figure 1

- q *does not simulate into d_1 since there is no mapping from the blank nodes of q to the URIs in d_1 (there are no blank nodes in d_1) such that q simulates into d_1.*

- q *does simulate into d_2 for the following reason: for the mapping $\mu := \{\_:X \to a, \_:Y \to b, \_Z \to :W\}$, $\mu(q) = d_2$. Hence the conditions of Definition 34 are (almost trivially) fulfilled.*

Theorem 6 (Simulation versus simple entailment). *Let G_1 and G_2 be two RDF graphs. If G_1 entails G_2 then all subgraphs of G_2 represented as query terms with double curly braces simulate into $\text{term}(G_1)$, where $\text{term}(G_1)$ is the representation of G_1 as a set of XCERPT^{RDF} data terms.*

Theorem 6 is a consequence of the Interpolation Lemma 5.

It would be nice to have a decision procedure for simple entailment based on term simulation. Unfortunately we can only have such a decision procedure for the negative case, i.e. we can show that a graph g_1 does not entail a graph g_2 by query term simulation based on the observation in Theorem 6. For the postive case we would need Theorem 6 to hold in both directions. To see that the "if" condition in Theorem 6 is not an "if and only if" condition consider the two RDF graphs $g_1 := \{(a, p, \_:X), (b, p, \_:X)\}$ and $g_2 := \{(a, p, \_:Y), (b, p, \_:Z)\}$. All query terms corresponding to subgraphs of g_1 simulate into g_2, however, g_2

---

[17] $\mu(q)$ denotes the query term obtained from q by substituting all blank nodes according to μ, and analogously for $\tau(\mu(q))$ and $\tau(\mathcal{D})$.

does not entail g_1. To obtain a characterization of simple entailment in terms of simulation, XCERPT^{RDF} terms would have to be extendend by *reverse predicates*, such that we could represent g_1 as a *single* term $\_{:}X\{\{p \leftarrow a, p \leftarrow b\}\}$. Alternatively, simulation could be defined between *sets* of XCERPT^{RDF} query terms and sets of XCERPT^{RDF} data terms. Both these extensions are straightforward, and thus omitted for the sake of brevity.

In the remainder of this section, ground term simulation is extended to the non-ground term simulation between the set of all query terms and the set of all construct terms in a similar way the extension to terms with blank nodes. While simulation of XCERPT^{RDF} terms containing blank nodes suffices for the specification of the stratified fix-point semantics and the well-founded semantics for XCERPT^{RDF} programs, for backward chaining the simulation of possibly non-ground query terms with possibly non-ground construct terms must be evaluated – i.e. bindings for the variables in both terms must be calculated. This section does not deal with the operational semantics of XCERPT^{RDF} programs, but it gives a *declarative* semantics for non-ground term simulation, since non-ground term simulation is important for the *evaluation* of XCERPT^{RDF} programs. Often, the simulation of a query term with a construct term yields constraints *besides* variable bindings. These constraints can be used to optimize backward chaining. This section does not elaborate on these constraints.

In contrast to the bindings for blank nodes, the bindings for variables in XCERPT^{RDF} are of interest to the author of a query term, and thus the notions of (typed) variable bindings, substitutions, substitution-sets, equivalence classes for substitution sets and the application of substitution sets to non-ground XCERPT^{RDF} terms are introduced. This procedure is in line with the definition of term simulation for Xcerpt^{XML} terms, but extends Xcerpt^{XML} simulation by the notions of *well-typed* bindings, substitutions and substitution sets. Variable types are introduced in XCERPT^{RDF} to avoid the construction of invalid RDF graphs, such as graphs that contain a triple in subject position or a blank node in predicate position. Moreover, XCERPT^{RDF} simulation is different from Xcerpt^{XML} simulation in that it must treat blank nodes as existentially quantified variables.

Definition 35 (XCERPT^{RDF} Binding, Substitution, Substitution Set). *An* XCERPT^{RDF} *binding is a pair* (V, T) *where* V *is an* XCERPT^{RDF} *variable or blank node and* t *is an* XCERPT^{RDF} *Term. An* XCERPT^{RDF} *binding* (V, t) *is well-typed if the following conditions hold:*

- *If* V *is a blank node, then* t *must be a URI or Literal or blank node itself.*

- *If* V *is a variable with type* $t(V) = $ node *– i.e.* V *is a node variable – then* t *must be an atomic* XCERPT^{RDF} *term.*

- *If* $t(V) = $ arc *– i.e.* V *is an arc variable – then* t *must be an* XCERPT^{RDF} *arc.*

- *If* $t(V) = $ predicate *– i.e.* V *is a predicate variable – then* t *must be an* XCERPT^{RDF} *predicate.*

- *If* $t(V) = $ graph *– i.e.* V *is a graph variable – then* t *must be an* XCERPT^{RDF} *term.*

- *If* $t(V) = \text{cbd}$ – *i.e.* V *is a concise bounded description variable – then* t *must be an* XCERPT^{RDF} *term representing a concise bounded description.*

An XCERPT^{RDF} *substitution over a set of* XCERPT^{RDF} *variables* $\mathcal{V}$ *is a set of bindings* $s = \{(v_1, t_1), \ldots, (v_n, t_n)\}$ *such that* $\mathcal{V} \supseteq \{v_1, \ldots, v_n\}$. $\{v_1, \ldots, v_n\}$ *is called the* domain $\text{dom}(s)$ *of* s, $\{t_1, \ldots, t_n\}$ *its* range $\text{range}(s)$. *An* XCERPT^{RDF} *substitution is well-typed, if each of its bindings is well-typed. An* XCERPT^{RDF} *substitution set over a set of variables* $\mathcal{V}$ *is a set of* XCERPT^{RDF} *substitutions over* $\mathcal{V}$. *An* XCERPT^{RDF} *substitution set* S *is well-typed if each of its substitutions is well-typed and for all substitutions* $s_i, s_j \in S$ *and each variable* $v \in \text{dom}(s_i) \cap \text{dom}(s_j)$ *the type of* v *in* s_i *and* s_j *coincides.*

Definition 36 (Equivalence Classes for Substitution Sets). *Let* S *be an* XCERPT^{RDF} *substitution set and* $\mathcal{V}$ *a set of* XCERPT^{RDF} *variables. The equivalence classes of* S *with respect to* $\mathcal{V}$ *is the* set of substitution sets $\Sigma(S, \mathcal{V}) = \{s \subseteq S \mid \forall s_i, s_j \in S \left(\forall v \in \mathcal{V} \left(s_i(v) = s_j(v)\right)\right) \wedge s \text{ is maximal}\}.$

Equivalence classes are introduced for grouping variable bindings within XCERPT^{RDF} construct terms according to the involved grouping constructs. As in [Scho4a] in the case of *implicit* grouping constructs, equivalence classes are computed with respect to the *free variables* of a term $FV(t)$. In the case of *explicit* grouping, equivalence classes are computed with respect to the free variables in a term plus the set of explicitly mentioned variables in the group-by clause. A variable X is free within a term t, if it does not appear within a grouping construct in t.

Free variables, bound variables, grouping

Definition 37 (Application of a substitution set to XCERPT^{RDF} terms). *Let* S *be an* XCERPT^{RDF} *substitution set, and* q *an* XCERPT^{RDF} *query term.* S *is* applicable *to* q *iff*

- S *is well-typed*
- *all non-optional variables in* q *are in* $\bigcap_{s \in S} \text{dom}(s)$[18]
- *for all variables* v *in* q, *the types of* v *in* S *and* q *coincide.*

If S *is not applicable to* q, *then the application* $S(q)$ *of* S *to* q *results in the empty set. Otherwise,* $S(q)$ *results in a multi-set of* XCERPT^{RDF} *query terms defined as follows:*

- *if* $|\Sigma(S, FV(q))| > 1$ *then* $S(q) = \{S'(q) \mid S' \in \Sigma(S, FV(q))\}$.
- *if* $|\Sigma(S, FV(q))| = 1$ *then*
  - *if* q *is an* XCERPT^{RDF} *variable, then* $S(q)$ *is the binding for* q *in* S *(by assumption there is only one binding for* q).
  - *if* q *is a URI, blank node identifier or RDF literal, then* $S(q) = \{q\}$
  - *if* q *is of the form* all q' *then* $S(q)$ *is* $S(q')$.[19]
  - *if* q *is a compound term of the form* label{{$t_1, \ldots, t_n$}} *or* label{$t_1, \ldots, t_n$} *with subterms (i.e. arcs, containers or collections)* $t_1, \ldots, t_n$ *then* $S(q) = $ label{{ $S(t_1), \ldots, S(t_n)$ }} *and* label{ $S(t_1), \ldots, S(t_n)$ }, *respectively.*

---
18 optional, negative and positive variables are defined as in [Scho4a].
19 Note that the set of free variables $FV(q)$ is in general a subset of $FV(q')$. Hence, the substitution set S' will be separated into equivalence classes before it is applied to q'.

Definition 38 (Non-ground XCERPT^{RDF} simulation). *Let q be an XCERPT^{RDF} query term and c an XCERPT^{RDF} construct term. q simulates into c iff there is some substitution ϕ and some substitution set Φ such that $\phi(q)$ and all terms in $\Phi(c)$ are ground and $\phi(q) \preceq t$ for some $t \in \Phi(c)$.*

A substitution μ is a unifier for q and c, iff for all grounding substitution sets Σ, and for all $t_1 \in \Sigma(\mu(q))$ there is some $t_2 \in \Sigma(\mu(c))$ with $t_1 \preceq t_2$.

Example 23. *Consider the query term* q = a{{ var X → var X }} *and the construct term* c = a{ var Y → d }. *q simulates into c since for* $\phi = \{X \to d\}$ *and* $\Phi = \{\{Y \to d\}\}$, $\phi(q) = $ a{{ d → d }} *simulates into the only element* a{ d → d } *in* $\Phi(c)$.

Example 24. *Let* q = a{{ arcVar X, arcVar Y }} *and* c = a { all arcVar Z }. *q simulates into c since for* $\phi = \{X \to (b \to d), Y \to (d \to e)\}$ *and* $\Phi = \{\{Z \to (b \to d)\}, \{Z \to (d \to e)\}\}$, $\phi(q)$ *is* a{{ b → d, d → e }} *and simulates into the only element* a{ b → d, d → e } *of* $\Phi(c)$.

5.5 XCERPT^{RDF} QUERIES, FACTS, RULES AND PROGRAMS

With the semantics of single XCERPT^{RDF} terms fixed in the previous section, this section builds upon XCERPT^{RDF} to build queries (Definition 39), facts (Definition 40), rules (Definition 41) and programs (Definition 42), which are defined in-line with the same notions for Xcerpt^{XML}.

XCERPT^{RDF} queries serve to express sophisticated conditions on RDF graphs available on the Web, on the local computer, or on graphs constructed as an intermediate result via a rule in the rule program. XCERPT^{RDF} queries can be formed based on XCERPT^{RDF} terms via conjunctions, disjunctions, negations and resource specifications. All XCERPT^{RDF} queries can be brought into disjunctive normal form, i.e. with disjunctions appearing only on the outermost level, not within one of the other constructors for queries. Therfore disjunctions are mere syntactic sugar notation for multiple rules with the same body. For the purpose of evaluation, the disjunctive normal form of queries can save considerable implementation efforts.

Definition 39 (XCERPT^{RDF} queries). *XCERPT^{RDF} queries are recursively defined as follows:*

- *any XCERPT^{RDF} query term is an XCERPT^{RDF} query*

- *if q is an XCERPT^{RDF} query and u is a URI, then* in{ resource{ u , q } } *is an XCERPT^{RDF} query.*

- *if $q_1, \ldots q_n$ are XCERPT^{RDF} queries, then* and$(q_1, \ldots, q_n)$ *is an XCERPT^{RDF} query, also called a conjunction.*

- *if $q_1, \ldots, q_n$ are XCERPT^{RDF} queries, then* or$(q_1, \ldots, q_n)$ *is an XCERPT^{RDF} query, also called a disjunction.*

- *if q is an XCERPT^{RDF} query, then* not(q) *is the negation of q, and also an XCERPT^{RDF} query.*

XCERPT^{RDF} facts are essentially equivalent to XCERPT^{RDF} named graphs and XCERPT^{RDF} data terms. Facts serve to specify the data that is known, or that is provided by some resource. In a forward chaining evaluation of XCERPT^{RDF} programs, facts are produced as intermediate results and saved in main memory as possible justifications for future rule applications. Any RDF graph on the Web[20] can be seen as an XCERPT^{RDF} fact, but to be accessible, graphs on the Web must be queried with the resource construct of Definition 39. In this way, the set of facts of Xcerpt programs is manageably small. If a graph that is not available on the Web or as a file is to be queried, it must be included between the Xcerpt key words CONSTRUCT and END.

Definition 40 (XCERPT^{RDF} facts). *If g is an* XCERPT^{RDF} *graph, and d is an* XCERPT^{RDF} *data term, then* CONSTRUCT g END *and* CONSTRUCT d END *are* XCERPT^{RDF} *facts.*

Construct terms within XCERPT^{RDF} rules serve to construct intermediate results. These results may be single terms, XCERPT^{RDF} graphs in the case of multiple root nodes, or XCERPT^{RDF} named graphs, if provenance information is to be encoded. XCERPT^{RDF} rules and goals are constructed from XCERPT^{RDF} queries and heads. In a forward chaining evaluation of XCERPT^{RDF} programs, the presence of XCERPT^{RDF} goals is not necessary, whereas a backward chaining evaluation requires the presence of exactly one goal. Goals serve to specify the information that a query author is interested in and can save their specification can save a considerable amount of computations, since they allow the goal-directed backward search for answers. In many circumstances, one is not interested in some fraction of information derivable from a given set of rules, but in the entire *closure* specified by the rules. Use cases for this situation are trueth maintenance systems, online analytical processing or the computation of the RDFS closure of an RDF graph. In these cases, forward chaining is the method of choice, and the XCERPT^{RDF} programs will not include any goals.

Definition 41 (XCERPT^{RDF} rules). *If* $c_1, \ldots, c_n$ *are* XCERPT^{RDF} *construct terms and* u *is an URI, then* c_1, RDFGRAPH { $c_1, \ldots, c_n$ } *and* RDFGRAPH u { $c_1, \ldots, c_n$ } *are* XCERPT^{RDF} *rule heads. If* h *is an* XCERPT^{RDF} *rule head and* q *is an* XCERPT^{RDF} *query, then* CONSTRUCT h FROM q END *is called an* XCERPT^{RDF} *rule, and* GOAL h FROM q END *is called an* XCERPT^{RDF} *goal.*

Definitions 39 and 41 do *not include* the syntax of versatile rules, i.e. those rules which query XML and RDF data at the same time, or convert XML to RDF or conversely. Versatile rules are obtained when allowing (i) XML query terms in XCERPT^{RDF} queries, (ii) XCERPT^{RDF} query terms within Xcerpt^{XML} queries, (iii) Xcerpt^{XML} construct terms within XCERPT^{RDF} rules, or (iv) XCERPT^{RDF} construct terms within Xcerpt^{XML} rules. For case (i) and (ii) equivalence between bindings for variables of different types must be defined – e.g. for the bindings of XCERPT^{RDF} node or predicate variables and Xcerpt^{XML} label variables. For (iii) a mapping from XCERPT^{RDF} substitution sets to Xcerpt^{XML} substitution sets must be defined, and for (iv) bindings for Xcerpt^{XML} variables must be converted in a standard way to bindings for XCERPT^{RDF} variables. The syntax of XCERPT^{RDF} programs is defined in the very same way as the one of Xcerpt^{XML} programs.

Definition 42 (XCERPT^{RDF} programs). *Let* p *be an XML namespace prefix [BHLT06], and* u *a URI. Then* ns-prefix p = "u" *is a namespace declaration and* ns-prefix = "u" *is a default namespace declaration. If* $d_1 \ldots, d_l$ *are namespace declarations with at most one default namespace declaration,*

---

20 Or on the Internet – the set of protocols available to the resource construct is not limited, but implementation dependent.

$f_1, \ldots, f_m$ *are* XCERPT^{RDF} *facts and* $r_1, \ldots, r_n$ *are* XCERPT^{RDF} *rules or goals (with at most one goal), then* $d_1, \ldots, d_l, f_1, \ldots, f_m, r_1, \ldots, r_m$ *is an* XCERPT^{RDF} *program. Namespace prefixes must precede facts and rules, but rules may also appear before facts.*

6 THE XCERPT^{RDF} REGULAR PATH LANGUAGE RPL

Contents

6.1 Design Goals of RPL 119
6.2 RPL by Example 120
6.3 Syntax of RPL 123
6.4 Compositional Semantics of RPL 124
6.5 Restrictions and Extensions of RPL 127
6.6 RPL compared to Lorel, SPARQLeR and nSPARQL 129
6.7 Further Complexity Results 132
6.8 Compilation of RPL to Prolog 135

Graph traversal operators play a crucial role in query languages for semi-structured data and for RDF query languages in particular. This need bas been acknowledged by the development of languages like Versa[Ogbo5] SPARQLeR[KJ07] and nested regular expressions (NRE) [PAG08] and underlined in [AGH04]. Moreover, the need for traversal of semi-structured data in general, and XML in particular is underscored by the huge success of XPath, arguably the most prominent XML query language.

The importance of path query languages for semi-structured data

XCERPT^{RDF} regular path expressions (RPEs) come in three flavors: *node-restricting*, *edge-restricting* and *path-restricting*, identified by the keywords NODES, EDGES, PATH, respectively. *Node-restricting* (*edge-restricting*) path expressions only place restrictions on the nodes (edges) appearing within a path. *Path-restricting* expressions may place restrictions on both, nodes and edges. RPEs evaluate to sets of pairs of nodes – i.e. binary relations over the set N of nodes of an RDF graph. The three unrestrictive RPEs [PATH _*], [EDGES _*] and [NODES _*] evaluate to N × N.

Three flavors of RPL

In this section we present the design goals of RPEs (Section 6.1), informally introduce their semantics by example (6.2) and formally define their syntax (Definition 45) and compositional semantics (Definition 49). Moreover we show that RPL can be evaluated in polynomial time in the size of the query and the data (Section 6.7), compare RPL to other path query languages (Section 6.6), show the intractability of RPL (and path query lanugages in general) extended by unordered paths (Section 6.5), and briefly describe an implementation of RPL by a translation to XSB Prolog (Section 6.8).

Overview of this section

6.1 DESIGN GOALS OF RPL

The Regular Path Language (RPL) was conceived with the following design goals in mind:

- *Usability* and *Intuitiveness*: Good language design includes the reuse of established and successful querying formalisms, and the precise reflection of the data model a user has in mind. Arguably, the most popular formalism for matching sequences of characters are regular expressions, and the data model of RDF are unordered, edge- and node-labeled directed graphs. RPEs build upon these concepts and are thus easy to learn for users acquainted with regular expressions and RDF.

- *Conciseness*: While regular expressions allow the concise description of sequencing, alternation and closure, URIs in path expressions may be abbreviated by qualified names. Namespace prefixes must be defined outside of the RPE, e.g. by a surrounding SPARQL or Xcerpt^{RDF} program.

- *Expressiveness*: While RPEs are designed as an extension to SPARQL graph patterns and Xcerpt^{RDF} query terms, they are quite expressive on their own. Restrictions can be placed on the paths themselves, on each of the edges or nodes on the path via regular expressions[1] or functions, and non-locally on the edges or nodes connected to one of the nodes on a path via *nested path expressions*.

- *Versatile navigation*: RDF queries taking into account the RDF Schema semantics, such as finding all direct and indirect instances of a given rdfs:Class or rdfs:Property ignore the nodes on the traversed path, but are only interested in the traversed predicates. Therefore SPARQLeR path expressions [KJ07] only consist of predicate names. Moreover RDF Schema queries require reverse navigation, i.e. navigation from the objects triples with predicate rdf:type, rdfs:subClassOf or rdfs:subPropertyOf to their subjects. RPEs allow both: navigation along predicates or nodes only, and navigation along paths consisting of predicates *and* nodes.

- *Easy integration*: RPEs are an independent sublanguage of Xcerpt^{RDF}, that can be used independently or in conjunction with other RDF query languages such as SPARQL. But only in conjunction with Xcerpt^{RDF}, they share its nice properties such as strong answer closedness and graph construction facilities.

6.2 RPL BY EXAMPLE

Before introducing RPL, we define the notions of RDF triples, graphs, and paths in RDF graphs.

Definition 43 (RDF triple, graph). *Let* U, B, L *be three disjoint sets of URIs, blank node identifiers and RDF literals. Then* $t = (s, p, o) \in U \cup B \times U \times U \cup B \cup L$ *is an RDF triple, and* $t_g \in U \times U \times U \cup L$ *is a ground RDF triple.* s, p, o *are the* subject, predicate *and* object *of* t, *respectively. A (ground) RDF graph is a set of (ground) RDF triples. The set of nodes* N *of an RDF graph* G *are all elements in* $U \cup B \cup L$ *that appear in subject or object position of a triple in* G.

Definition 44 (Path in an RDF graph). *Let* G *be an RDF graph. The sequence* $n_1, \ldots, n_k$ *is a path in* G, *iff the triples* (n_1, n_2, n_3), (n_3, n_4, n_5), $\ldots$, (n_{k-2}, n_{k-1}, n_k) *are in* G.

Example 25. *[PATH _ _ (eg:/.*/ _)* rdf:type]: All pairs* (n_1, n_2) *of nodes connected over intermediate nodes of the namespace eg. Additionally, the last*

---

1 While regular expressions and RPEs share many syntactic notations, they are clearly separated by delimiters

edge on the connecting path must correspond to the qualified name rdf:type. This first example demonstrates the following points:

- RPEs come in three flavors, indicated by the keywords NODES, EDGES and PATH, and lay restrictions on the nodes, edges or nodes *and* edges appearing on a path in an RDF graph, respectively.

- As in SPARQL, XPath, XQuery, XSLT and XCERPT[RDF], URIs may be abbreviated by qualified names.

- Wildcards (_) and regular string expressions[2] (e.g. /.*/) play an important role within RPEs. Together with qualified names, URIs and literals, they constitute the atomic building blocks of RPEs, called *atomic RPEs*.

- From atomic RPEs, *compound* RPEs can be built via *sequencing* (denoted by whitespace), *alternation* (|), *Kleene closure* (* and +), *optionality* (?), and *negation* (not(...)). If the RPE e evaluates to the binary relation r over the RDF graph G with node set N, then the RPE e* evaluates to the transitive-reflexive closure of r, e+ to the transitive closure of r, and e? to $r \cup \{(n,n) \mid n \in N\}$.

- Path flavored RPEs are expected to start with a subexpression that describes (amongst others) the initial node on the path, and expected to end with a subexpression that describes the last edge on the path. The first and third subexpression (and all other subexpression at an even position) describe a node on the path.

Example 26. *The expression [PATH _ eg:p (_[not(PATH eg:p1)] eg:p)*] collects all pairs of nodes connected over a path with at least one predicate with URI eg:p. All intermediate nodes must not have an outgoing eg:p1 edge. Thus, evaluated over the RDF graph G in Figure 2, this expression would yield the set of tuples $\{(n_0,n_1),(n_1,n_2),(n_1,n_3),(n_2,n_3)\}$, but not the tuples (n_0,n_2) or (n_0,n_3).*

Figure 2: An example RDF graph

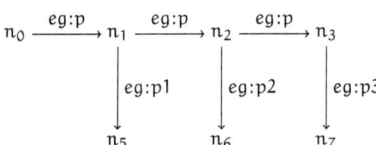

This second example introduces *path predicates* and demonstrates the following points:

- Path expressions may be nested via *path predicates*, which roughly correspond to XPath predicates. While URIs, qualified names or regular expressions within RPEs represent *local restrictions* only, predicates allow the specification of *non-local* restrictions, i.e., restrictions that are not directly enforced on nodes or edges on

---

2 We use the term *regular string expressions* to differntiate ordinary regular expressions from regular path expressions.

the path, but on nodes or edges connected via a nested path expression. Predicates may be made up of *positive* expresssions that *require the existence* of some nodes or predicates not directly on the path connecting the returned nodes, or of *negative* expressions that require the *absence* of certain branches in the graph.

- The expression $e_1 := (\_[\text{not}(\text{EDGES eg:p1})] \text{ eg:p})$ evaluates to all pairs of nodes (n_1, n_2) such that n_1 does not have an outgoing path starting with predicate eg:p1, and n_1 is connected to n_2 over an edge named eg:p. The expression $e_2 := (\_[\text{not}(\text{EDGES eg:p1})] \text{ eg:p})*$ evaluates to the transitive-reflexive closure of e_1. The purely transitive closure is obtained by using + instead of *.

Example 27. *The edge-flavored query [EDGES rdf:type (rdfs:subClassOf) *] evaluates to all pairs of nodes connected via one rdf:type edge and zero or more rdfs:subClassOf edges (in this order).*

This query determines the direct or indirect class membership of resources under the RDFS semantics. Note that also for many other RDF queries, only the edges along a path are relevant. The reverse relation is obtained by the query [EDGES (<rdfs:subClassOf)* <rdf:type].

Example 28. *The node-flavored expression [NODES (eg:a eg:b)] finds all pairs of nodes that are connected over nodes eg:a and eg:b (in this order), with arbitrary predicates on the path. The query [NODES (eg:/.*/ | foaf:/.*/)*] on the other hand, finds all pairs of nodes connected over a path of length zero or more which contains only intermediate nodes belonging to the namespaces eg or foaf. The predicates on the path are irrelevant, as indicated by the keyword NODES.*

Example 29 (RDFS querying with RDFLog augmented by RPL). *This example shows how RDF rule languages can be augmented by RPL path expressions to immitate the RDFS semantics.*

Due to its simplicity, we choose RDFLog [BFL+*08a] as the rule language to be extended. But similar embeddings can be given for most RDF rule languages, including the various SPARQL extensions with rules [Pol07, SS04, BFL*+*09b]. The RDFLog rule*[3]

$$\forall x \, p \, y \, p_1 \, z \, . \, (x \, p \, y) \leftarrow (x \, p_1 \, z), (p_1 \, [\textit{EDGES sp* }] \, y) \quad (6.1)$$

can be used to materialize the extension of the predicate p *under the RDFS semantics. In a backward chaining evaluation of an RDFLog program, materialization is only carried out on demand, and is thus more efficient than computing the RDFS closure of the queried graph. If only single rules or queries are allowed (such as in SPARQL), then the body of Equation 6.1 can simply be used in the query at the place of* p.

The extension of predicates with a special semantics under the RDFS model theory deserve special treatment. E.g the extension of rdf:type *is computed by the following RDFLog rules with RPL predicates:*

$$\forall x \, y \, . \, (x \, \text{type} \, y) \leftarrow (x \, [\textit{EDGES type sc*}] \, y)$$
$$\forall x \, y \, p_1 \, z \, . \, (x \, \text{type} \, y) \leftarrow (x \, p_1 \, z), (p_1 \, [\textit{EDGES sp* dom sc*}] \, y)$$
$$\forall x \, y \, p_1 \, z \, . \, (x \, \text{type} \, y) \leftarrow (z \, p_1 \, x), (p_1 \, [\textit{EDGES sp* range sc*}] \, y)$$

Querying RDF graphs under the RDFS semantics at the aid of RPL

---

[3] rdf:type, rdfs:subClassOf, rdfs:subPropertyOf, rdfs:range, and rdfs:domain are abbreviated by type, sc, sp, range and dom, respectively.

It can be shown that also extensions of the remaining RDFS predicates subclassOf, subPropertyOf, domain and range can be encoded as RDFLog or SPARQL rule bodies augmented with RPL. The encoding is analogous to the one presented in [PAG08] and is omitted here for the sake of brevity.

Example 30 (RQL query primitives translated to RPL). *As a final example, we show that all RQL query primitives (except for the nearest common ancestor relation) presented in Section 3.4 can be easily expressed in RPL.*

- *direct subclasses:* PATH Artist <rdfs:subClassOf _
- *direct and indirect subclasses:* PATH Artist (<rdfs:subClassOf _)+
- *direct subproperties:* PATH paints <rdfs:subPropertyOf _
- *direct and indirect subproperties:*
  PATH paints (<rdfs:subPropertyOf _)+
- *direct superclasses:* PATH Artist rdfs:subClassOf _
- *direct and indirect superclasses:* PATH Artist (rdfs:subClassOf _)+
- *direct superproperties:* PATH paints rdfs:subPropertyOf _
- *direct and indirect superproperties:*
  PATH paints (rdfs:subPropertyOf _)+
- *leaf classes:* PATH _[not(EDGES >rdfs:subClassOf)]
- *top classes:* PATH _[not(EDGES rdfs:subClassOf)]
- *leaf properties:* PATH _[not(EDGES >rdfs:subClassOf)]
- *top properties:* PATH _[not(EDGES rdfs:subClassOf)]

6.3 SYNTAX OF RPL

Definition 45 (Abstract syntax of RPEs). *The abstract syntax of RPL is recursively defined as follows:*

- *A URI* u, *regular expression* re, *qualified name* q, *literal* l *and wild card* _ *is an atomic RPE. Moreover, a qualified name* prefix:localpart *where* localpart *is a regular expression, is an atomic RPE.*
- *If* p *is an atomic path expression, then* p, < p, > p *and* ^p *are directed path expressions.*
- *if* p_1 *is an atomic RPE, and* $q_1, \ldots q_n$ *are RPL predicates (see below), then* p_1 *and* $p_1[q_1]\ldots[q_n]$ *are predicated RPEs.*
- *If* p *is a predicated or concatenated RPE, then* p, p∗, p+ *and* p? *are adorned RPEs.*
- *If* $p_1, \ldots p_n$ *are adorned or disjunctive (see below) RPEs, then* $(p_1 \ldots p_n)$ *with* $n \geqslant 1$ *is a concatenated RPE.*
- *If* $p_1, \ldots p_n$ *are concatenated RPEs, then* $(p_1 \mid \ldots \mid p_n)$ *with* $n \geqslant 1$ *is a disjunctive RPE.*
- *If* p *is a concatenated RPE,* PATH p, EDGES p, NODES p *are flavored RPEs. They are called path-restricting, edge-restricting and node-restricting expressions, respectively.*

Figure 3: Relationships among subexpressions of RPEs

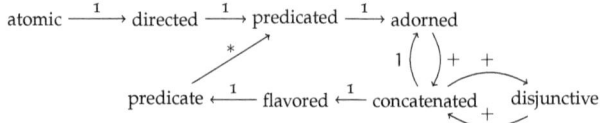

- If p *is a flavored RPE, then* p *and* not(p) *are RPL predicates.*

Figure 3 summarizes the relationships between the different types of subexpressions in RPL. An arrow labeled with 1, + or ∗ from type A to type B means that expressions of type B are made up of exactly one, at least one, or zero or more expression of type A, respectively. It holds that any atomic RPL expression is also a directed subexpression, which are in turn also predicated subexpressions, which are in turn adorned subexpressions. As in XQuery, a concatenated expression (called sequence in XQuery) of one element is equivalent to the element itself. Also a disjunctive RPE of one element is equivalent to the element itself.

The following remarks clarify Definition 45.

- Atomic RPEs correspond to the building blocks of ground RDF graphs with the following exceptions: (i) qualified names are allowed as shorthand notations for URIs, (ii) regular expressions are allowed as a means for matching URIs and Literals[4], (iii) the local part of a qualified name may be expressed by a regular expression, (iv) wildcards can be used to match any blank node, URI or literal.

- RPEs do not provide any means for selecting RDF literals based on their types or based on their language tags, other than using a regular expression for this purpose.

- Just as with ordinary regular (string) expressions, parentheses are used to influence operator precedence. The operators Kleene star (∗), Kleene plus (+), optionality (?) are mutually exclusive and have precedence over all other operators. The concatenation operator (denoted by whitespace) binds stronger than the disjunctive operator |, i.e. a b | c is equivalent to (a b) | c. Parentheses may be omitted, if they do not alter operator precedence.

6.4 COMPOSITIONAL SEMANTICS OF RPL

The intuitive presentation of the RPEs is now formalized by a compositional semantics, which is given by the function $[\![\cdot]\!]$ and its four helper functions $[\![\cdot]\!]^P$ for path-restricting expressions, $[\![\cdot]\!]^E$ for edge-restricting expressions, $[\![\cdot]\!]^N$ for node-restricting expressions and $[\![a]\!]^V$ for atomic expressions a that are evaluated in *vertex position*. While the functions

---

[4] matching blank nodes with regular expressions is not allowed, since this would mean *syntactic* matching of RDF graphs, i.e. the semantics of an RPE would be dependent on the syntactic representation of the RDF graph that is being queried.

6.4 COMPOSITIONAL SEMANTICS OF RPL

$[\![\cdot]\!]$, $[\![\cdot]\!]^P$, $[\![\cdot]\!]^E$ and $[\![\cdot]\!]^N$ evaluate to subsets of $N \times N$, i.e. binary relations on the set N of nodes of the queried RDF graph, the function $[\![\cdot]\!]^V$ evaluates to subsets of N.

In order to present the semantics in an easily digestible manner, we split the entire definition according to the flavor of the RPE to be formalized. Definition 46 gives the semantics for *edge-restricting* RPEs, Definitions 47, 48 and 49 add the necessary equations for *node-restricting*, *path-restricting* and arbitrary RPEs, respectively. The three flavors of RPEs differ in the way subexpressions are concatenated. In contrast, most equations for evaluating atomic RPEs, alternatives and Kleene closures are independent of the flavor and are only given once.

In the following, let G be an RDF graph over the vocabulary $U \cup B \cup L$, u a URI, l an RDF Literal, re a regular expression, a an atomic RPE, pe a predicated RPE, $f_1, \ldots f_k$ flavored RPEs, and e, $e_1, \ldots, e_k$ arbitrary RPEs.

Definition 46 (Semantics of edge-restricting RPEs). *The semantics of edge-restricting RPEs is given by the function $[\![\cdot]\!]^E$ defined as follows:*

$$[\![u]\!]^{E,P} = \{(n_1, n_2) \mid (n_1, u, n_2) \in G\} \quad (6.2)$$

$$[\![\_]\!]^{E,P} = \{(n_1, n_2) \mid \exists p . (n_1, p, n_2) \in G\} \quad (6.3)$$

$$[\![/re/]\!]^{E,P} = \{(n_1, n_2) \mid \quad (6.4)$$
$$\exists p \in \mathcal{L}(re) . (n_1, p, n_2) \in G\} \quad (6.5)$$

$$[\![>pe]\!]^X = [\![pe]\!]^X \text{ for } X \in \{E, P\} \quad (6.6)$$

$$[\![<pe]\!]^X = \{(n_2, n_1) \mid \quad (6.7)$$
$$(n_1, n_2) \in [\![>pe]\!]^X\} \text{ for } X \in \{E, P\} \quad (6.8)$$

$$[\![e_1 \ldots e_k]\!]^E = \{(n_1, n_{k-1}) \mid \exists n_2, \ldots n_k (\quad (6.9)$$
$$\forall 1 \leq i \leq k ((n_i, n_{i+1}) \in [\![e_i]\!]^E)) \} \quad (6.10)$$

$$[\![(e_1 \mid \ldots \mid e_k)]\!]^X = [\![e_1]\!]^X \cup \ldots \cup [\![e_k]\!]^X \text{ for } X \in \{P, E, N\} \quad (6.11)$$

$$[\![a[f_1] \ldots [f_k]]\!]^E = \bigcup_{a' \in [\![a[f_1] \ldots [f_k]]\!]^V} [\![a']\!]^E \quad (6.12)$$

$$[\![\epsilon]\!]^{E,P} = \{(n, n) \mid n \in N\} \quad (6.13)$$

$$[\![e+]\!]^X = [\![e]\!]^X \cup [\![e \; e+]\!]^X \text{ for } X \in \{P, E, N\} \quad (6.14)$$

$$[\![e*]\!]^X = [\![\epsilon]\!] \cup [\![e+]\!]^X \text{ for } X \in \{P, E, N\} \quad (6.15)$$

$$[\![e?]\!]^X = [\![\epsilon]\!] \cup [\![e]\!]^X \text{ for } X \in \{P, E, N\} \quad (6.16)$$

The centerpiece of Definition 46 is Equation 6.9. It states that the semantics of a sequence of edge-restricting RPEs is a binary relation of nodes (n_1, n_2) such that there is a path from n_1 to n_2 over arbitrary intermediate nodes $n_2, \ldots n_{k-1}$ such that these intermediate nodes are connected via the subexpressions $e_1, \ldots, e_k$.

The other equations in Definition 46 do not only hold for edge-restricting RPEs, but also for path-restricting ones, and some hold also for node-restricting expressions, as indicated by X.

Equations 6.2, 6.3 and 6.4 establish that a URI u evaluates to the pairs of nodes connected via a predicate of name u, the wildcard character _ to all pairs of nodes connected via an arbitrary predicate, and a regular string expression re to those pairs of nodes which are connected via a predicate that is in the language $\mathcal{L}(re)$ defined by re. Note that when part of a node-restricting expression, the semantics of URIs, wildcards and regular string expressions is different (see Definition 47).

Equations 6.6 and 6.7 formalize the specification of edge traversal in forward or reverse direction with the directions < and >. If no direction is given, then Equations 6.2, 6.3 and 6.4 hold, i.e. forward traversal is assumed.

Equations 6.13, 6.14, 6.15 and 6.16 define the semantics of the Kleene star, Kleene plus and optional parts of RPEs.

Formalizing the semantics of predicates within edge-restricting expressions, Equation 6.12 references Definition 47. Here the idea is to also allow the formulation of queries that use the same URI in predicate and subject or object position. An example for such queries from [PAG08] is finding all pairs of cities that are connected via some transportation service, given a hierarchy of transportation services and connections among cities using instances of this hierarchy.

Definition 47 (Semantics of node-restricting RPEs). *The semantics for node-restricting RPEs is defined as follows:*

$$
\begin{align}
\llbracket \_ \rrbracket^V &= N & (6.17) \\
\llbracket /re/ \rrbracket^V &= N \cap \mathcal{L}(re) & (6.18) \\
\llbracket u \rrbracket^V &= \{u\} \cap N & (6.19) \\
\llbracket l \rrbracket^V &= \{l\} \cap N & (6.20) \\
\llbracket pe \rrbracket^N &= \{(n,n) \mid n \in \llbracket pe \rrbracket^V\} & (6.21) \\
\llbracket a[f_1]\ldots[f_k] \rrbracket^V &= \llbracket a \rrbracket^V \cap \{n_1 \mid \exists n_2 . (n_1,n_2) \in \llbracket f_1 \rrbracket\} \cap & (6.22) \\
&\quad \ldots \cap \{n_1 \mid \exists n_2 . (n_1,n_2) \in \llbracket f_k \rrbracket\} & (6.23) \\
\llbracket e_1 \ldots e_k \rrbracket^N &= \{(n_1, n_{2k}) \mid & (6.24) \\
&\quad \exists n_2, \ldots n_{2k-1}, p_1, \ldots, p_{k-1} . \\
&\quad \forall 1 \leqslant i \leqslant k \, ((n_{2i-1}, n_{2i}) \in \llbracket e_i \rrbracket^N) \wedge \\
&\quad \forall 1 \leqslant i \leqslant k-1 \, ((n_{2i}, p_i, n_{2i+1}) \in G)\}
\end{align}
$$

While many RDFS queries only respect the predicates on a path between two resources and are therefore best expressed as edge-restricting RPEs, some path queries may only be interested in the traversed nodes and are better expressed as node-restricting RPEs. An example for this type of query is finding all pairs of persons in a social graph that are somehow connected over the resources anna and new_york. This query could be answered by the RPE NODES (anna new_york)| (new_york anna). Definition 47 formalizes node-restricting RPEs.

In this setting, a URI, regular string expression, wildcard or qualified name is evaluated in node position (Equation 6.21), and is thus treated differently from the evaluation within edge-restricting RPEs (Equation 6.2).

The core of Definition 47 is the formalization of node concatenation in Equation 6.24. Concatenations may involve arbitrary RPEs, i.e. atomic, predicated, directed, alternatives, Kleene closures and concatenations themselves. While the nodes on the path described by a node-restricting concatenation are given by the subexpressions of the concatenation, the predicates are arbitrary. Equation 6.24 makes use of the binary helper function $\llbracket \cdot \rrbracket^N$ defined on subexpressions, and the unary function $\llbracket \cdot \rrbracket^V$, which is part of the formalization of path-restricting RPEs.

Path-restricting RPEs are needed whenever constraints shall be laid both on the predicates and nodes on a path within an RDF graph. Equation 6.26 is the centerpiece of Definition 48. Path-restricting RPEs are expected to start and end with restrictions on the first and last *edge* of an RDF graph, because they are designed for easy integration with

6.5 RESTRICTIONS AND EXTENSIONS OF RPL   127

RDF query languages such as SPARQL and XCERPT^{RDF} where they are used at the place of RDF predicates. If the first and/or last restriction is laid on a node instead, this must be indicated with a '^' symbol, and Equations 6.27 and 6.28 apply.

Definition 48 (Semantics of path-restricting RPEs). *The semantics of path-restricting RPEs is defined as follows:*

$$[\![\hat{}a]\!] = [\![a]\!]^V \tag{6.25}$$

$$[\![e_1 \ldots e_k]\!]^P = \{(n_1, n_j) \mid \exists n_2, \ldots, n_{j-1} \;.\; \tag{6.26}$$
$$(n_1, n_2) \in [\![e_1]\!]^P \wedge n_2 \in [\![e_2]\!]^V \wedge$$
$$\ldots \wedge n_{j-1} \in [\![e_{k-1}]\!]^V \wedge (n_{j-1}, n_j) \in [\![e_k]\!]^P\}$$

$$[\![\hat{}pe\; e]\!]^P = \{(n_1, n_2) \in [\![e]\!]^P \mid n_1 \in [\![pe]\!]^V\} \tag{6.27}$$

$$[\![e\; \hat{}pe]\!]^P = \{(n_1, n_2) \in [\![e]\!]^P \mid n_1 \in [\![pe]\!]^V\} \tag{6.28}$$

Definition 49 (Semantics of flavored RPEs).

$$[\![\text{PATH } e]\!] = [\![e]\!]^P \tag{6.29}$$
$$[\![\text{EDGES } e]\!] = [\![e]\!]^E \tag{6.30}$$
$$[\![\text{NODES } e]\!] = \{(n_1, n_4) \mid \exists n_2, n_3, p_1, p_2 \;.\; \tag{6.31}$$
$$(n_2, n_3) \in [\![e]\!]^N \wedge (n_1, p_1, n_2), (n_3, p_2, n_4) \in G\}$$
$$[\![\text{not}(u)]\!] = [\![\_]\!] \setminus [\![u]\!] \tag{6.32}$$

6.5 RESTRICTIONS AND EXTENSIONS OF RPL

In order to compare RPL to other regular path languages over ordinary graphs and RDF graphs, and to study the complexity of RPL fragments, we introduce the following set of sublanguages:

Definition 50 (RPL sublanguages). *Besides the operators +, ? and ∗, RPL makes use of the following features:*

- *regular string expressions (denoted by RSE)*
- *the EDGE keyword (denoted by →)*
- *the NODE keyword (denoted by ○)*
- *the PATH keyword (denoted by -->)*
- *predicates (denoted by [])*
- *concatenation (denoted by /)*
- *disjunction (denoted by |)*
- *predicate negation (denoted by ¬)*
- *direction modifiers (denoted by μ)*

$RPL^{f_1,\ldots,f_k}$ *with* $f_1, \ldots, f_k \in \{RSE, \to, \circ, \dashrightarrow, [], /, |, \neg, \mu\}$ *denotes the sublanguage of RPL making use of the operators +, ?, and ∗ and the features* $f_1, \ldots, f_n$ *only.*

Languages such as XPath and Xcerpt allow queries to be incompletely specified in depth, or with respect to order. Incompleteness in depth is specified via the descendant axis in XPath and via the desc keyword in Xcerpt. Incompleteness with respect to order is the default querying mode in XPath and can be overridden by using the << operator; in Xcerpt it is specified via curly braces.

An obvious extension of RPL is thus to introduce *unordered* and *incomplete* paths. While the order in Xcerpt query terms is enforced/relaxed with respect to the *sibling* axis of an XML document, the order in RPEs may be relaxed with respect to the paths traversed, i.e. the *descendant* axis. Also the concept of *incomplete* specification of *siblings* in Xcerpt query terms may be transferred to the *descendant* axis by allowing double brackets within RPL. We denote the extensions of the sublanguages of RPL by unordered paths, incomplete paths and both by adding the symbols {}, [[ ]] or both to the feature list of the sublanguage. The RPL expression NODES { x y z } thus evaluates to all pairs of nodes that are connected by a path containing only the intermediate nodes x, y, and z in an arbitrary order. The RPL expression NODES [[x y]] on the other hand evaluates to all pairs of nodes that are connected via a path that contains the nodes x and y with x appearing before y, and an arbitrary number of nodes before x, between x and y and following y.

The semantics of {} is formalized by the functions $\llbracket \cdot \rrbracket^{UN}$, $\llbracket \cdot \rrbracket^{UE}$, and $\llbracket \cdot \rrbracket^{UP}$ for unordered node-flavored, edge-flavored and path-flavored expressions, respectively. The semantics of [[ ]] is given by the functions $\llbracket \cdot \rrbracket^{IN}$, $\llbracket \cdot \rrbracket^{IE}$, and $\llbracket \cdot \rrbracket^{IP}$.

Definition 51 (Semantics of unordered and incomplete RPEs).

$$\llbracket e \rrbracket^{UN} = \bigcup_{p \in Perm(e)} \llbracket p \rrbracket^{N} \qquad (6.33)$$

$$\llbracket e \rrbracket^{UE} = \bigcup_{p \in Perm(e)} \llbracket p \rrbracket^{E} \qquad (6.34)$$

$$\llbracket e \rrbracket^{UP} = \bigcup_{p \in Perm(e)} \llbracket p \rrbracket^{P} \qquad (6.35)$$

$$\llbracket e \rrbracket^{IN} = \bigcup_{c \in Comp(e)} \llbracket c \rrbracket^{N} \qquad (6.36)$$

$$\llbracket e \rrbracket^{IE} = \bigcup_{c \in Comp(e)} \llbracket c \rrbracket^{E} \qquad (6.37)$$

$$\llbracket e \rrbracket^{IP} = \bigcup_{c \in Comp(e)} \llbracket c \rrbracket^{P} \qquad (6.38)$$

A completion *of a sequence* $e := e_1, \ldots, e_n$ *is a sequence c that contains all elements of e plus an arbitrary number of wildcards. A completion of e is called* order-respecting, *iff for* $e_i, e_j \in e$ *with* $i < j$, e_i *appears in c before* e_j. Perm(e) *and* Comp(e) *denotes the set of all permutations and order respecting completions of e, respectively.*

Both extensions of RPL – to unordered paths and to incomplete paths – are mere syntactic sugar. The RPE NODES { x y } can be rewritten to the equivalent RPE NODES (x y)| (y x) and the RPE NODES [[x y]] can be rewritten to NODES _* x _* y _*. Observe that whereas the rewriting of incomplete path expressions is linear in the size of the original expression, the rewriting of unordered paths is exponential in the size of the original expression. We chose not to include incomplete RPEs in standard RPL, since one can easily do without them. On the other hand we chose not to include unordered RPEs in standard RPL, because it would make evaluation of RPL NP-hard as shown in Section 6.7.

The semantics of RPEs that are both unordered and incomplete (denoted by {{ }}) is easily defined at the aid of non-order-respecting permutations. For the sake of brevity, we omit this extension of RPL.

6.6 RPL COMPARED TO LOREL, SPARQLER AND NSPARQL

[ABE09] extends SPARQL by regular expression patterns which may occur at the place of predicates in RDF graphs. These regular expression patterns include amongst others Kleene closure, disjunction, concatenation, but not predicate negation and regular string expressions. Moreover, node labels are are not considered part of the path to be matched by the regular expression pattern.

The Lorel query language [AQM$^+$97] is an offspring of the XML database system Lore, but can be used to query all kinds of semistructured data. It has received considerable attention in the research community, partially due to its incorporation of regular path expressions.

RPEs compare to Lorel path expressions as follows:

- The data model of Lorel is an edge-labeled graph, without node labels. Therefore Lorel does not distinguish the three flavors of RPEs.

- Both languages provide the unary operators Kleene plus (+), Kleene star (*) and optionality (?), and the binary operators concatenation (denoted by '.' in Lorel), and alternative.

- Lorel allows the use of the character '%' to match 0 or more characters within a label. RPL on the other hand allows regular string expressions. Wildcards for entire labels are denoted by '#' in Lorel and '_' in RPL.

- Lorel allows the extraction of values from traversed paths by so-called path variables. RPEs do not use variables since they may be embedded in RDF query language such as SPARQL or XCERPT^{RDF}, that provide themselves variables.

- RPEs allow the restriction of paths based on path predicates, Lorel does not. Hence Example 26 is not expressible in Lorel.

In [MW95] the evaluation of regular expressions over the alphabet σ of an edge-labeled graph g is studied. Compared to RPEs, [MW95] considers the labels of edges to be atomic, i.e. they do not consider regular string expressions on node or edge-level. Moreover, non-local restrictions on paths (i.e. predicates) and traversal in reverse direction are not expressible. Since nodes in the queried graphs are unlabelled, only the edge labels are relevant, i.e. the path expressions in [MW95] correspond to a subset of edge-flavored RPEs.

[MW95] considers the problems *Regular Simple Path*, *Fixed Regular Path (R)*, and *Regular Path*. The problem Regular Simple Path takes a regular expression e, a graph g over the same alphabet Σ, and a pair of nodes (x,y) as input, and returns true iff g contains a directed simple path from x to y that satisfies e. A path is called *simple*, if it does not contain the same vertex twice. The problem Fixed Regular Path is the same as regular simple path, but e is not considered as input. Regular Path is the same as Regular Simple Path, but the path is not required to be simple.

[MW95] show that Fixed Regular Simple Path is NP-complete and Regular Simple Path is NP-hard by a simple reduction from the problems Even Path and Disjoint Paths treated in [LP84] and [FHW78], respectively. Regular Path, however, is decidable in polynomial time in the size of the data and query (combined complexity) – shown by the construction of a product automaton of the NFA of a regular path expression and the database graph interpreted as a NFA. In RPL we choose to accept arbitrary paths, including non-simple paths as possible connections among two nodes. RPEs are more expressive than the regular path expressions of [MW95] in three respects: (i) They allow the specification of predicates on nodes, (ii) regular expressions for matching edge and node labels, and (iii) in that they take into account also the labels of *nodes*. Therefore, the results of [MW95] leave the question, if there is a polynomial time algorithm for the evaluation problem of RPEs, open. The following result for the complexity of RPL$^{\rightarrow,/,|,\mu}$ expressions is a direct consequence of the complexity *Regular Path*.

Corollary 1. *RPL$^{\rightarrow,/,|,\mu}$ can be evaluated in time $O(|E||G|)$, where $|E|$ is the size of the path expression and $|G|$ is the size of the queried RDF graph.*

[PAG08] propose the regular path language nested regular expressions (NRE) with the following syntax:

$$\text{exp} := \text{axis} \mid \text{axis::a} \ (a \in U) \mid \text{axis::[exp]} \mid \text{exp/exp} \mid \text{exp|exp} \mid \text{exp}^* \quad (6.39)$$

where $\text{axis} \in \{\text{self}, \text{next}, \text{next}^{-1}, \text{node}, \text{node}^{-1}, \text{edge}, \text{edge}^{-1}\}$ and U denotes the set of URIs. The axes next, edge and node are used to navigate from one node in an RDF graph to an adjacent one, from a node to one of its outgoing edges and from an edge to its sink. If the starting node is left unspecified, next, edge and node can be interpreted as binary relations over an RDF graph G. Node tests following the axes next, edge and node constrain the label of a traversed edge, the object of an arc, and the subject, respectively. The semantics of the predicates [], alternatives |, Kleene star *, and concatenation / are as expected.

In this section we briefly give an intuitive semantics of NRE by translating Examples 25, 26, 27 and 28 to NREs.

We abbreviate URIs in a NRE by qualified names to shorten the examples.

Example 31 (Nested regular expressions). • *Example 25 is contained in the NRE (next)*/next::rdf:type. An exact translation is not possible due to the absence of regular string expressions for matching nodes or edges of RDF graphs.*

- *Example 26 is contained in the NRE (next::eg:p)$^+$. An exact translation is not possible due to the absence of negation in NRE predicates.*

- *Example 27 is equivalent to next::rdf:type/(next::rdfs:subClassOf)*.*

- *The first RPL expression in Example 28 is equivalent to the NRE next/self::eg:a/next/self::eg:b.*

- *The NRE*

  $$next::a/(next::[next::a/self::b])^*/(next::[node::b] \mid next::a)^+ \quad (6.40)$$

  *from [PAG08] is contained in the RPE [EDGES a(_[PATH a b]) * _].
  An exact translation to an RPE is not possible, since RPEs always
  evaluate to pairs of nodes of an RDF graph. In contrast, NREs may
  also evaluate to pairs of edges and nodes, as the subexpression "node::b"
  of Expression 31 does. Expression 31 can, however, be translated to
  an equivalent* XCERPT^{RDF} *query term or SPARQL query pattern that
  makes use of a single RPE.*

Given an NRE exp, an RDF graph G, and a pair of nodes (n_1, n_2), the problem whether there is a path from n_1 to n_2 matching exp within G, can be decided in $O(|G| \cdot |exp|)$.

Corollaries 2 and 3 shed light on the expressive relationship between fragments of RPL and NREs. An immediate consequence of corollary 2 is corollary 4.

Corollary 2. *Any RPE* $r \in RPL^{\rightarrow,\circ,--\rightarrow,[],/,|,\mu}$ *can be translated to an equivalent NRE of length* $\mathcal{O}(|r|)$.

Proof. The translation function from $RPL^{\rightarrow,\circ,--\rightarrow,[],/,|,\mu}$ to nested regular expressions (NRE) is given in Listing 6.1. Obviously, the size of to _nSPARQL(exp) is linear in the size of exp for any RPL expression in $RPL^{\rightarrow,\circ,--\rightarrow,[],/,|,\mu}$.

Listing 6.1: Translation from RPL to NREs

```
to_NRE(EDGES exp)               = to_NRE(exp, edges)
to_NRE(NODES exp)               = next/to_NRE(exp, nodes)/next
to_NRE(PATH  exp)               = to_NRE(exp, path)
to_NRE(exp*, mode)              = to_NRE(exp, mode)*
to_NRE(exp+, mode)              = to_NRE(exp, mode)+
to_NRE(exp?, mode)              = self | to_NRE(exp, mode)

to_NRE(_, edges)                = next
to_NRE(u, edges)                = next::u
to_NRE(>u, edges)               = next::u
to_NRE(<u, edges)               = next⁻¹::u
to_NRE(u[p₁]...[pₙ], edges)     =
  next::u[to_NRE(p₁)]...[to_NRE(pₙ)]
to_NRE(exp₁ |...| expₙ, mode)   =
  to_NRE(exp₁, mode) |...| to_NRE(expₙ, mode)
to_NRE(exp₁ ... expₙ, edges)    =
  to_NRE(exp₁, edges)/.../to_NRE(expₙ, edges)

to_NRE(_, nodes)                = self
to_NRE(u, nodes)                = self::u
to_NRE(exp₁ ... expₙ, nodes)    =
  to_NRE(exp₁, nodes)/next/.../next/to_NRE(expₙ, nodes)
to_NRE(a[p₁] ... [pₙ], nodes)   =
  self::a[to_NRE(p₁)] ... [to_NRE(pn)]

to_NRE(^a, path)                = self::a
to_NRE(>a, path)                = next::a
to_NRE(<a, path)                = next⁻¹::a
to_NRE(exp₁ ... exp_n, path)    =
  to_NRE(exp₁, edges)/to_NRE(exp₂,nodes)/.../
  to_NRE(expₙ₋₁,nodes)/to_NRE(expₙ,edges)
```

NREs do not support the Kleene optionality operator ?. Nevertheless RPL expressions with ? can be translated to a NRE by using the self axis without a node test, which has the same semantics as the empty path expression in RPL.

Note that some syntactically correct RPL expressions are not given a semantics in Section 6.4. Among these expressions are EDGES ^a, NODES >a, NODES <a or PATH >a >b. Similarly, these expressions are not handled by the translation function. For implementations, there are two possible ways of treating such expressions: Raising a syntax error at parse time, or evaluation to the empty relation over all possible input graphs.

Corollary 3. *Any NRE p_n excluding the axes* node, node^{-1}, edge, *and* edge^{-1} *can be translated to an equivalent RPE p_c of length $O(|p_n|)$.*

Proof. For the translation of nested regular expression (NRE) including only the axes next, next^{-1} and self, the expression is first normalized by inserting steps along the self axis without node tests. The resulting expression e does not contain consecutive steps along the axes next and next^{-1}, but the axis next and next^{-1} on the one hand and the axis self on the other hand alternate. This transformation is done for both the expression itself and for any subexpression appearing within a predicate. For example the NRE

$$\text{next}^{-1}\text{::b/next[next::a/next::b]/next}^{-1}\text{::c}$$

is normalized to

$$\text{next}^{-1}\text{::b/self/next[next::a/self/next::b]/self/next}^{-1}\text{::c} \, .$$

Obviously, this transformation preserves the semantics of the expression. Subsequently, the transformed expression is translated to RPL according to the function to_rpl in Listing 6.2. Obviously size of the resulting expression is linear in the size of the original.

Listing 6.2: Translation of NREs to RPL.

```
to_rpl(step₁/.../stepₙ) = PATH to_rpl(step₁) ... to_rpl(stepₙ)
to_rpl(next) = >_
to_rpl(next::a) = >a
to_rpl(next⁻¹) = <_
to_rpl(next⁻¹::a) = <a
to_rpl(self) = ^_
to_rpl(sefl::a) = ^a
```

□

Corollary 4. *A RPE p_c in RPL$^{\rightarrow,\circ,--\rightarrow,[],/,|,\mu}$ can be evaluated in $O(|G| \cdot |p_c|)$.*

6.7 FURTHER COMPLEXITY RESULTS

The comparison of RPL to related path query languages in the last section has already brought up some complexity results for sublanguages of RPL. In this section we establish the tractability of RPL as a whole and the intractability of RPL with unordered paths.

6.7 FURTHER COMPLEXITY RESULTS   133

Theorem 7 (Tractability of RPL and $NRE^{RSE,\neg}$). *RPL and the extension of NRE by regular string expressions and predicate negation (denoted by $NRE^{RSE,\neg}$) can be evaluated in time $O(|exp| \cdot |G|)$.*

Proof. (Sketch) Theorem 7 builds upon Corollary 4, that establishes that the evaluation of $RPL^{\rightarrow,\circ,--\ast,[],/,|,\mu}$ is in $O(|exp| \cdot |G|)$. The only features missing in $RPL^{\rightarrow,\circ,--\ast,[],/,|,\mu}$ when compared to full RPL are predicate negation ($\neg$) and regular string expressions (RSE). The evaluation of regular string expressions by *deterministic* finite automata (DFAs) is linear. However, conversion of a regular string expression r into a DFA may yield a DFA whose size is exponential in the size of r. If r does not contain any * and ? operators (but may contain + operators), r can be directly converted into a DFA in linear time. Thus, defining the size of an RDF graph as the total length of the characters appearing within its nodes and edges, the complexity remains in $O(|exp| \cdot |G|)$ when regular string expressions (without * and ?) are added to the language.

Showing that predicate negation has no effect on evaluation complexity is a little more tricky: Consider the proof of the tractability of NRE in [PAG08]. It involves the construction of product automata $G \times \mathcal{A}_p$ for each predicate p appearing in the expression exp to be evaluated. We can extend NRE to $NRE^{\neg}$ by allowing predicate negation in the same way as RPL allows predicate negation. A RPE p_c with predicate negation can then be translated to an $NRE^{\neg}$ expression p_n in linear time, such that the size of p_n remains linear in the size of p_c.

It remains to be shown that $NRE^{\neg}$ is in $O(|exp| \cdot |G|)$. For this end, we adapt the algorithm LABEL(G, exp) from [PAG08] to label both positive and negative predicates appearing in exp. For each negative predicate not(p) we introduce the label not_p which is attached to each node n in G *not* matching with p. Then, for each negative predicate not(p) in exp, we replace not(p) by not_p, thereby obtaining an ordinary NRE expression exp^+. exp^+ evaluates to true over G with the adapted labeling algorithm if and only if exp evaluates to true over G with the original labeling algorithm.   □

Theorem 8 (NP-Completeness of $RPL^{\circ,/,\{\}}$). *The evaluation problem for $RPL^{\circ,/,\{\}}$ is NP-complete.*

Proof. Obviously the evaluation problem for $RPL^{\circ,/,\{\}}$ is in NP. We show its NP-hardness by a reduction from the directed Hamiltonian path problem. Let G be an arbitrary RDF graph with nodes $\{n_1, \ldots, n_k\}$. Then G has a directed Hamiltonian path if and only if the RPE { NODES $n_1, \ldots n_k$ } has a non-empty solution over G.
                                                                         □

Theorem 9. *The evaluation problem for $RPL^{\rightarrow,/,\{\}}$ is in $O(n \cdot \sigma^w \cdot e)$ where n is the number of nodes of the RDF graph, e the number of edges, σ the number of edge labels, and w is the length of the path expression.*

Corollary 5. *The evaluation problem for $RPL^{\rightarrow,/}$ is in $O(e \cdot w)$ where w is the length of the regular path expression and e is the number of edges in the RDF graph.*

Proof. Theorem 9 only gives an upper bound for the evaluation of $RPL^{\rightarrow,/,\{\}}$, therefore it suffices to give an algorithm that runs in $O(n \cdot \sigma^w \cdot e)$ time.

Let G be an RDF graph, and $p \in RPL^{\rightarrow,/,\{\}}$. The idea of the algorithm is to view G as a non-deterministic finite automaton, and p as a word to be checked by the automaton. p is checked from the first element to the last, and the set of valid states in the automaton is remembered in each step, starting out from the set of all nodes in the RDF graph. For RPL$^{\rightarrow,/}$ (i.e. only ordered edge-flavored expressions), this view gives us an algorithm in $O(e \cdot w)$, where e is the number of edges in G, and w is the length of p (Corollary 5).

For unordered edge-flavored path expressions, a naive implementation would compute all possible permutations, and check the RDF graph for correspondence with each of these permuations. Since there $w!$ permutations for a path of length w, this procedure has a complexity of $O(w! \cdot e)$. The following algorithm is more efficient:

Again, the RDF graph G is viewed as a finite automaton, which is traversed using symbols occurring in the path expression p. In step i of the computation, each node n in G is labeled with all paths p of length i such that n is reachable over p from some other node m in G. Initially, all nodes are labeled with the empty path ϵ. After w steps (or earlier), the algorithm terminates and exactly the set of labeled nodes in G is reachable over p. In Listing 6.3 we use set notation to represent paths, since the order of traversal is irrelevant; however we must think of paths as multisets, because the same edge label may occur multiple times in p. For this reason, the set difference operator \ and the union operator $\cup$ in Listing 6.3 are the set difference and the union operator for *multisets*, not *sets*, respectively.

Listing 6.3: Evaluation algorithm for expressions in RPL$^{\rightarrow,/,\{\}}$

```
for each node n in G do labels(n) = {ε} end
for i = 1 to w do          // w is the length of path p
  for each e in E do       // follow every edge
    for each l in labels(source(e)) do
      if label(e) is in p\l then
        labels(sink(e)).add({l}∪label(e))
      end
    end
  end
  remove all labels of length i − 1
end
```

In the i-th iteration of the outermost loop of Listing 6.3, the set of labels for the nodes in G is bounded by $\sigma^i \cdot |n|$. Thus, the number of edge traversals in step i is bounded by $\sigma^i \cdot |n|$. The total number of edge traversals is thus $\sigma^{w+1} \cdot |n|$ (geometric series). □

Theorem 10 (NP-Completeness of RPL$^{\rightarrow,/,\{\}}$). *The evaluation problem of* RPL$^{\rightarrow,/,\{\}}$ *is NP-complete.*

Proof. For the proof of Theorem 10 we use a reduction from the Hamiltonian Cycle Problem. The idea of the proof is illustrated in Figure 4. Let $G = (V, E)$ be a directed labeled graph with nodes $\{1, \ldots, k\}$. G has a Hamiltonian Cycle if and only if the RPE { EDGES $1_{in}, 1_{out}, \ldots, k_{in}, k_{out}$ } has a non-empty solution over the *edge expansion graph* of G, which is defined as follows:

Definition 52 (Edge expansion graph). *Let $G = (V, E)$ with $V = 1, \ldots, k$ be a graph. The edge expansion graph $F = (V', E', \mu)$ of G is an edge labeled graph with the following properties:*

- $V \subseteq V'$

- *For each edge $(u,v) \in E$ there is some node n in V' and edges $(u,n), (n,v) \in E'$ with $\mu(u,n) = u_{out}$ and $\mu(n,v) = v_{in}$. There are no other edges in E' involving n.*

- *These are all nodes and edges in F.*

The edge expansion graph F of a given Graph G with v vertices and e edges contains $v + e$ vertices and $2 \cdot e$ edges. Obviously, F can be constructed from G in polynomial time.

□

Figure 4: Reduction from the Hamilton Cycle Problem to RPL$^{\to,/,()}$ evaluation

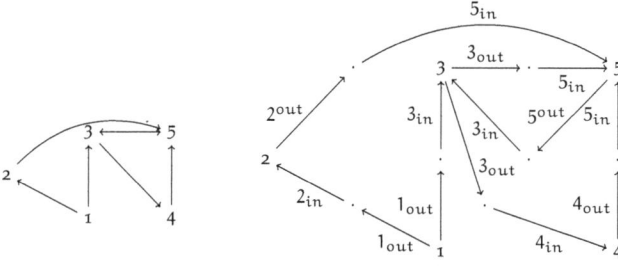

6.8 COMPILATION OF RPL TO PROLOG

In this section we show how RPL can be easily and efficiently implemented by a compilation to Prolog. Before giving the translation, we first hihglight three challenges that must be met by the translation process.

1. Since regular expressions make intense use of the kleene closure operators + and *, which must be translated to recursive rules in Prolog, non-termination must be avoided. Non-termination of transitive closure computations in Prolog can often be resolved by term permutation in rule bodies, or clause permutation in programs. But in the presence of cyclic data, transitive closure computations may still not terminate, due to infinitely many paths between nodes. There are two ways of dealing with this issue: (a) keeping track of the path that is traversed during the computation of the transitive closure or (b) tabling of the predicates that are used for transitive closure computation. Solution (b) eases the translation process, but requires evaluation by a Prolog engine that supports tabling such as XSB.

2. A second challenge in the translation process arises from the use of regular string expressions in RPL. This challenge is most easily met by translation to a Prolog engine that takes care of regular expression matching such as Ciao Prolog or XSB Prolog.

3. A third challenge arises from the fact that most Prolog engines are not prepared to dealing with RDF data, with the notable exception of SWI Prolog. Again, there are (at least) two solutions

for dealing with this situation: (a) use SWI Prolog or (b) assume that RDF graphs are encoded as ternary terms with some distinguished predicate name such as triple. This assumption is not as farfetched as it might seem, since the well-known N-Triples serialization of RDF is simply a collection of triples, and can be easily imported into Prolog engines. Moreover, there are conversion utilities from RDF/XML, Notation3 or Turtle to N-Triples.

We deal with the issues 1 and 2 by a translation to XSB Prolog and resolve issue 3 by assuming a native Prolog encoding of RDF graphs as ternary atoms with predicate name triple.

Let u be a URI, $pr_1, \ldots$ RPL predicates, $a_1, \ldots$ adorned or disjunctive RPEs, and c a concatenated or predicated RPE. The translation of RPL expressions to Prolog is given by the following function to_prolog. Each translation rule yields at least one Prolog rule, and may recursively call other translation rules. The predicate name of the head of the rule to be generated is given as an argument to the translation function.

$$\text{to\_prolog}(\text{flavor } c, p) = \begin{cases} \text{edges}(c, p) & \text{if flavor} = \text{EDGES.} \\ \text{path}(c, p) & \text{if flavor} = \text{PATH.} \\ \text{nodes}(c, p) & \text{if flavor} = \text{NODES.} \end{cases} \quad (6.41)$$

$$\text{edges}(u, p) = p(X, Y) \text{ :- triple}(X, u, Y). \quad (6.42)$$
$$\text{edges}(<u, p) = p(X, Y) \text{ :- } p_1(Y, X). \quad R \quad (6.43)$$

with p_1 a fresh predicate name and $\text{edges}(u, p_1) = R$. Predicated RPL expressions are translated by Equations 6.44 and 6.45.

$$\text{edges}(u[pr_1] \ldots [pr_n], p) = \quad (6.44)$$
$$p(X, Y) \text{ :- triple}(X, u, Y), p_1(u, \_), \ldots, p_n(u, \_). \quad R_1 \ldots R_n$$

with p_i fresh predicate names and $\text{edges}(pr_i, p_1) = R_i$ for $1 \leq i \leq n$. The corresponding rule for $<u$ is obtained by switching X and Y in the term triple(X,u,Y).

$$\text{edges}(\_[pr_1] \ldots [pr_n], p) = \quad (6.45)$$
$$p(X, Y) \text{ :- triple}(X, P, Y), p_1(P, \_), \ldots, p_n(P, \_). \quad R_1 \ldots R_n$$

with p_i fresh predicate names and $\text{to\_prolog}(pr_i, p_i) = R_i$ for $1 \leq i \leq n$. The corresponding rule for a regular expression re instead of an underscore is obtained by inserting the term re_match(re, P, _, _) after the term triple(X, P, Y) into the rule defining p. Note that this translation only works for XSB Prolog when the module regmatch is included. Again, the corresponding rules for the reverse edges < _ or < re is obtained by switching X and Y in the term triple(X,u,Y).

$$\text{nodes}(u[pr_1] \ldots [pr_n], p) = \quad (6.46)$$
$$p(u, u) \text{ :- node}(u), p_1(u, \_), \ldots, p_n(u, \_). \quad R_1 \ldots R_n$$

with $p_1, \ldots, p_n$ fresh predicate names, and $\text{to\_prolog}(pr_i) = R_i$ for $1 \leqslant i \leqslant n$. Wildcards and literals at the place of u are translated in the same way. A regular expression re at the place of u requires binding the node n to a variable, and testing if n is in the language defined by re with the XSB predicate re_match as follows:

$$\text{nodes}(u[pr_1]\ldots[pr_n], p) = \quad (6.47)$$
$$p(P,P) \text{ :- node}(P), \text{re\_match}(re, P, \_, \_, \_), p_1(P,\_), \ldots, p_n(P,\_).$$
$$R_1 \ldots R_n$$

$$\text{edges}(c?, p) = p(X,X) \text{ :- node}(X). \quad p(X,Y) \text{ :- } p_1(X,Y). \ R \quad (6.48)$$

with p_1 a fresh predicate name and $\text{edges}(c, p_1) = R$, and the predicate node defined by the following rules:

$$\text{node}(X) \text{ :- triple}(X, \_, \_). \quad \text{node}(X) \text{ :- triple}(\_, \_, X). \quad (6.49)$$

$$\text{edges}(c+, p) = \quad (6.50)$$
$$p(X,Y) \text{ :- } p_1(X,Y). \quad p(X,Y) \text{ :- } p_1(X,Z), p(Z,Y). \ R$$

with p_1 a fresh predicate name and $\text{edges}(c, p_1) = R$. The kleene star operator $*$ is translated in a very similar fashion.

$$\text{edges}((a_1 \ldots a_n), p) = \quad (6.51)$$
$$p(X,Y) \text{ :- } p_1(Z_0, Z_1), \ldots, p_n(Z_{n-1}, Z_n). \ R_1 \ldots R_n$$

with $p_1, \ldots p_n$ fresh predicate names and $\text{edges}(a_i, p_i) = R_i$ for $1 \leqslant i \leqslant n$.

$$\text{nodes}((a_1 \ldots a_n), p) = \quad (6.52)$$
$$p(X,Y) \text{ :- } p_1(Z_0, Z_1), \text{triple}(Z_1, \_, Z_2), \ldots,$$
$$\text{triple}(Z_{2n-2}, \_, Z_{2n-1}), p_n(Z_{2n-1}, Z_{2n}). R_1 \ldots R_n$$

with $p_1, \ldots p_n$ fresh predicate names and $\text{nodes}(a_i, p_i) = R_i$ for $1 \leqslant i \leqslant n$.

$$\text{path}((a_1 \ldots a_n), p) = \quad (6.53)$$
$$p(X,Y) \text{ :- } p_1(Z_0, Z_1), \ldots, p_n(Z_{n-1}, Z_n). \ R_1 \ldots R_n$$

with $p_1, \ldots p_n$ fresh predicate names and $\text{edges}(a_i, p_i) = R_i$ for odd i and $\text{nodes}(a_i, p_i) = R_i$ for even i in $\{1, \ldots, n\}$.

$$\text{edges}((c_1 | \ldots | c_n), p) = \quad (6.54)$$
$$p(X,Y) \text{ :- } p_1(X,Y). \quad \ldots \quad p(X,Y) \text{ :- } p_n(X,Y). \ R_1 \ldots R_n$$

with $p_1, \ldots p_n$ fresh predicate names and $\text{edges}(c_i, p_i) = R_i$ for $1 \leqslant i \leqslant n$. Disjunctive RPEs within edge- and path-flavored RPEs are translated in exactly the same way.

$$\text{to\_prolog}(\text{not}(f), p) = p(X,Y) \text{ :- not } p_1(X,Y). \ R \quad (6.55)$$

where p_1 is a fresh predicate name and $\text{to\_prolog}(f, p_1) = R$.

Part III

XCERPT MULTI-RULE SEMANTICS AND
TERM SUBSUMPTION

7 XCERPT TERM SIMULATION AND MULTI-RULE SEMANTICS

Contents

7.1 Simulation as the Foundation for Versatile Querying   141
7.2 Simulation and Negation: Local Stratification   146
7.3 Well-Founded Semantics for Xcerpt   150
7.4 Grouping versus Negation Stratification   156
    7.4.1 Elimination of Single Grouping Constructs   157
    7.4.2 Elimination of Nested Grouping Constructs   159

Having given an informal, example-driven introduction to the language Xcerpt, its evaluation principles and intuitive semantics in the preceding sections, this section introduces the precise semantics for Xcerpt *query terms* through a formal definition of *query term simulation* (Section 7.1), and *programs* through an iterative fixpoint procedure (Section 7.2). Previous publications on the semantics of Xcerpt have considered the class of *stratifiable Xcerpt programs* only. Section 7.2 also extends the semantics of Xcerpt programs to the class of *locally stratifiable programs*, which is a true superset of the set of stratifiable Xcerpt programs, and which is inspired by the notion of local stratification in logic programming [CB94]. In Section 7.3 the well-founded semantics for general logic programs is adapted to Xcerpt, thereby also giving a semantics to programs that are not locally stratified. Although not formally proven, we conjecture that locally stratifiable Xcerpt programs have a two-valued well-founded model which coincides with the model computed by the iterative fixpoint procedure over its local stratification.

While this section transfers the notion of local stratification and well-founded semantics to Xcerpt only, the proposed method can be applied to any other rule language that has a term-based model theory, and a notion of assymetric matching between queries and data. In particular, this semantics also applies to $\textsc{Xcerpt}^{RDF}$.[1]

7.1 SIMULATION AS THE FOUNDATION FOR VERSATILE QUERYING

Simulation between Xcerpt terms is inspired by rooted graph simulation [Mil71, HHK95], but is by far more involved since Xcerpt terms feature constructs for specifying incompleteness in depth, breadth, and order, allow variables, regular expressions and negated subterms. This section formally defines a subset of Xcerpt^{XML}[2] variables, descendant constructs, subterm negation, incompleteness in breadth and with respect

---

[1] Although $\textsc{Xcerpt}^{RDF}$ allows blank nodes in rule heads, this semantics is not a general semantics for RDF rule languages with blank nodes in rule heads. In particular, this semantics does not deal with leanness and simple RDF entailment. Instead it is based on the term-based semantics of Xcerpt.
[2] Chapter 4 introduces both $\textsc{Xcerpt}^{RDF}$ and Xcerpt^{XML} query, construct and data terms. In this section we concentrate on Xcerpt^{XML} terms, but most of the results and design principles also apply to $\textsc{Xcerpt}^{RDF}$ terms. We write "Xcerpt term" to denote the abstract

to order, multiple variables, multiple occurrences of the same variable, and variable restrictions. In comparison to full Xcerpt^{XML} query terms as described in [Furo8a, Scho4a] and for the sake of brevity, this definition does not include term identifiers and references, non-injective subterm specifications, optional subterms, qualified descendants, label variables, and the new syntax for XML attributes. Based on this definition of Xcerpt^{XML} query, construct and data terms, ground and non-ground query term simulation is defined as the formal semantics for the evaluation of Xcerpt^{XML} query terms on semi-structured data.

Definition 53 (Xcerpt^{XML} query term). *Query terms over a set of labels* $\mathcal{N}$, *a set of variables* $\mathcal{V}$, *and a set of regular expressions* $\mathcal{R}$ *are inductively defined as follows:*

- for each label $l \in \mathcal{N}$, l{{ }}, l{ }, l[ ] and l[[ ]] are atomic query terms. l is a short hand notation for l{{ }}.

- for each variable $X \in \mathcal{V}$, var X is a query term

- for each regular expression $r \in \mathcal{R}$, /r/{{ }}, /r/{ }, /r/[[ ]] and /r/[ ] are query terms. /r/ is a shorthand notation for /r/{{ }}. With $\mathcal{L}(r)$ we denote the set of labels matched by r, i.e. the language defined by the regular expression.

- for each variable $X \in \mathcal{V}$ and query term t, var X as t is a query term. t is called a *variable restriction* for X.

- for each query term t, desc t is a query term and called *depth-incomplete* or *incomplete in depth*.

- for each query term t, without t is a query term and called a *negated subterm*.

- for each query term t optional t is an *optional query term*.

- for each label or regular expression l and query terms $t_1, \ldots, t_n$ with $n \geq 1$,

$$q_1 = l\{\{ t_1, \ldots, t_n \}\}$$
$$q_2 = l\{ t_1, \ldots, t_n \}$$
$$q_3 = l[[t_1, \ldots, t_n]]$$
$$q_4 = l[t_1, \ldots, t_n]$$

are query terms. q_1 and q_3 are said to be *specified incompletely in breadth*, or simply *breadth-incomplete*, whereas q_2 and q_4 are *specified completely in breadth*, or simply *breadth-complete*. q_1 and q_2 are specified *incomplete with respect to order* or simply *order-incomplete*, whereas q_3 and q_4 are *order-complete*.

A variable X is said to *appear positively* in an Xcerpt^{XML} query term q, if it is included in q not in the scope of a without construct. It *appears negatively* within q if it is included within the scope of a without construct. Note that the same variable may appear both positively and negatively within q – e.g. X within a{{ var X, without var X }}.

---
concept of terms in both XCERPT^{RDF} and Xcerpt^{XML}, and "Xcerpt^{XML} term" to refer to Xcerpt^{XML} terms only.

7.1 SIMULATION AS THE FOUNDATION FOR VERSATILE QUERYING

Definition 54 (Xcerpt^{XML} data terms). *An Xcerpt^{XML} data term is a ground Xcerpt^{XML} query term that does not contain the constructs* without, optional, desc, *regular expression and double braces or double brackets.*

Definition 55 (Xcerpt^{XML} construct terms). Xcerpt^{XML} *construct terms over a set of variables* $\mathcal{V}$ *and a set of labels* $\mathcal{N}$ *are defined as follows:*

- *an Xcerpt^{XML} data term* d *over* $\mathcal{N}$ *is a construct term*
- *for each variable* $X \in \mathcal{V}$, var X *is a construct term*
- *for a construct term* c, all c *is a construct term*
- *for a construct term* c, optional c *is a construct term*
- *for a construct term* c, *and a sequence of variables* $X_1, \ldots, X_k \in \mathcal{V}$ all c group by $\{X_1, \ldots, X_k\}$ *is a construct term*
- *for a label* $l \in \mathcal{N}$ *and set of construct terms* $c_1, \ldots, c_n$, $l\{c_1, \ldots, c_n\}$ *is a construct term.*

In the following, we let $\mathcal{D}$ and $\mathcal{Q}$ denote the set of all Xcerpt^{XML} data and query terms, respectively.

A query term and a data term are in the simulation relation, if the query term "matches" the data. Matching Xcerpt^{XML} query terms with data terms is very similar to matching XPath queries with XML documents – apart from the variables and the injectivity requirement in query terms. The formal definition of simulation of a query term with semi-structured data is somewhat involved. To shorten the presentation, we first introduce some notation:

Definition 56 (Injective, bijective and monotone mappings). [3]
Let $I := \{t_1^1, \ldots, t_k^1\}$, $J := \{t_1^2, \ldots, t_n^2\}$ *be sets of query terms and* $\pi : I \Rightarrow J$ *be a mapping.*

- π *is* **injective**, *if all* $t_i^1, t_j^1 \in I$ *satisfy* $t_i^1 \neq t_j^1 \Rightarrow \pi(t_i^1) \neq \pi(t_j^1)$.

- π *is* **bijective**, *if it is injective and for all* $t_j^2 \in J$ *there is some* $t_i^1 \in I$ *such that* $\pi(t_i^1) = t_j^2$.

- π *is* **monotone**, *if for all* $t_i^1, t_j^1 \in I$ *with* $i < j$, $\pi(t_i^1) = t_k^2$ *and* $\pi(t_j^1) = t_l^2$ *holds* $k < l$.

We use the following abbreviations to reference parts of a query term q:

l(q): the string or regular expression used to build the query term. For a variable v, l(v) is undefined.

childt(q): the set of direct subterms of q

childt$^+$(q): the set of positive direct subterms (i.e. those direct subterms which are not of the form without ...),

---

[3] This definition of injectivity and bijectivity concerns the subterms – or nodes – of a query term only. Therefore it is also referred to as *node injectivity*. In previous publications about Xcerpt, we have used *position injectivity* instead, which concerns the edges between parent and child terms. In the absence of references (as in Definition 55), however, node and position injectivity are semantically equivalent. Therefore, and for the sake of simplicity, we use node injectivity in this contribution.

childt$^-$(q): the set of negated direct subterms (i.e. the direct subterms of the form without...),

desc(q): the set of direct descendant subterms of q (i.e. those of the from desc...),

subt(q): the direct or indirect subterms of q, i.e. all direct subterms as well as their subterms.

ss(q): the subterm specification of q. It can either be *complete* (single curly braces) or *incomplete* (double curly braces).

vars(q): the set of variables occurring somewhere in q.

pos(q): q$'$, if q is of the form without q$'$, q otherwise.

Definition 57 (Label subsumption). *A term label l_1 subsumes another term label l_2 iff l_1 and l_2 are strings and $l_1 = l_2$, or l_1 is a regular expression and l_2 is a string such that l_1 matches with l_2, or l_1 and l_2 are both regular expressions and l_1 matches with any label that l_2 matches with.*

Theorem 11 (Decidability of Label Subsumption). *Label subsumption is decidable.*

Proof. The only interesting case is the one with the two labels being both regular expressions. For any two regular expressions e_1 and e_2, a regular expression e that accepts the union $\mathcal{L}(e_1) \cup \mathcal{L}(e_2)$ of the languages of e_1 and e_2 is given by $e_1 \mid e_2$. Any regular expression e can be converted to a deterministic finite automaton that accepts the same language (see e.g. [HU79][Section 3.2.3] for a proof). This conversion involves the construction of a deterministic finite automaton from a non-deterministic one, which may result in an exponential blow up. For two deterministic finite automatons one can test their equivalence with the table filling algorithm (see [HU79][Section 4.4.2]). Obviously e_1 subsumes e_2 iff the deterministic finite automatons of e_1 and $e_1 \mid e_2$ are equivalent. □

Definition 58 (Ground query term simulation). *Let q be a ground query term[4] and d a data term. A relation $S \subseteq (\mathrm{SubT}(q) \cup \{q\}) \times (\mathrm{SubT}(d) \cup \{d\})$ is a simulation of q into d if the following holds:*

- *q S d*

- *if $q := l_1\{\{q_1,\ldots,q_n\}\}$ S $l_2\{d_1,\ldots,d_m\} =: d$ then l_1 must subsume l_2, and there must be an injective mapping $\pi : \mathrm{ChildT}^+(q) \to \mathrm{ChildT}^+(d)$ such that q_i S $\pi(q_i)$ for all $i \in \mathrm{ChildT}^+(q)$. Moreover, there must not be a $q_j \in \mathrm{ChildT}^-(q)$ and $d_l \in \mathrm{ChildT}^+(d) \setminus \mathrm{range}(\pi)$ such that $\mathrm{pos}(q_j) \preceq d_l$ (note the recursive reference to '$\preceq$' here),*

- *if $q := l_1[[q_1,\ldots,q_n]]$ S $l_2[d_1,\ldots,d_m] =: d$ then l_1 must subsume l_2, and there must be monotone mapping $\pi : \mathrm{ChildT}^+(q) \to \mathrm{ChildT}^+(d)$ such that q_i S $\pi(q_i)$ for all $i \in \mathrm{ChildT}^+(q)$. Moreover, there must not be a $q_j \in \mathrm{ChildT}^-(q)$ and $d_l \in \mathrm{ChildT}^+(d) \setminus \mathrm{range}(\pi)$ such that $\mathrm{pos}(q_j) \preceq d_l$ (note the recursive reference to '$\preceq$' here) and the extension of π with the pair (q_j, d_l) is monotone.*

---

4 For the sake of brevity we assume that q does not contain optional subterms.

- *if* $q := l_1\{q_1,\ldots,q_n\} \mathcal{S} l_2\{d_1,\ldots,d_m\} =: d$ *then* l_1 *must subsume* l_2, *and there must be a bijective mapping* $\pi : \mathsf{ChildT}^+(q) \to \mathsf{ChildT}^+(d)$ *such that* $q_i \mathcal{S} \pi(q_i)$ *for all* $i \in \mathsf{ChildT}^+(q)$. *We impose no further requirements on the set* $\mathsf{ChildT}^-(q)$ *of negated direct subterms of* q. *The totality of* π *already ensures that there is no extension of* π *to some element* $q_j \in \mathsf{ChildT}^-(q)$ *such that* $\mathsf{pos}(q_j) \preceq d_l$ *for some* $d_l \in \mathsf{ChildT}^+(d) \setminus \mathsf{range}(\pi)$. *Therefore the semantics of query terms is independent from the presence of negated direct subterms within breadth-complete query terms.*

- *if* $q := l_1[q_1,\ldots,q_n] \mathcal{S} l_2[d_1,\ldots,d_m] =: d$ *then* l_1 *must subsume* l_2, *and* $q_i \mathcal{S} d_i$ *for all* $q_i \in \mathsf{ChildT}^+(q)$.

- $\mathcal{S}$ *does not contain any pair* (q, d) *such that* q *is order-complete and* d *is order-incomplete.*

- *if* $q = \mathsf{desc}\ q'\ \mathcal{S}\ d$ *then* $q'\ \mathcal{S}\ d$ *or* $q'\ \mathcal{S}\ d'$ *for some subterm* d' *of* d.

We say that q *simulates into* d *(short:* $q \preceq d$) *if and only if there is a relation* $\mathcal{S}$ *that satisfies the above conditions. To state the contrary we write* $q \npreceq d$.

Since every Xcerpt^{XML} data term is also a query term, the above definition of simulation between a query term and a data term can be extended to a relation between pairs of query terms. For the sake of brevity this full definition of *extended ground query term simulation* is given in the appendix of [BFL07].

The existence of a ground query term simulation states that a given data term satisfies the conditions encapsulated in the query term. Many times, however, query authors are not only interested in checking the structure and content of a document, but also in extracting data from the document, and therefore query terms may contain logical variables. To formally specify the data that is extracted by matching a query term with a data term, the notion of non-ground query term simulation is introduced (Definition 59). Substitutions are defined as usual, and the application of a substitution to a query term is the consistent replacement of the variables by their images in the substitution.

Definition 59 (Non-ground query term simulation). *Let* v *be a variable with restriction* r. *A substitution* σ *respects* r, *iff* $r \preceq \sigma(v)$. *A query term* q *with variables simulates into a data term* d *iff there is a substitution* $\sigma : \mathsf{Vars}(q) \to \mathcal{D}$ *such that* $q\sigma$ *simulates into* d *and such that* σ *respects the variable restrictions of all variables in* q.

In some cases query terms are not expressible enough or inconvenient for specifying a query in the body of a rule. Conjunctions of query terms are needed if more than one resource is queried and the results are to be joined. Disjunctions of query terms are convenient to extract data from different resources and wrap them into a common XML fragment or RDF graph. Finally the absence of data simulating with a given query term is tested by query negation. The notion of a query combines conjunctions, disjunctions and negations of query terms:

Definition 60 (Xcerpt query). *Xcerpt queries are recursively defined as follows:*

- *an Xcerpt query term is an Xcerpt query*

- *for a set of Xcerpt queries* $q_1, \ldots, q_n$, *the conjunction* $\mathcal{C} :=$ and($q_1, \ldots, q_n$), *the disjunction* $\mathcal{D} :=$ or($q_1, \ldots, q_n$) *and the negation* $\mathcal{N} :=$ not(q_1) *are Xcerpt queries. If a variable X appears positively within a* q_i ($1 \leqslant i \leqslant n$) *then it also appears positively within* $\mathcal{C}$ *and* $\mathcal{D}$, *but negatively within* $\mathcal{N}$. *If X appears negatively within* q_i, *it also appears negatively within* $\mathcal{C}$, $\mathcal{D}$ *and* $\mathcal{N}$.

Definition 61 (Xcerpt rule, goal, fact, program). *Let q be a query over a set of labels* $\mathcal{L}$, *a set of variables* $\mathcal{V}$ *and a set of regular expressions* $\mathcal{R}$ *and c a construct term over* $\mathcal{L}$ *and* $\mathcal{V}$. *Then* CONSTRUCT c FROM q END *is an Xcerpt rule*, GOAL c FROM q END *is an Xcerpt goal, and* CONSTRUCT c END *is an Xcerpt fact. An Xcerpt program is a sequence of range-restricted Xcerpt rules, goals and facts.*[5]

The construct term c is called the *head* of an Xcerpt rule or goal, the query q is called its *body*. An Xcerpt fact can also be written as an Xcerpt rule with an empty body. An Xcerpt rule, goal or fact is called *range restricted*, if all variables that appear in its head also appear positively in its body. In a forward chaining evaluation of a program, the distinction between goals and facts is unnecessary. In a backward chaining evaluation, however, the goals are the starting point of the resolution algorithm. In contrast to Logic programming, goals are not a single term only, but an entire rule to ensure answer closedness of Xcerpt programs. Especially for the task of information integration on the Web, answer closedness is indispensable.

7.2 SIMULATION AND NEGATION: LOCAL STRATIFICATION

While Section 7.1 defines the semantics of single query terms and queries, this section defines the semantics of Xcerpt rules and programs. Special attention is laid on the interplay between simulation unification and non-monotonic negation in rule bodies.

The problem of evaluating rule based languages with non-monotonic negation has received wide-spread attention throughout the logic programming community (See [AB94] and [BEE+07] for surveys). A multitude of semantics have been proposed for such languages (program completion semantics, stable-model semantics [GL88], well-founded semantics [vRS91b], inflationary semantics [KP88]). Especially the well-founded and stable-model semantics have been found to comply with the intuition of program authors and are therefore implemented by logic programming engines such as XSB [SSW93] and DLV [EFK+00]. Several classes of logic programs have been defined for which some of the above mentioned semantics coincide. Among these classes are definite programs, stratifiable programs, locally stratifiable programs [Prz88] and modularly stratifiable programs [Ros90]. The well-founded semantics and the stable model semantics coincide on the class of locally stratifiable programs.

In the following we introduce stratifiable and locally stratifiable Xcerpt programs. In adapting these concepts to Xcerpt, one has to pay close attention to the differences introduced by the richer kind of unification employed.

---

[5] Since facts and goals are a kind of rules, we refer to Xcerpt programs as a sequence of rules in the following.

Figure 5: Social graph corresponding to the facts in Listing 7.1

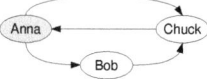

Definition 62 (Stratification). *A stratification of an Xcerpt program P consisting of the rules $r_1, \ldots r_n$ is a partitioning of $r_1, \ldots r_n$ into strata $S_1, \ldots, S_k$, such that the following conditions hold:*

- *All terms asserted by facts in P are in S_1.*

- *If a rule r_1 contains a positive query term q that simulates with the construct term c of another rule r_2, then r_1 positively depends on r_2, and r_1 is in the same or a higher stratum than r_2.*

- *If a rule r_1 contains a negated query term not q such that q simulates with the construct term c of another rule r_2, then r_1 negatively depends on r_2 and is in a strictly higher stratum than r_2.*

Given the stratification of a program P, its semantics can be defined by the iterative fixpoint procedure suggested for general logic programs. For finite programs, stratification is decidable. However, there are Xcerpt programs, such as the one in Listing 7.1, that are not stratifiable, but which may be evaluated bottom up.

Listing 7.1 is a formulation of the single source shortest path problem over a directed social graph, which is given by the facts (lines 1 to 5) in Listing 7.1 and which is depicted in Figure 5. The program computes for each node n in a directed graph the shortest distance to some source node s, in this case anna.

This program uses a slight extension of Xcerpt's term syntax. The term

$$\text{Acquaintance[anna, } \leqslant \text{i]}$$

simulates with the data terms Acquaintance[anna, j] if and only if i and j are natural numbers and $j \leqslant i$. Furthermore, the terms Acquaintance [anna, $\leqslant$ j] and Acquaintance[anna, i] simulate with Acquaintance[anna, > j] if and only if $i > j$. The symbol '>' can be interpreted as a hint by the programmer to the evaluation engine, that a rule can only be used to derive atoms with integer values greater than a certain natural number. The example in Listing 7.1 serves to illustrate the problems and challenges for defining the semantics and evaluation of possibly recursive rule programs with non-monotonic negation and rich unification. These challenges are encountered independent of the specific kind of rich unification, be it SPARQL query evaluation, Xcerpt query term simulation, or XPath query evaluation.

To see that Program P in Listing 7.1 is not stratifiable, consider the negated query term not q, with q = Acquaintance [var P, $\leqslant$ var D] in the body of the only rule of P. q simulates with the head h = Acquaintance [var P, D + 1 > 0] of the same rule. Thus the rule should be in a strictly higher stratum than itself, which is a contradiction.

Listing 7.1: Single source shortest path problem for the source node 'anna'

```
CONSTRUCT knows[ anna, bob ] END
CONSTRUCT knows[ bob, chuck] END
CONSTRUCT knows[ anna, chuck ] END
CONSTRUCT knows[ chuck, anna ] END

CONSTRUCT Acquaintance[ anna, 0 ] END

CONSTRUCT
  Acquaintance[ var P, var D + 1 ]
FROM
  and (
    Acquaintance[ var P', var D ],
    knows[ var P, var P'],
    not ( Acquaintance[ var P, ≤ D ] )
END
```

To see that P can nevertheless be evaluated in a bottom up manner, consider a ground instance g of the recursive rule in Listing 7.1. The term constructed by the head of g contains an integer value i which is exactly by one larger than the integer values of terms that may simulate with (negated or positive) query terms in the body of g. Thus, in a bottom up evaluation of the program, we may first compute the fixpoint of the program considering only terms containing the integer value zero, followed by the fixpoint computation for terms with the value 1, and so on. Since a valid rule application will only construct terms containing the value $n + 1$ using terms with values n, it may never be the case that the body of a rule once found true is invalidated by the derivation of a fact at a later point in time. Figure 6 visualizes the resulting stratification.

Figure 6: Local stratification for Listing 7.1

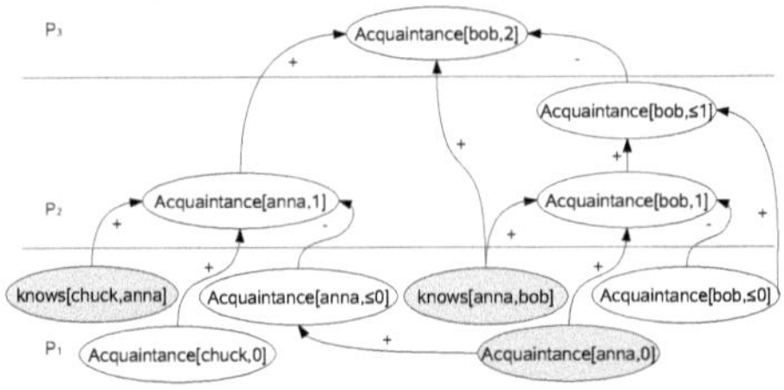

With the concept of *local stratification* we distinguish the class of *locally stratifiable Xcerpt programs*, which is a true superset of the class of stratifiable Xcerpt programs, and thereby introduce a more general characterization of Xcerpt programs that guarantees that these programs can be evaluated by an iterative fixpoint procedure in a bottom up manner. A local stratification partitions the *Herbrand universe* of an Xcerpt program rather than the *rules* of the program into strata.

Definition 63 (Xcerpt Herbrand universe, Xcerpt Herbrand base, Xcerpt Herbrand instantiation). *The Herbrand universe of an Xcerpt program P are all Xcerpt data terms that can be constructed over the vocabulary of P.*[6] *Since Xcerpt programs consist only of terms without predicate symbols,*

---
6 The vocabulary of P is the set of labels appearing in P.

the Herbrand base *of* P *is defined to be the same as the Xcerpt Herbrand universe.*

Let r *be a rule in* P. *A rule* r′ *obtained from* r *by consistently replacing variables in* r *by terms of the Herbrand Universe of* P *is a* Herbrand instantiated rule *of* P. *The* Herbrand instantiation *of* P *is the set of all Herbrand instantiated rules of* P.

Note that the above definition deviates from the Herbrand universe for logic programs as follows: While Prolog function symbols have always an associated arity, Xcerpt labels may be used to construct terms with arbitrary many children. Thus a program over the vocabulary $V = \{a\}$ has the Herbrand universe { a{ }, a{ a }, a{ a{ a } }, a{ a, a } ...}. In the following discussion of the well-founded semantics we will, however, not consider the entire Herbrand universe for computing unfounded sets, but restrict them to the terms that occur in ground instances of the rules.

Definition 64 (Local stratification of Xcerpt programs). *A local stratification of an Xcerpt program* P *is a partitioning of the Herbrand universe of* P *into strata such that the following conditions hold:*

- *All facts of* P *are in stratum 1.*

- *If a term* q *appears* positively *in the body of a rule* r *with head* c *in the Herbrand instantiation of* P, *then* q *must be in the same or a higher stratum than* c.

- *If a term* q *appears* negatively *within the body of a rule* r *with head* c *in the Herbrand instantiation of* P, *then* q *is in a strictly higher stratum than* c.

- *If a term* q *simulates into a term* c, *then* q *is in the same or in a higher stratum than* q.

The definition of local stratification of Xcerpt programs coincides with the definition of local stratification for general logic programs in the first three points. The fourth condition is necessitated by the richer unification relation induced by simulation unification in Xcerpt. While in logic programming two ground terms unify if and only if they are syntactically identical, this is not true for Xcerpt terms (consider e.g. the terms a{{ }}, a[[ ]] and a{ b }).

Example 7.2 underlines the necessity of the fourth condition in Definition 64: By Definition 64, Program P in Listing 7.2 is not locally stratifiable, but it would be, if the last condition were not part of the definition. In fact, the semantics for P is unclear, and it cannot be evaluated by an iterative fixpoint procedure. Figure 7 shows the dependency graph for Listing 7.2, which contains a cycle including a negative edge. The dependency graph for a ground Xcerpt program simply includes all rule heads and body literals as nodes, and all simulation relations between query and construct terms and negative and positive dependencies of rule heads on their body literals. The dependency graph for a non-ground Xcerpt program is the dependency graph of its Herbrand Instantiation. An Xcerpt program P is locally stratifiable, if its dependency graph does not contain any negative cycles (i.e. cycles including at least one negative edge).

Figure 7: Dependency graph for Listing 7.2

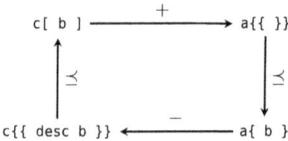

Listing 7.2: An Xcerpt program that is not locally stratifiable

```
CONSTRUCT a{ b } FROM not(c{{ desc b{{ }} }}) END
CONSTRUCT c[ b ] FROM a{{ }} END
```

Since Listing 7.2 is not locally stratifiable, its semantics cannot be defined by a fixpoint procedure over its stratification. Similar programs – except for the simulation relation – have been studied in logic programming. For example, the logic program $\{(a \leftarrow \neg c), (c \leftarrow a)\}$ is not locally stratifiable, still the well-founded semantics of the program is given by the empty interpretation $\{\}$. To give Xcerpt programs a semantics, no matter if they are locally stratified or not, we adapt the well-founded semantics to Xcerpt programs in the Section 7.3.

7.3 WELL-FOUNDED SEMANTICS FOR XCERPT

For the sake of simplicity this section only considers Xcerpt programs without the grouping constructs all – Section 7.4 proposes a way to reduce grouping stratification to negation stratification, giving rise for an integrated semantics for Xcerpt programs containing both grouping constructs and negation. Moreover, in this section queries are assumed to be either simple query terms, negations of query terms or conjunctions of positive or negated query terms. In the absence of grouping constructs or aggregate functions, a rule involving a disjunction in the rule body can be rewritten into an equivalent set of rules that are disjunction free. Also negations of conjunctions can be rewritten to conjunctions with only positive or negative query terms as conjuncts.[7]

Definition 65 (Xcerpt literal). *An Xcerpt literal is either an Xcerpt data (in this case it is called a* positive literal*) term or the negation not* d *of some Xcerpt data term* d *(i.e. a negative literal). For a set* S *of Xcerpt literals,* $pos(S)$ *denotes the positive literals in* S, $neg(S)$ *the negative ones.*

Definition 66 (Consistent sets of Xcerpt literals). *For a set of Xcerpt literals* S *we denote with* $\neg \cdot S$ *the set of terms obtained by negating each element in* S. *Let* p *and* n $=$ not d *be a positive and negative literal, respectively, and let* S *be a set of literals.* p *and* S *are consistent, iff not* p *is not in* S. n *and* S *are consistent iff* d *is not in* S. S *is consistent, if it is consistent with each of its elements.*

Definition 67 (Partial Xcerpt interpretations (adapted from [vRS91a])).

Let P *be an Xcerpt program, and* $HB(P)$ *its Herbrand base. A partial interpretation* I *is a consistent subset of* $HB(P) \cup \neg \cdot HB(P)$.

---
7 This normalization of Xcerpt rules is similar to finding the disjunctive normal form of logical formulae.

7.3 WELL-FOUNDED SEMANTICS FOR XCERPT

Definition 68 (Satisfaction of Xcerpt terms). *Let I be a partial interpretation for a program P. The model relationship between I and an Xcerpt term is defined as follows.*

- *Let q be a positive query term.*
    - *I satisfies q $(I \vDash q)$ iff there is some data term $d \in pos(I)$ with $q \preceq d$*
    - *I falsifies q $(I \nvDash q)$ iff for all data terms $d \in HB_P$ holds $q \preceq d \Rightarrow d \in neg(I)$.*
    - *Otherwise, q is undefined in I.*
- *Let $q = not\ q'$ be a negative query term.*
    - *I satisfies q $(I \vDash q)$ iff for all data terms d holds $q' \preceq d \Rightarrow d \in neg(I)$.*
    - *I falsifies q $(I \nvDash q)$ iff there is some data term $d \in pos(I)$ with $q' \preceq d$.*
    - *Otherwise, q is undefined in I.*

Definition 69 (Satisfaction of Xcerpt queries). *Let I be a partial interpretation and q a conjunction of Xcerpt terms. I satisfies q if I satisfies each conjunct in q.*[8]

Definition 70 (Xcerpt Unfounded Sets (adapted from [vRS91a])). *Let P be an Xcerpt program, HB_P its Herbrand base, and I a partial interpretation. We say $A \subseteq HB_P$ is an* unfounded set *of P with respect to I if each atom $p \in A$ satisfies the following condition. For each instantiated rule R of P with head p and body Q at least one of the following holds:*

1. *For some positive literal $q \in Q$ holds that for all $d \in HB_P$ holds $q \preceq d \Rightarrow d \in A \lor d \in neg(I)$.*
2. *Some negative literal $q \in Q$ is satisfied in I.*

The greatest unfounded set *of P with respect to an interpretation I is the union of all unfounded sets of P with respect to I.*

Definition 71 (Well-founded semantics of an Xcerpt program). *The wellfounded semantics of an Xcerpt program P is defined as the least fixpoint of the operator $W_P(I) := T_P(I) \cup \neg \cdot U_P(I)$ where U_P and T_P are defined as follows:*

- *a postive Xcerpt literal l is in $T_P(I)$ iff there is some ground instance R_g of some rule R in P with construct term l and query Q such that $I \vDash Q$.*
- *$U_P(I)$ is the greatest unfounded set of P with respect to I.*

Consider the program P in Listing 7.3. Its Herbrand base is $HB(P) = \{a\{\ \}\}$. Starting with the empty interpretation I_0, $T_P(I_0) = \emptyset$, $U_P(I_0) = \emptyset$, and $I_1 := W_P(I_0) = \emptyset = I_0$. Thus the well-founded semantics of P is $\emptyset$.

Listing 7.3: Simple Negation through recursion and simulation (A)
```
CONSTRUCT a{ } FROM not( a{{ }} ) END
```

---

[8] Xcerpt rules are assumed to be in disjunctive normal form. Therefore disjunctions need not be considered here. Satisfaction of negations is treated in Definition 68 above.

Listing 7.4: Simple Negation through recursion and simulation (B)
```
CONSTRUCT a{ } FROM not( a{{ }} ), not( b{ } ) END
CONSTRUCT a{ b } END
```

As a second example, consider program Q in Listing 7.4 with Herbrand base $HB(Q) = \{\, a\{\ b\ \},\ a\{\ \},\ b\{\ \}\,\}$. We obtain the following fix point calculation:

- $I_0 = \emptyset$
- $\mathbf{T}_Q(I_0) = \{\, a\{\ b\ \}\,\}$
- $\mathbf{U}_Q(I_0) = \{\, a\{\ \},\ b\{\ \}\,\}$
- $I_1 = \mathbf{W}_Q(I_0) = \{\, a\{\ b\ \},\ \text{not}\ a\{\ \},\ \text{not}\ b\{\ \}\,\}$
- $\mathbf{T}_Q(I_1) = \{\, a\{\ b\ \}\,\}$
- $\mathbf{U}_Q(I_1) = \{\, a\{\ \},\ b\{\ \}\,\}$
- $I_2 = \mathbf{W}_Q(I_1) = \{\, a\{\ b\ \},\ \text{not}(\ a\{\ \}\ ),\ \text{not}(\ b\{\ \}\ )\,\} = I_1$

As a final example, consider the stratified and locally stratified program R in Listing 7.5 with Herbrand universe $HB(R) = \{\, b\{\ \},\ a\{\ b\ \},\ a\{\ \},\ c\{\ c\ \}\,\}$.

Listing 7.5: Simple Negation through recursion and simulation (C)
```
CONSTRUCT b{ } FROM not( a{{ }} ) END
CONSTRUCT a{ b } FROM not( c{{ }} ) END
CONSTRUCT a{ } FROM not( c{{ }} ) END
CONSTRUCT c{ c } END
```

We obtain the following fixpoint calculation:

- $I_0 = \emptyset$
- $\mathbf{T}_R(I_0) = \{\, c\{\ c\ \}\,\}$
- $\mathbf{U}_R(I_0) = \emptyset$
- $I_1 = \mathbf{W}_R(I_0) = \{\, c\{\ c\ \}\,\}$
- $\mathbf{T}_R(I_1) = \{\, c\{\ c\ \}\,\}$
- $\mathbf{U}_R(I_1) = \{\, a\{\ \},\ a\{\ b\ \}\,\}$
- $I_2 = \mathbf{W}_R(I_1) = \{\, c\{\ c\ \},\ \text{not}(\ a\{\ \}\ ),\ \text{not}(\ a\{\ b\ \}\ )\,\}$
- $\mathbf{T}_R(I_2) = \{\, c\{\ c\ \},\ b\{\ \}\,\}$
- $\mathbf{U}_R(I_2) = \{\, a\{\ \},\ a\{\ b\ \}\,\}$
- $I_3 = \mathbf{W}_R(I_2) = \{\, c\{\ c\ \},\ b\{\ \},\ \text{not}(\ a\{\ \}\ ),\ \text{not}(\ a\{\ b\ \}\ )\,\}$
- $\mathbf{T}_R(I_3) = \mathbf{T}_R(I_2)$
- $\mathbf{U}_R(I_3) = \mathbf{U}_R(I_2)$
- $\mathbf{W}_R(I_3) = \mathbf{W}_R(I_2)$

It is immediate that the well-founded semantics of R coincides with the fixpoint calculated over the stratification of R – a fact that is true for every locally stratified Xcerpt program.

Theorem 12. *For a locally stratified Xcerpt program* P, *the well-founded semantics of* P *is total and coincides with the fixpoint calculated over the local stratification of* P.

In [PP90] the class of weakly stratified logic programs is introduced, which is a true superset of the class of locally stratified programs and has a well-defined, two-valued intended semantics. Put briefly, to decide whether a logic program is locally stratifiable one considers the dependency graph constructed from the *entire* Herbrand instantiation of the logic program. In contrast, the decision for weak stratification is based on the absence of negative cycles within the dependency graph constructed *from a subset* of the Herbrand interpretation. This subset excludes instantiated rules containing literals of extensional predicate symbols that are not given in the program. The standard example for a program that is weakly stratified but not locally stratified is the following:

$$win(X) : -move(X, Y) \land \neg win(Y)$$

A position X is a winning position of a game, if there is a move from X to position Y and Y is a losing position. As mentioned above, weak stratification depends on the extension of extensional predicate symbols (move in the above example), and the program above is only weakly stratifiable in the case that move has an acyclic extension. With Xcerpt not distinguishing between predicate symbols and function symbols, weak stratification cannot be direclty transferred to Xcerpt. Still, some term t in the Herbrand universe of an Xcerpt program can only be constructed extensionally (as facts), but not intentionally (by rules), since there may not be a rule with head h such that the outermost label of h and t coincide. We call such terms, in analogy with logic programming, as *extensionally defined*, and terms constructed by rules *intentionally defined*.

Weak stratification for Xcerpt is defined just as local stratification for Xcerpt programs, with the small deviation that not the entire Herbrand instantiation is considered in the construction of the dependency graph, but only those rules of the Herbrand instantiation which are valid, in the sense that they do not contain extensional atoms that are not given as facts of the program. We call this set of rules the *Reduced Herbrand Instantiation* of an Xcerpt program P.

Definition 72 (Reduced Herbrand Instantiation). *Let* P *be an Xcerpt program,* H_P *ist Herbrand instantiation and* $r \in H_P$. *Then* r *is in the* reduced Herbrand instantiation *of* P, *if and only if all extensional atoms in the body of* r *also occur as facts in* P.

Definition 73 (Weak stratification of Xcerpt programs). *A weak stratification of an Xcerpt program* P *is a partitioning of the Herbrand universe of* P *into strata such that the following conditions hold:*

- *All facts of* P *are in stratum 1.*

- *If a term* q *appears* positively *in the body of a rule* r *with head* c *in the reduced Herbrand instantiation of* P, *then* q *must be in the same or a higher stratum than* c.

- *If a term* q *appears* negatively *within the body of a rule* r *with head* c *in the reduced Herbrand instantiation of* P, *then* q *is in a strictly higher stratum than* c.

- If a term q simulates into a term c, then q is in the same or in a higher stratum than q.

A logic program with rich unification, which is weakly stratifiable, but not locally stratifiable is the program S in Listing 7.6. It computes the longest path relationship between the nodes in a social network and the source node anna. The recursive rule in S can be read as "The longest path from anna to a person P is n(D) if and only if there is some other person P1 who knows P, and whose longest path from anna is D, and if there is no longer path from anna to P than n(D)". The terms $n(0), n(n(0)), \ldots$ are interpreted as the natural numbers $1, 2, \ldots$.

Listing 7.6: The longest path problem as a logic program with rich unification.

```
longest_path(anna, 0).
knows(anna, bob). knows(bob, chuck). knows(anna, chuck).
longest_path(P, n(D)) ←
   knows(P1, P), longest_path(P1, D), not(longest_path(P, > n(D))).
```

Figure 8: Weak stratification for Listing 7.6

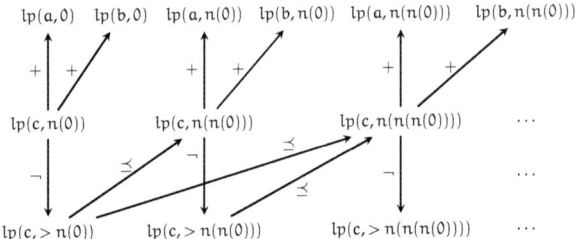

Unification of terms in Listing 7.6 is defined as standard Prolog unification with the following semantics for the '>' symbol: a query a(>i) unifies with a term a(j) if and only if i, j are natural numbers with j > i. By Definition 71, the well-founded semantics of Listing 7.6 is indeed the longest-path relationship with source anna, as Figure 9 shows.

Program S is not locally stratified, because in the presence of cycles in the data – e.g. a fact knows(anna, anna) – the dependency graph of S contains a cycle through negation. However, in the case of cycles in the data, also the intuitive semantics of S is unclear, as paths may be infinitely long. For all acyclic knows relationships, S is *weakly stratified*.

Listing 7.7 shows part of the reduced Herbrand instantiation of Listing 7.6. It shows only rules where terms of the form $n(n(\ldots 0 \ldots))$ are substituted for D, and only the atomic terms anna, bob and chuck are substituted for the variables P and P1. But also in consideration of such non-intended rules, the program remains weakly stratifiable.

Listing 7.7: Reduced Herbrand instantiation of Listing 7.6

```
longest_path(anna, 0).
knows(anna, bob). knows(bob, chuck). knows(anna, chuck).
longest_path(chuck, n(0)) ←
   knows(anna, chuck), longest_path(anna, 0),
   not(longest_path(chuck, > n(0))).
longest_path(chuck, n(n(0))) ←
```

Figure 9: Computation of the well-founded semantics for the program S in Listing 7.6

$$\begin{aligned}
I_0 &= \emptyset \\
\mathbf{T}_S(I_0) &= \{k(a,b), k(b,c), k(a,c), lp(a,0)\} \\
\mathbf{U}_S(I_0) &= \{lp(a,n(0)), lp(a,n(n(0))), \ldots, \\
&\quad lp(b,0), lp(b,n(0)), lp(b,n(n(0))), \ldots, \\
&\quad lp(c,0), lp(c,n(0)), lp(c,n(n(0))), \ldots, k(b,a), k(c,a), k(c,b)\} \\
\mathbf{W}_S(I_0) &= \{k(a,b), k(b,c), k(a,c), lp(a,0), \\
&\quad not(lp(a,n(0))), not(lp(a,n(n(0)))), \ldots, \\
&\quad not(lp(b,0)), not(lp(b,n(0))), \ldots, \\
&\quad not(lp(c,0)), not(lp(c,n(0))), \ldots, \\
&\quad not(k(b,a)), not(k(c,a)), not(k(c,b))\} = I_1 \\
\mathbf{T}_S(I_1) &= \{k(a,b), k(b,c), k(a,c), lp(a,0), lp(b,n(0)), lp(c,n(0))\} \\
\mathbf{U}_S(I_1) &= \{lp(a,n(0)), lp(a,n(n(0))), \ldots, \\
&\quad lp(b,0), lp(b,n(n(0))), lp(b,n(n(n(0)))), \ldots, \\
&\quad lp(c,0), lp(c,n(n(0))), lp(c,n(n(n(0)))), \ldots, \\
&\quad k(b,a), k(c,a), k(c,b)\} \\
\mathbf{W}_S(I_1) &= \{k(a,b), k(b,c), k(a,c), lp(a,0), lp(b,n(0)), lp(c,n(0)) \\
&\quad not(lp(a,n(0))), not(lp(a,n(n(0)))), \ldots, \\
&\quad not(lp(b,0)), not(lp(b,n(n(0)))), not(lp(b,n(n(n(0))))), \ldots, \\
&\quad not(lp(c,0)), not(lp(c,n(n(0)))), not(lp(c,n(n(n(0))))), \ldots, \\
&\quad not(k(b,a)), not(k(c,a)), not(k(c,b))\} = I_2 \\
\mathbf{T}_S(I_2) &= \{k(a,b), k(b,c), k(a,c), lp(a,0), lp(b,n(0)), lp(c,n(0)), \\
&\quad lp(c,n(n(0)))\} \\
\mathbf{U}_S(I_2) &= \{lp(a,n(0)), lp(a,n(n(0))), \ldots, \\
&\quad lp(b,0), lp(b,n(n(0))), lp(b,n(n(n(0)))), \ldots, \\
&\quad lp(c,0), lp(c,n(n(n(0)))), \ldots, \\
&\quad k(b,a), k(c,a), k(c,b)\} \\
\mathbf{W}_S(I_2) &= \{k(a,b), k(b,c), k(a,c), lp(a,0), lp(b,n(0)), lp(c,n(0)), \\
&\quad lp(c,n(n(0))), \\
&\quad not(lp(a,n(0))), not(lp(a,n(n(0)))), \ldots, \\
&\quad not(lp(b,0)), not(lp(b,n(n(0)))), not(lp(b,n(n(n(0))))), \ldots, \\
&\quad not(lp(c,0)), not(lp(c,n(n(n(0))))), \ldots, \\
&\quad not(k(b,a)), not(k(c,a)), not(k(c,b))\} = I_3 \\
\mathbf{T}_S(I_3) &= \{k(a,b), k(b,c), k(a,c), lp(a,0), lp(b,n(0)), lp(c,n(0))\} \\
\mathbf{U}_S(I_3) &= \{lp(a,n(0)), lp(a,n(n(0))), \ldots, \\
&\quad lp(b,0), lp(b,n(n(0))), lp(b,n(n(n(0)))), \ldots, \\
&\quad lp(c,0), lp(c,n(0)), lp(c,n(n(n(0)))), \ldots, k(b,a), k(c,a), k(c,b)\} \\
\mathbf{W}_S(I_3) &= \mathbf{T}_S(I_3) \cup \neg \cdot \mathbf{U}_S(I_3) \\
\mathbf{W}_S(I_4) &= \mathbf{W}_S(I_3)
\end{aligned}$$

```
knows(anna, chuck), longest_path(anna, n(0)),
not(longest_path(chuck, > n(n(0)))).
...
longest_path(bob, n(0)) ←
  knows(anna, bob), longest_path(anna, 0),
  not(longest_path(bob, > n(0))).
longest_path(bob, n(n(0))) ←
  knows(anna, bob), longest_path(anna, n(0)),
  not(longest_path(bob, > n(n(0)))).
...
longest_path(chuck, n(0)) ←
  knows(bob, chuck), longest_path(bob, 0),
  not(longest_path(chuck, > n(0))).
longest_path(chuck, n(n(0))) ←
  knows(bob, chuck), longest_path(bob, 0),
  not(longest_path(chuck, > n(n(0)))).
...
```

The most interesting section of the dependency graph of program S is shown in Figure 8 – the terms $lp(b, > n(0)), lp(b, n(n(0))), \ldots$, the facts $knows(a, b), knows(b, c), knows(a, c)$ and their dependencies with other literals are omitted for the sake of conciseness. Also only rule instantiations which are valid under the given extensional data are reflected in the graph, as weak stratification suggests. Even under these restrictions, the dependency graph of Listing 7.6 has an infinite weak stratification, and does not have a lowest stratum, which makes the program unamenable to an iterated fixpoint calculation over the strata. Nevertheless, the well-founded semantics for Listing 7.6 is well-defined and coincides with its intuitive semantics. The well-founded semantics being declarative, we leave the search for an operational semantics of weakly stratified programs with an infinite stratification as an open question.

7.4 ON THE RELATION OF GROUPING STRATIFICATION WITH NEGATION STRATIFICATION

The Xcerpt grouping constructs all and some are used to collect sets of bindings for the same variable within a term. Grouping constructs are useful for constructing all kinds of collections, such as the list of all European capitals from a binary relation containing the capitals of countries as in Example 32. According to the fixpoint semantics given in [Scho4a], Example 32 entails the Xcerpt data term capitals{Berlin, Paris, Rome}, but it *does not* entail the data term capitals{Berlin, Paris}.

Example 32 (A simple Xcerpt program with a grouping construct).

capitals{all var City} ← capital[var Country, var City].
capital[Germany, Berlin].
capital[France, Paris].
capital[Italy, Rome].

As pointed out in [Scho4a], grouping constructs allow the specification of programs whose semantics is unclear or unintended by the query author. To exclude such programs and to determine the correct order of evaluation of rule programs, grouping stratification has been introduced as a syntactic criterion for asserting that the semantics of a program is clear. Moreover, the semantics of an Xcerpt program P with grouping constructs is iteratively defined over the stratification of P. Any Xcerpt program that is grouping stratifiable is guaranteed to have a well-defined meaning. There are, however, Xcerpt programs that are not grouping stratifiable, and still have a well defined meaning. In [Esto8] the set of *locally grouping stratifiable* programs is introduced, which generalizes the set of grouping stratifiable programs, and a semantics for this class of programs is given which coincides with the semantics of [Scho4a] on the class of grouping stratifiable programs.

In this section we show that (i) grouping stratification is in fact the same thing as negation stratification, (ii) that Xcerpt programs with grouping constructs can be mapped to Xcerpt programs without grouping constructs, but with negation, such that the evaluation of the transformed program, and a canonical transformation of the results is equivalent to the evaluation of the program with grouping constructs. In practice, this transformation immediately gives rise to an evaluation algorithm for Xcerpt programs that is easier to implement, since it does not depend on the notion of grouping stratification.

7.4.1 Translation of Programs with Single Grouping Constructs to Grouping-free Xcerpt Programs

We start out by evaluating a simple Xcerpt program P with a single all construct by a translation to an Xcerpt program $T(P)$ without grouping constructs, evaluation of $T(P)$ to obtain the result $Eval(T(P))$, and inverse transformation of $Eval(T(P))$ to $T^{-1}(Eval(T(P)))$. $T^{-1}(Eval(T(P)))$ yields the same result as the direct evaluation $Eval(P)$ of P.

Example 33. *A simple Xcerpt program P with the grouping construct* all

g{all var X} ← f{X}.
f{a}. f{b}. f{c}.

Consider the Xcerpt program P in Example 33. First we consider direct evaluation of P: the rule body f{X} is unified with all facts of the program (f{a}, f{b}, and f{c}), yielding the following substitution set σ.

$$\sigma = \{\{X \mapsto a\}, \{X \mapsto b\}, \{X \mapsto c\}\}$$

σ is then applied to the head of the rule, yielding the term g{a, b, c}. With indirect evaluation, P is first translated to $T(P)$ (Example 34), which is evaluated to $Eval(T(P))$ in Example 7, and finally the result is transformed back to $T^{-1}(Eval(T(P)))$, yielding the final result g{c, b, a}, which is simulation-equivalent to g{a, b, c}, obtained by the direct evaluation.

The idea of the transformation in the first step is not to compute the maximum instantiation of a rule head h with grouping constructs at once, but to iteratively compute larger instantiations of the head until the maximum instantiation is reached. For this end, we use recursive list structures of the form list[F, R] where F is an Xcerpt term, and R is either itself a compound list or the empty list nil. In this representation, the term g{a, b, c} appears as g{list[a, list[b, list[c, nil]]]}. In contrast to flat collections of terms, list terms have a fixed arity of 2, but can also contain arbitrary numbers of elements.

Since we are only interested in the maximum instantiation of the rule head g{all var X}, a helper label helper is used to compute the intermediate results. Finally, only the largest atom with outermost label helper is transformed to the same atom with outermost label g. To avoid confusion with the vocabulary of the original programs, the vocabulary list, nil and helper should be prefixed by a reserved namespace, e.g. the Xcerpt namespace http://www.xcerpt.org.

The literals not(helper{desc F}) and not(helper{list[var _, var R]}) ensure that newly added elements are not already contained in a list, and that list tails are only used once in the construction. In this way, an order over the elements in the list is fixed. The rewritten program additionally contains a fact helper{nil} as the minimally instantiated rule head to initiate the iterative construction of the result.

Example 34. *Grouping-free rewriting* T(P) *of the program* P *in Example 33*

helper{list[var F, var R]} ←
    f{varF}, helper{var R}, not(helper{desc F}),
    not(helper{list[var_, var R]}).
f{a}. f{b}. f{c}.
helper{nil}.
g{var List} ← helper{var List}, not(helper{list[var _, var List]}).

The evaluation of the above program proceeds as in Table 7: on the left hand side, the substitution sets obtained from evaluating rule bodies are shown, the right hand side shows the result of the application of these substitution sets to the respective rule heads.

Table 7: Evaluation of the program T(P) in Example 34

{var F ↦ a, var R ↦ nil}	⇒ helper{list[a, nil] }
{var F ↦ b, var R ↦ list[a, nil] }	⇒ helper{list[b, list[a, nil]] }
{var F ↦ c, var R ↦ list[b, list[a, nil]] }	⇒ helper{list[c, list[b, list[a, nil]]] }
{var List ↦ list[c, list[b, list[a, nil]]] }	⇒ g{list[c, list[b, list[a, nil]]] }

After the transformed program is evaluated, all but the maximal instantiated rule head m = g{list[c, list[b, list[a, nil]]]} are discarded, and m is transformed back into the ordinary Xcerpt term notation g{c, b, a} without lists.

With the method informally described by the above example, Xcerpt rules with single grouping constructs can be evaluated without determination of the grouping stratification of the program. For the sake of brevity, we leave the determination of a general transformation algorithm for Xcerpt programs with simple grouping constructs to grouping-free Xcerpt programs as future work. Moreover we do not cover the question about how Xcerpt rules containing both negation and grouping constructs are translated to grouping-free Xcerpt programs. In fact, the semantics of such rules has been left unspecified in [Scho4a], and the approach taken in this section seems to be a promising way for achieving a unified negation- and grouping-semantics for Xcerpt.

Rewriting of rules with grouping constructs and negation

7.4.2 Translation of Programs with Nested Grouping Constructs to Grouping-free Xcerpt Programs

Grouping constructs are often used in a nested manner as in Example 35, which groups cities according to the countries they are located in, and wraps the result in a single Xcerpt term with root label db (for database). The semantics of nested grouping constructs in Xcerpt is non-trivial, but in line with grouping in XCERPT^{RDF} (Definition 37). This subsection shows how rules with nested grouping constructs can be translated to rules with simple, unnested grouping constructs, retaining the semantics of the original program. Together with the algorithm sketched in the previous subsection, both techniques allow the rewriting of arbitrary Xcerpt programs to Xcerpt programs without grouping constructs.

Example 35 (An Xcerpt program Q with nested grouping constructs).

>   db{all country{var Country, cities{all var City} } } ←
>   located_in[var City, var Country].
>   located_in[Barcelona, Spain].
>   located_in[Madrid, Spain].
>   located_in[Warsaw, Poland].

Evaluation of Q yields the Xcerpt term

> Eval(Q) = db{country{Spain, cities{Barcelona, Madrid} },
>   country{Poland, cities{Warsaw} } }

Xcerpt rules with nested grouping constructs can be rewritten to sequences of rules without nested grouping constructs as follows: Let r be a rule with nested grouping constructs contained in an Xcerpt program P. Let l_h be the outermost label of the head of r. Let r_1 be the rule obtained from r by omitting the outermost grouping construct, and substituting the outermost label by a fresh label l_1.[9] Let r_2 be a rule of the form of Equation 7.1. Then the result of the evaluation of the program P' which is obtained from P by substituting the rule r by the sequence of rules r_1, r_2 restricted to the vocabulary of P.

$$l_h\{\text{all var Item}\} \leftarrow l_1\{\text{var Item}\} \qquad (7.1)$$

Example 36 (Rewriting nested grouping constructs to simple grouping constructs). *The program Q of example 35 is rewritten to the following Xcerpt program R(Q). Observe that R(Q) does not contain nested grouping constructs.*

>   item{country{var Country, cities{all var City}}} ←
>   located_in[var City, var Country].
>   db{all var Item} ← item{var Item}
>   located_in[Barcelona, Spain].
>   located_in[Madrid, Spain].
>   located_in[Warsaw, Poland].

---
9 Freshness of the label l_1 can be ensured by using a reserved namespace such as http://www.xcerpt.org.

R(Q) *is evaluated as shown below. All terms with outermost label* item *are only intermediate results and can be discarded after the evaluation. The term with outermost label* db *is considered as the final result and coincides with the direct evaluation of* Q.

$$\sigma_1 = \{\,\{City \mapsto Barcelona, Country \mapsto Spain\},$$
$$\{City \mapsto Madrid, Country \mapsto Spain\},$$
$$\{City \mapsto Warsaw, Country \mapsto Poland\}\,\}$$
$$\Rightarrow item\{country\{Spain, cities\{Barcelona, Madrid\}\}\},$$
$$item\{country\{Poland, cities\{Warsaw\}\}\}$$
$$\sigma_2 = \{\,\{Item \mapsto country\{Spain\ldots\}\},$$
$$\{Item \mapsto country\{Poland\ldots\}\}\,\}$$
$$\Rightarrow db\{country\{Spain\ldots\}, country\{Poland\ldots\}\}$$

As for the rewriting of simple grouping constructs to grouping-free Xcerpt programs, we do not give a general algorithm for the task of rewriting nested grouping constructs to simple grouping constructs. Yet the specification of such an algorithm seems to be straightforward.

Once all nested grouping constructs have been eliminated, the resulting rule set can be rewritten to an Xcerpt program completely free of grouping constructs as shown in Section 7.4.1.

Example 37 (Grouping-free version of Example 35). *Example 35 can be rewritten to the following (almost) equivalent program without grouping constructs:*

$helper_1\{country\{var\ Country, cities\{list[var\ City, var\ Rest]\}\}\} \leftarrow$
    $located\_in[var\ City, var\ Country],$
    $helper_1\{country\{var\ Country, cities\{var\ Rest\}\}\},$
    $not(helper_1\{country\{var\ Country, desc\ var\ City\}\}),$
    $not(helper_1\{country\{var\ Country, cities\{list[var\ \_, var\ Rest]\}\}\})).$
$helper_1\{country\{var\ Country, cities\{nil\}\}\} \leftarrow$
    $located\_in[var\ \_, var\ Country].$
$item\{country\{var\ Country, cities\{var\ List\}\}\} \leftarrow$
    $helper_1\{country\{var\ Country, cities\{var\ List\}\}\},$
    $not(helper_1\{country\{var\ Country, cities\{list[var\ \_, var\ List]\}\}\})$
$helper_2\{list[var\ Item, var\ Rest]\} \leftarrow$
    $item\{var\ Item\}, helper_2\{var\ Rest\}, not(helper_2\{desc\ var\ Item\}),$
    $not(helper_2\{list[var\ \_, var\ Rest]\}).$
$helper_2\{nil\}.$
$db\{var\ List\} \leftarrow helper_2\{var\ List\}, not(helper_2\{list[var\ \_, var\ List]\})$
$located\_in[Barcelona, Spain].$
$located\_in[Madrid, Spain].$
$located\_in[Warsaw, Poland].$

Figure 10 shows the dependency graph of the program above. While Q is a grouping stratifiable program, its transformation to a grouping-free program yields an Xcerpt program with negation that is not negation-stratifiable. It is, however, weakly negation stratifiable.

Figure 10: Dependency graph of the grouping-free transformation of Q

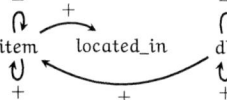

While the transformation of the Xcerpt program with nested grouping constructs in 35 results in a weakly grouping stratifiable program, this might not always be the case. We leave this question open for future work.

8
XCERPT QUERY TERM SUBSUMPTION

Contents

8.1 Xcerpt^{XML} Query Terms and Simulation   165
8.2 Simulation Subsumption   165
8.3 Simulation Subsumption by Rewriting   167
8.4 Properties of the Rewriting System   170
     8.4.1 Subsumption Monotonicity and Soundness   170
     8.4.2 Completeness   172
     8.4.3 Decidability and Complexity   173
8.5 Complexity for Xcerpt Fragments   174
8.6 Future Work in the Area of Xcerpt Query Term Subsumption   185

This section deals with the subsumption relationship between Xcerpt query terms. Deciding subsumption has traditionally been an important means for optimizing multiple queries against the same set of data and can be used for improving termination of Xcerpt programs in a backward chaining evaluation engine.

Xcerpt query terms (Definition 53) are an answer to accessing Web data in a rule-based query language. Like most approaches to querying Web data (or semi-structured data, in general), Xcerpt query terms differ from relational query languages such as SQL by a set of query constructs specifically attuned to the less rigid, often diverse, or even entirely schema-less nature of Web data. As Definitions 53 (Xcerpt Query Term) and 58 suggest, Xcerpt terms are similar to normalized forward XPath (see [OMFB02]) but extended with variables, deep-equal, a notion of injective match and regular expressions. Thus, they achieve much of the expressiveness of XQuery without sacrificing the simplicity and pattern-structure of XPath.

When used in the context of Xcerpt, query terms serve a similar role to terms of first-order logic in logic languages. Therefore, the notion of unification has been adapted for Web data in [Sch04a], there called "simulation unification". Simulation for Xcerpt^{XML} terms is recapitulated in Definition 59. This form of unification is capable of handling all the extensions of query terms over first-order terms that are needed to support Web data: selecting terms at arbitrary depth (desc), distinguishing partial from total terms, regular expressions instead of plain labels, negated subterms (without), etc.

The notions of query term, simulation and substitution sets are exemplified in Section 4.1 and formally defined in 7.1. In this section, we consider query containment between two Xcerpt terms.

Subsumption or containment of two queries (or terms) is an established technique for optimizing query evaluation: a query q_1 is said to be *subsumed* by or *contained* in a query q_2 if every possible answer to q_1 against every possible data is also an answer to q_2. Thus, given all answers to q_2, we can evaluate q_1 only against those answers rather than against the whole database.

For first-order terms, subsumption is efficient and employed for guaranteeing termination in tabling (or memoization) approaches to backward chaining of logic [TS86, CW96]. However, when we move from first-order terms to Web queries, subsumption (or containment) becomes quickly less efficient or even intractable. Xcerpt query terms have, as pointed out above, some similarity with XPath queries. Containment for various fragments of XPath is surveyed in [Scho4b], both in absence and in presence of a DTD. Here, we focus on the first setting, where no additional information about the schema of the data is available. However, Xcerpt query terms are a strict super-set of (navigational) XPath as investigated in [Scho4b]. In particular, the Xcerpt query terms may contain (multiple occurrences of the same) variables. This brings them closer to *conjunctive queries* (with negation and deep-equal), as considered in [WL03] on general relations, and in [BMS07] for tree data. Basic Xcerpt query terms can be reduced to (unions of) conjunctive queries with negation. However, the injectivity of Xcerpt query terms (no two siblings may match with the same data node) and the presence of deep-equal (two nodes are deep-equal iff they have the same structure) have no direct counterpart in conjunctive query containment. Though [Klu88b] shows how inequalities in general affect conjunctive query containment, the effect of injectivity (or all-distinct constraints) on query containment has not been studied previously. The same applies to deep-equal, though the results in [Koco5] indicate that in *absence* of composition deep-equal has no effect on evaluation and thus likely on containment complexity.

For Xcerpt query terms, subsumption is, naturally, of interest for the design of a terminating, efficient Xcerpt engine. Beyond that, however, it is particularly relevant in a Web setting. Whenever we know that one query subsumes another, we do not need to access whatever data the two queries access twice, but rather can evaluate both queries with a single access to the basic data by evaluating the second query on the answers of the first one. This can be a key optimization also in the context of search engines, where answers to frequent queries can be memorized so as to avoid their repeated computation. Even though today's search engines are rather blind of the tree or graph structure of HTML, XML and RDF data, there is no doubt that some more or less limited form of structured queries will become more and more frequent in the future (see Google scholar's "search by author, date, etc."). Query subsumption, or containment, is key to a selection of queries, the answers to which are to be stored so as to allow as many queries as possible to be evaluated against that small set of data rather than against the entire search engine data. Thus, the notion of simulation subsumption proposed in this chapter can be seen as a building block of future, structure-aware search engines.

Therefore, we study in this section subsumption of Xcerpt query terms. The main building blocks of this section are the following.

- we introduce and formalize a notion of subsumption for Xcerpt query terms, called *simulation subsumption*, in Section 8.2. To the best of our knowledge, this is the first notion of subsumption for queries with injectivity of sibling nodes and deep-equal.

- we show, also in Section 8.2, that simulation on ground query terms is equivalent to simulation subsumption.[1] This shows that ground query term simulation as introduced in [Scho4a] captures the intuition that a query term that simulates into another query term subsumes that term.

- we define, in Section 8.3, a *rewriting system* that allows us to reduce the test for subsumption of q in q' to finding a sequence of syntactic transformations that can be applied to q to transform it into q'.

- we show, in Section 8.4, that this rewriting system gives rise to an algorithm for testing subsumption that is sound and complete and can determine whether q subsumes q' in time $\mathcal{O}(n!^n)$. In particular, this shows that simulation subsumption is decidable.

8.1 XCERPT^{XML} QUERY TERMS AND SIMULATION

Query terms are an abstraction for queries that can be used to extract data from semi-structured trees. In contrast to XPath queries, they may contain (multiple occurrences of the same) variables and demand an *injective mapping* of the child terms of each term. For example, the XPath query /a/b[c]/c demands that the document root has label a, and has a child term with label b that has itself a child term with label c. The subterm c that is given within the predicate of b can be mapped to the same node in the data as the child named c of b. Therefore, this XPath query would be equivalent to the query term a{{b{{c}}}}, but not to a{{b{{c, c}}}}. Simulation could be, however, easily modified to drop the injectivity requirement.

8.2 SIMULATION SUBSUMPTION

In this section, we first introduce simulation subsumption (Definition 74), then for several query terms we discuss whether one subsumes the other to give an intuition for the compositionality of the subsumption relationship. Subsequently, the transitivity of the subsumption relationship is proven (Lemma 1), some conclusions about the membership in the subsumption relationship of subterms, given the membership in the subsumption relationship of their parent terms are stated. These conclusions formalize the compositionality of simulation subsumption and are a necessary condition for the completeness of the rewriting system introduced in Section 8.3.

In tabled evaluation of logic programs, solutions to subgoals are saved in a solution table, such that for equivalent or subsumed subgoals, these sets do not have to be recomputed. As mentioned before, this avoidance of re-computation does not only save time, but can, in certain cases be crucial for the termination of a backward chaining evaluation of a program. In order to classify subgoal as solution or look-up goals, boolean subsumption as specified by Definition 74 must be decided. Although Xcerpt query terms may contain variables, n-ary subsumption as defined in [Scho4b] would be too strict for our purposes. To see this, consider the Xcerpt query terms $q_1 := a\{\{var\ X\}\}$ and $q_2 := a\{\{c\}\}$.

---

[1] With small adaptions of the treatment of regular expressions and negated subterms in query term simulation.

Although all data terms that are relevant for q_2 can be found in the solutions for q_1, q_1 and q_2 cannot be compared by n-ary containment, because they differ in the number of their query variables.

Definition 74 (Simulation Subsumption). *A query term q_1 subsumes another query term q_2 if all data terms that q_2 simulates with are also simulated by q_1.*

Example 38 (Examples for the subsumption relationship). *Let the query terms $q_1, \ldots q_5$ be given by:*

- $q_1 := a\{\{\}\}$
- $q_2 := a\{\{desc\ b, desc\ c, d\}\}$
- $q_3 := a\{\{desc\ b, c, d\}\}$
- $q_4 := a\{\{without\ e\}\}$
- $q_5 := a\{\{without\ e\{\{without\ f\}\}\}\}$

Then the following subsumption relationships hold:

- *q_2 subsumes q_3 because it requires less than q_3: While q_3 requires that the data has outermost label a, subterms c and d as well as a descendant subterm b, q_2 requires not that there is a direct subterm c, but only a descendant subterm. Since every descendant subterm is also a direct subterm, all data terms simulating with q_3 also simulate with q_2.*

  But the subsumption relationship can also be decided in terms of simulation: q_2 subsumes q_3, because there is a mapping π from the direct subterms ChildT(q_2) of q_2 to the direct subterms ChildT(q_3) of q_3, such that q_i subsumes $\pi(q_i)$ for all q_i in ChildT(q_2).

- *q_3 does not subsume q_2, since there are data terms that simulate with q_2, but not with q_3. One such data term is $d := a\{b, e\{c\}, d\}$.*

  Again, the subsumption relationship between q_3 and q_2 (in this order) can be decided by simulation. There is no mapping π from the direct subterms of q_3 to the direct subterms of q_2, such that a simulates into $\pi(a)$.

- *q_1 subsumes q_4 since it requires less than q_4. All data terms that simulate with q_4 also simulate with q_1.*

- *q_4 does not subsume q_1, since the data term $a\{\{e\}\}$ simulates with q_1, but does not simulate with q_4.*

- *q_5 subsumes q_4, but not the other way around.*

Proposition 1. *The subsumption relationship between query terms is transitive, i.e. for arbitrary query terms q_1, q_2 and q_3 it holds that if q_1 subsumes q_2 and q_2 subsumes q_3, then q_1 subsumes q_3.*

Proposition 1 immediately follows from the transitivity of the subset relationship. Query term simulation and subsumption are defined in a way such that, given the simulation subsumption between two query terms, one can draw conclusions about subsumption relationships that must be fulfilled between pairs of subterms of the query terms. Lemma 10 formalizes these sets of conclusions.

Lemma 10 (Subterm Subsumption). *Let q_1 and q_2 be query terms such that q_1 subsumes q_2. Then there is an injective mapping π from $\text{ChildT}^+(q_1)$ to $\text{ChildT}^+(q_2)$ such that q_1^i subsumes $\pi(q_1^i)$ for all $q_1^i \in \text{ChildT}^+(q_1)$.*

Furthermore, if q_1 and q_2 are breadth-incomplete, then there is a (not necessarily injective) mapping σ from $\text{ChildT}^-(q_1)$ to $\text{ChildT}^-(q_2)$ such that $\text{pos}(\sigma(q_1^j))$ subsumes $\text{pos}(q_1^j)$ for all $q_1^j \in \text{ChildT}^-(q_1)$.

If q_1 is breadth-incomplete and q_2 is breadth-complete then there is no q_1^j in $\text{ChildT}^-(q_1)$ and $q_2^k \in \text{ChildT}^+(q_2) \setminus \text{range}(\pi)$ such that $\text{pos}(q_1^j) \preceq q_2^k$.

Lemma 10 immediately follows from the equivalence of the subsumption relationship and the extended query term simulation (see Lemma 15 in the appendix).

8.3 SIMULATION SUBSUMPTION BY REWRITING

In this section, we lay the foundations for a proof for the decidability of subsumption between query terms according to Definition 74 by introducing a rewriting system from one query term to another, which is later shown to be sound and complete. Furthermore, this rewriting system lays the foundation for the complexity analysis in Section 8.4.3.

The transformation of a query term q_1 into a subsumed query term q_2 is exemplified in Figure 8.3.

Definition 75 (Subsumption monotone query term transformations). *Let q be a query term. The following is a list of so-called* subsumption monotone *query term transformations.*

- *if q has incomplete subterm specification, it may be transformed to the analogous query term with complete subterm specification.*

$$\frac{a\{\!\{q_1,\ldots,q_n\}\!\}}{a\{q_1,\ldots,q_n\}}, \qquad \frac{a[\![q_1,\ldots,q_n]\!]}{a[q_1,\ldots,q_n]} \qquad (8.1)$$

- *if q has unordered subterm specification, it may be transformed to the analogous query term with ordered subterm specification.*

$$\frac{a\{\!\{q_1,\ldots,q_n\}\!\}}{a[\![q_1,\ldots,q_n]\!]}, \qquad \frac{a\{q_1,\ldots,q_n\}}{a[q_1,\ldots,q_n]} \qquad (8.2)$$

- *if q is of the form $\text{desc } q'$ then the descendant construct may be eliminated or it may be split into two descendant constructs separated by the regular expression /.*/, the inner descendant construct being wrapped in double curly braces.*

$$\frac{\text{desc } q}{q}, \qquad \frac{\text{desc } q}{\text{desc } /.*/\{\!\{\text{desc } q\}\!\}} \qquad (8.3)$$

- *if q has incomplete-unordered subterm specification, then a fresh variable X may be appended to the end of the subterm list. A fresh variable is a variable that does not occur in q_1 or q_2 and is not otherwise introduced by the rewriting system.*

$$X \text{ fresh} \Rightarrow \frac{a\{\!\{q_1,\ldots,q_n\}\!\},}{a\{\!\{q_1,\ldots,q_n,\text{var } X\}\!\}} \qquad (8.4)$$

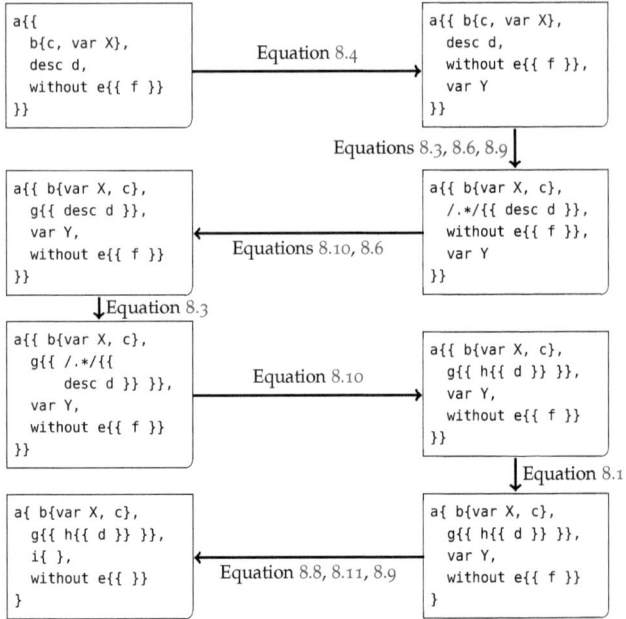

- *if q has incomplete-ordered subterm specification, then a fresh variable may be inserted at the beginning, at the end, or in between two subterms of q:*

$$\frac{X \text{ fresh}, i \in \{1,\ldots,n\} \Rightarrow}{a[[q_1,\ldots,q_i, \text{var } X, q_{i+1},\ldots,q_n]]} \quad (8.5)$$

- *if q has unordered subterm specification, then the subterms of q may be arbitrarily permuted.*

$$\pi \in \text{Perms}(\{1,\ldots,n\}) \Rightarrow \frac{a\{\{q_1, \ldots, q_n\}\}}{a\{\{q_{\pi(1)}, \ldots, q_{\pi(n)}\}\}} \quad (8.6)$$

$$\pi \in \text{Perms}(\{1,\ldots,n\}) \Rightarrow \frac{a\{q_1, \ldots, q_n\}}{a\{q_{\pi(1)}, \ldots, q_{\pi(n)}\}} \quad (8.7)$$

- *if q contains a variable var X, which occurs in q at least once in a positive context (i.e. not within the scope of a without) then all occurrences of var X may be substituted by another Xcerpt query term.*

$$X \in \text{PV}(q), t \in \text{QTerms} \Rightarrow \frac{q}{q\{X \mapsto t\}} \quad (8.8)$$

This rule may only be applied, if q contains all occurrences of X in q_1. Furthermore, no further rewriting rules may be applied to the replacement term t.

If a variable appears within q only in a negative context (i.e. within the scope of a without*), the variable cannot be substituted by an arbitrary term to yield a transformed term that is subsumed by q. The query terms* a{{ without var X }} *and* a{{ without b{ } }} *together with the data term* a{ c } *illustrate this characteristic of the subsumption relationship. For further discussion of substitution of variables in a negative context see Example 39.*

- *if q has a subterm q_i, then q_i may be transformed by any of the transformations in this list except for Equation 8.8 to the term $t(q_i)$, and this transformed version may be substituted at the place of q_i in q, as formalized by the following rule:* [23]

$$\frac{q_i}{t(q_i)} \Rightarrow \frac{a\{\{q_1, \ldots, q_n\}\}}{a\{\{q_1, \ldots, q_{i-1}, t(q_i), q_{i+1}, \ldots q_n\}\}} \tag{8.9}$$

- *if the label of q is a regular expression e, this regular expression may be replaced by any label that matches with e, or any other regular expression e' which is subsumed by e (see Definition 57).*[2]

$$e \in RE, e \text{ subsumes } e' \Rightarrow \frac{e\{\{q_1, \ldots, q_n\}\}}{e'\{\{q_1, \ldots, q_n\}\}} \tag{8.10}$$

- *if q contains a negated subterm $q_i =$ without r and r' is a query term such that $t(r') = r$ (i.e. r' subsumes r) for some transformation step t, then q_i can be replaced by $q_i' :=$ without r'.*[4]

$$(q_i = \text{without } r) \wedge \frac{r'}{r} \wedge (q_i' = \text{without } r')$$
$$\Rightarrow \frac{a\{\{q_1, \ldots, q_i, \ldots, q_n\}\}}{a\{\{q_1, \ldots, q_i', \ldots q_n\}\}} \tag{8.11}$$

- *if q is breadth-complete and contains a negated subterm, this subterm may simply be omitted:*[5]

$$(q_i = \text{without } r), i \in \{1, \ldots, n\}$$
$$\Rightarrow \frac{a\{q_1, \ldots, q_i, \ldots, q_n\}}{a\{q_1, \ldots, q_{i-1}, q_{i+1} \ldots q_n\}} \tag{8.12}$$

---
[2] The respective rules for complete-unordered subterm specification, incomplete-ordered subterm specification and complete-ordered subterm specification are omitted for the sake of brevity.
[3] The exclusion of Equation 8.8 ensures that variable substitutions are only applied to entire query terms and not to subterms. Otherwise the same variable might be substituted by different terms in different subterms.
[4] The respective transformation rule for ordered-incomplete query terms is omitted for the sake of brevity. Since negated subterms in complete query terms are irrelevant, we assume complete subterms to not contain negated subterms. Alternatively, these terms can be transformed by Rule 8.12
[5] The respective rule for ordered-complete query term specification is omitted for the sake of brevity.

- if q is breadth-incomplete and contains two negated subterms $s_1 =$ without s_1' and $s_2 =$ without s_2' such that $s_1' = t(s_2')$ for some transformation step t, then s_1 can be omitted from q.

8.4 PROPERTIES OF THE REWRITING SYSTEM

In this section, we show that the rewriting system introduced in the previous section is sound (Section 8.4.1) and complete (Section 8.4.2). Furthermore, we study the structure of the search tree induced by the rewriting rules, show that it can be pruned without losing the completeness of the rewriting system and conclude that simulation subsumption is decidable. Finally we derive complexity results from the size of the search tree in Section 8.4.3.

8.4.1 *Subsumption Monotonicity and Soundness*

Lemma 11 (Monotonicity of the transformations in Definition 75). *All of the transformations given in Definition 75 are subsumption monotone, i.e. for any query term q and a transformation from Definition 75 which is applicable to q, q subsumes* t(q).

The proof of Lemma 11 is straight-forward since each of the transformation steps can be shown independently of the others. For all of the transformations, inverse transformation steps t^{-1} can be defined, and obviously for any query term q it holds that $t^{-1}(q)$ subsumes q.

Lemma 12 (Transitivity of the subsumption relationship, monotonicity of a sequence of subsumption monotone query term transformations). *For a sequence of subsumption monotone query term transformations* $t_1, \ldots, t_n$, *and an arbitrary query term q, q subsumes* $t_1 \circ \ldots \circ t_n(q_1)$.

The transitivity of the subsumption relationship is immediate from its definition (Definition 74) which is based on the subset relationship, which is itself transitive.

As mentioned above, the substitution of a variable X in a negative context of a query term q by a query term t, which is not a variable, results in a query term $q' := q[X \mapsto t]$ which is in fact more general than q. In other words $q[X \mapsto t]$ subsumes q for any query term q if X only appears within a negative context in q. On the other hand, if X only appears in a positive context within q, then q' is less general – i.e. q subsumes q'. But what about the case of X appearing both in a positive and a negative context within q? Consider the following example:

Example 39. *Let* q := a{{ var X, without b{{ var X }} }}. *It may be tempting to think that substituting X by* c[] *to give* q' = a{{ c[], without b{{ c[] }} }} *makes the first subterm of q less general, but the second subterm of q more general. In fact, the subterm* b[d] *within the data term* d := a[b[d]] *would cause the subterm* without b{{ var X }} *of q to fail, but the respective subterm of* q' *to succeed, suggesting that there is a data term that simulation unifies with* q', *but not with q, meaning that q does not subsume* q'. *However, there is no such data term, which is due to the fact that the second occurrence of X within q is only a consuming occurrence. When this part of the query term is evaluated, the variable X is already bound.*

8.4 PROPERTIES OF THE REWRITING SYSTEM   171

In Definition 76 the normalized form for Xcerpt query terms is introduced, because for an unnormalized query term q_1 that subsumes a query term q_2 one cannot guarantee that there is a sequence of subsumption monotone query term transformations $t_1, \ldots, t_n$ such that $t_n \circ \ldots \circ t_1(q_1) = q_2$. To see this, consider example 40.

Example 40 (Impossibility of transforming an unnormalized query term). *Consider* $q_1 := a\{\{var\ X\ as\ b\{\{c\}\}, var\ X\ as\ b\{\{d\}\}\}\}$ *and* $q_2 := a\{\{b\{\{c,d\}\}, b\{\{c,d\}\}\}\}$. q_2 *subsumes* q_1, *in fact both terms are even simulation equivalent. But there is no sequence of subsumption monotone query term transformations from* q_2 *to* q_1, *since one would have to omit one subterm from both the first subterm of* q_2 *and from the second one. But such a transformation would in general not be subsumption monotone.*

Besides opening up the possibility of specifying restrictions on one subterm non-locally, duplicate restrictions for the same variable also allow the formulation of *unsatisfiable* query terms, as the following example shows:

Example 41 (Unsatisfiable query terms due to variable restrictions). *Consider the query terms* $q_1 := a\{\{var\ X\ as\ b, var\ X\ as\ c\}\}$ *and* $q_2 := b\{\{\}\}$. *It is easy to see that* q_1 *is unsatisfiable, and thus* q_2 *subsumes* q_1. *However, there is no transformation sequence from* q_2 *to* q_1.

Also single variable restrictions may in some cases be problematic, because they allow the specification of infinite, or at least graph structured data terms as example 42 shows:

Example 42 (Nested variable restrictions). *Consider the query terms* $q_1 := a\{\{var\ X\ as\ b\{\{var\ X\}\}\}\}$ *and* $q_2 := a\{\{var\ Y\ as\ b\{\{b\{\{var\ Y\}\}\}\}\}\}$. *Both* q_1 *and* q_2 *simulate (among others) with the graph structured data terms* $d_1 := a\{\ \&1^{\wedge}b\ \{\ \&1\ \}\ \}$, $d_2 := a\{\ \&1^{\wedge}b\ \{\ b\{\ \&1\ \}\ \}\ \}$, *etc. Xcerpt data terms and query terms as defined in [BS02] may include defining occurrences of subterms (such as* $\&1^{\wedge}b\{\ \}$*) and referring ones (such as* $\&1$*), and thus represent true graph structures. In the absence of such graph structured data terms (as considered in this thesis) and in the absence of infinite data terms,* q_1 *and* q_2 *are simply unsatisfiable, and thus useless. Therefore we assume Xcerpt query terms to be free of such cyclic variable restrictions. Cyclic variable restrictions may also slightly harder to recognize such as in the query term* $q_3 := a\{\ var\ X\ as\ b\{\ var\ Y\ \},\ var\ Y\ as\ c\{\ var\ X\ \}\ \}$.

To overcome these issues, query terms are assumed to be in normalized form (Definition 76). In fact, almost all Xcerpt query terms can be transformed into normalized form.

Definition 76 (Query terms in normalized form). *A query term that contains only a single variable restriction for each variable, and that is free of cyclic variable restrictions, is a query term in* normalized *form. A query term which can be converted into an equivalent query term in normalized form is said to be* normalizable.

Not all Xcerpt query terms are normalizable, as Example 43 shows:

Example 43 (Unnormalizable Xcerpt query terms). *Consider the Xcerpt query term* $q := a\{\ var\ X\ as\ b\{\{\ c\ \}\},\ var\ X\ as\ b[[\ d,\ e]]\ \}$. *The first variable restriction for X requires that the binding for X has a subterm with label* c. *The second variable restriction for X requires its binding to have two subterms* d *and* e *with* d *preceding* e. *The term* $r := a\{\ var\ X\ as\ b\{\{\ c,\ d,\ e\ \}\},\ var\ X\ \}$ *is* *more general than* q *since it does not specify that* d *must precede* e *in the binding of* X. *On the other hand, the term* s := a { var X as b[[c, d , e]], var X } *is less general than* q, *since it fixes an order between the pairs* (c, d) *and* (c, e). *While* q *is equivalent to the query*[6] *in Listing 8.1 there is no query term with a single variable restriction that is equivalent to* q.

Listing 8.1: A disjunction of normalized query terms equivalent to q

```
or{
    a { var X as b[[ c, d , e ]], var X },
    a { var X as b[[ d, c , e ]], var X },
    a { var X as b[[ d, e , c ]], var X }
}
```

Unsatisfiability of query terms makes the decision procedure for subsumption more complex, and thus it is to be avoided whenever possible. Allowing the specification of unsatisfiable query terms does not add expressive power to a query language, and should thus be disallowed. Apart from the normal form, also *subterm injectivity* is a means for preventing the user of the Xcerpt query language from specifying unsatisfiable queries.

Example 44 (Unsatisfiability due to non-injectivity). *In this example we use triple curly braces to state that the mapping from the siblings enclosed within the braces need not be injective. With this notation queries become less restrictive as the number of braces in the subterm specification increases. Let* $q_1 := a\{\{\{b, \text{without } b\}\}\}$. *Since* q_1 *both requires and forbids the presence of a subterm with label* b, *it is clearly unsatisfiable. Let* $q_2 := b\{\{\}\}$. *Although* q_2 *subsumes* q_1, *we cannot find a subsumption monotone transformation sequence from* q_2 *to* q_1.

The above example shows that the the proof for the decidability of the subsumption relationship given in this section relies on the injectivity of the subterm mapping. Since there is no injectivity requirement for multiple consecutive predicates in XPath, the proof cannot be trivially used to show decidability of subsumption of XPath fragments.

8.4.2 Completeness

Theorem 13 (Subsumption by transformation). *Let* q_1 *and* q_2 *be two query terms in normalized form such that* q_1 *subsumes* q_2. *Then* q_1 *can be transformed into* q_2 *by a sequence of subsumption monotone query term transformations listed in Definition 75.*

Proof. We distinguish two cases:

- q_1 and q_2 are subsumption equivalent (i.e. they subsume each other)

- q_1 strictly subsumes q_2

The first case is the easier one. If q_1 and q_2 are subsumption equivalent, then there is no data term t, such that t simulates with one, but not the other. Hence q_1 and q_2 are merely syntactical variants of each other. Then q_1 can be transformed into q_2 by consistent renaming of variables (Equation 8.9), and by reordering sibling terms within subterms of q

---
6 Recall that a query is a conjunction, disjunction or negation of query terms.

(Equation 8.6). This would not be true for unnormalized query terms as Example 40 shows.

The second is shown by structural induction on q_1.

For both the induction base and the induction step, we assume that q_1 subsumes q_2, but that the inverse is false. Then there is a data term d, such that q_1 simulates into d, but q_2 does not. In both the induction base and the induction step, we give a distinction of cases, enumerating all possible reasons for q_1 simulating into d but q_2 not. For each of these cases, a sequence of subsumption monotone transformations $t_1, \ldots t_n$ from Definition 75 is given, such that $q_1' := t_n \circ t_{n-1} \circ \ldots \circ t_1(q_1)$ does *not* simulate into d. By Lemmas 11 and 12, q_1' still subsumes q_2. Hence by considering d and by applying the transformations, q_1 is brought "closer" to q_2. If q_1' is still more general than q_2, then one more dataterm d' can be found that simulates with q_1', but not with q_2, and another sequence of transformations to be applied can be deduced from this theorem. This process can be repeated until q_1 has been transformed into a simulation equivalent version of q_2. For the proof, see the appendix of [BFL07]. □

8.4.3 Decidability and Complexity

In the previous section, we establish that, for each pair of query terms q_1, q_2 such that q_1 subsumes q_2, there is a (possibly infinite) sequence of transformations $t_1, \ldots, t_k$ by one of the rules in Section 8.3 such that $t_k \circ \ldots \circ t_1(q) = q_2$.

However, if we reconsider the proof of Theorem 13, it is quite obvious that the sequence of transformations can in fact not be infinite: Intuitively, we transform at each step in the proof q_1 further towards q_2, guided by a data term that simulates in q_1 but not in q_2. In fact, the length of a transformation sequence is bounded by the sum of the sizes of the two query terms. As size of a query term we consider the total number of its subterms.

Proposition 2 (Length of Transformation Sequences). *Let q_1 and q_2 be two Xcerpt query terms such that q_1 subsumes q_2 and n the sum of the sizes of q_1 and q_2. Then, there is a sequence of transformations $t_1, \ldots, t_k$ such that $t_k \circ \ldots \circ t_1(q_1) = q_2$ and $k \in \mathcal{O}(n)$.*

Proof. We show that the sequences of transformations created by the proof of Theorem 13 can be bounded by $\mathcal{O}(n+m)$ if computed in a specific way: We maintain a mapping μ from subterms of q_1 to subterms of q_2 indicating how the query terms are mapped. μ is initialized with (q_1, q_2). In the following, we call a data term d *discriminating* between q_1 and q_2 if q_1 simulates in d but not q_2.

(1) For each pair (q, q') in μ, we first choose a discriminating data term that matches case 1 in the proof of Theorem 13. If there is such a data term, we apply Equation (8.10), label replacement, once to q obtaining t(q) and update the pair in μ by $(t(q), q')$. This step is performed at most once for each pair as $(t(q), q')$ have the same label and thus there is no more discriminating data term that matches case 1.

(2) Otherwise, we next choose a discriminating data term that matches case 2.a.i or 2.b.i. In both cases, we apply Equation (8.4), variable insertion, to insert a new variable and update the pair in μ. This step is performed at most $|q_2| - |q_1| \leqslant n$ times for each pair.

(3) Otherwise, we next choose a discriminating data term that matches case 2.a.ii and apply Equation (8.1), complete term specification and update the pair in μ. This step is performed at most once for each pair.

(4) Finally, the only type of discriminating data term that remains is one with the same number of positive child terms as q_2. We use an oracle to guess the right mapping σ from child terms of q_1 to child terms of q_2. Then we remove the pair from μ and add $(c, \sigma(c))$ to μ for each child term of q_1. This step is performed at most once for each pair in μ.

Since query subterms have a single parent, we add each subterm only once to μ in a pair. Except for case 2, we perform only a constant number of transformations to each pair. Case 2 allows up to n transformations for a single pair, but the total number of transformations (over all pairs) due to case 2 is bound by the size of q_2. Thus in total we perform at most $4 \cdot n$ transformations where n is the sum of the number of the sizes of q_1 and q_2. □

Though we have established that the length of a transformation sequence is bound by $\mathcal{O}(n)$, we also have to consider how to *find* such a transformation sequence. The proof of Proposition 2, already spells out an algorithm for finding such transformation sequences. However, it uses an oracle to guess the right mapping between child terms of two terms that are to be transformed. A naive deterministic algorithm needs to consider all possible such mappings whose number is bound by $\mathcal{O}(n!)$. It is worth noting, however, that in most practical cases the actual number of such mappings is much smaller as most query terms have fairly low breadth and the possible mappings between their child terms are severely reduced just by considering only mappings where the labels of child terms simulate. However, in the worst case the $\mathcal{O}(n!)$ complexity for finding the right mapping may be reached and thus we obtain:

Theorem 14 (Complexity of Subsumption by Rewriting). *Let q_1 and q_2 be two Xcerpt query terms. Then we can test whether q_1 subsumes q_2 in $\mathcal{O}(n!^n)$ time.*

Proof. By proposition 2 we can find a $\mathcal{O}(n)$ length transformation sequence in $\mathcal{O}(n!^n)$ time and by Theorem 13 q_1 subsumes q_2 if and only if there is such a sequence. □

8.5 COMPLEXITY OF SUBSUMPTION FOR VARIOUS LESS EXPRESSIVE FRAGMENTS OF XCERPT

In this section we consider the Xcerpt query term fragment with descendant axis, incompleteness in breadth and label wild cards. We denote this fragment by Xcerpt({{}}, desc, ∗) and show that subsumption for this fragment is CoNP hard, and CoNP-complete if simulation for Xcerpt({{}}) is in P. Along the lines, we derive several complexity results for other, mostly less expressive fragments, of Xcerpt. The proof is inspired, and in large parts analogous to [MS02], which considers $XP^{\{\},*,//}$, i.e. the fragment of XPath containing branching, the descendant axis and label wildcards. Xcerpt({{}}, desc, ∗) is equivalent to $XP^{\{\},*,//}$ except for two points: (i) the injectivity requirement for Xcerpt subterms and (ii) the consideration of unordered data in Xcerpt term simulation.

The proof requires the notion of *canonical models* for Xcerpt query terms. Since the definition of subsumption is based on simulation between query terms and the set of *all* data terms, it does not give rise to an algorithm for testing subsumption. For a given query term q, the set of canonical models of q is a subset of all data terms that is tested for simulation with another query term q' in order to decide if q' subsumes q. To minimize computation, we are generally interested in minimal canonical models. In some cases, the set of canonical models is finite when q' is known, but infinite when q' is unknown. If the set of canonical models of a query term is finite, we immediately obtain an algorithm for query term subsumption.

Definition 77 (Canonical models of a query term). *Given two query terms q and q', a set of data terms $\mathcal{M}(q)$ is a set of canonical models of q with respect to q', if the following condition holds: q is subsumed by q' if and only if $q' \preceq d \; \forall d \in \mathcal{M}(q)$. $\mathcal{M}(q)$ is a minimal set of canonical models for q with respect to q', if there is no smaller set $\mathcal{D}$ which is a set of canonical models of q with respect to q'.*

Example 45 (Canonical models for Xcerpt({{}})). *Consider the query term $q_1 := a\{\{b, c, b\}\}$. Can we fix a set of canonical models $\mathcal{M}(q_1)$ for q_1 such that we can reduce subsumption between q_1 and some arbitrary query term q (not necessarily in Xcerpt({{}})) to simulation between q_2 and $\mathcal{M}(q_1)$? Intuitively, the data term $d := a\{b, c, b\}$ encodes exactly the minimal information that is required by q_1. Hence, any other query term that simulates with d should subsume q_1. Obviously, $q_2 := a\{\{b, c\}\}$ simulates with d and also subsumes q_1. On the other hand $q_3 := a\{\{b, c\{\{d\}\}\}\}$, $q_4 := a\{\{b, c, d\}\}$ and $q_5 := a\{\{c, c\}\}$ do neither simulate into d nor contain q_1. d is equivalent to $d' := a\{c, b, b\}$ and any data term that is obtained from d by subterm permutation. So instead of fixing the set $\mathcal{M}(q_1)$ as the singular set $\{d\}$ we could just as well take $\{d'\}$. Obviously, $\{d\}$ is a minimal set of canonical models for q_1.*

One might expect that the set of canonical models for a query term with unordered subterm specification must also include *ordered* data terms. We know, however, that if some unordered query term simulates with an unordered data term, then it will also simulate with its ordered version. Hence there is no need for ordered data terms in the set of canonical models for unordered queries.

Corollary 6 (Canonical models for Xcerpt({{}})). *Let q be an Xcerpt query term in Xcerpt({{}}). Then the singular set $\{d\}$ where d is obtained from q by substituting single curly braces for double ones, is a minimal set of canonical models for q.*

Xcerpt({{}}) is a very restricted version of Xcerpt query terms, but it is not the simplest one. Xcerpt({}), i.e. the set of ground Xcerpt query terms with only unordered, complete term specification is even easier to handle for subsumption. The set of canonical models for an Xcerpt query term $q \in$ Xcerpt({}) is the unary set $\{q\}$.[7] Simulation between an Xcerpt query term in Xcerpt({}) and an Xcerpt data term in Xcerpt({}) is the same problem as *tree isomorphism for node-labeled trees*, a problem which has been shown to be solvable in linear time in [AHU74]. Also simulation between an Xcerpt query term in Xcerpt({}) and an Xcerpt data term in Xcerpt([]) is equivalent to tree isomorphism.

---
7 Since q does not contain any constructs specific to query terms, q is also a data term.

Also Xcerpt($[]$), i.e. the set of Xcerpt query terms with only ordered, complete subterm specification is an easier fragment than Xcerpt($\{\{\}\}$). Simulation between Xcerpt($[]$) query terms and Xcerpt($[]$) data terms can be decided in linear time, e.g. by a simultaneous depth first traversation of both terms, comparing node labels and node depth at each step. As a result, also subsumption between Xcerpt($[]$) query terms is in $O(n)$. We thus have:

Corollary 7 (Subsumption for simple breadth complete Xcerpt query terms). *Subsumption for* Xcerpt($[]$) *and* Xcerpt($\{\}$) *can be decided in linear time.*

After this short intermezzo on the complexity of subsumption for less expressive fragments of Xcerpt query terms, let us return back to the discussion of Xcerpt($\{\{\}\}$) subsumption.

Corollary 6 gives us a reduction from Xcerpt($\{\{\}\}$) subsumption to Xcerpt query term simulation. Since the mapping from Xcerpt query terms in Xcerpt($\{\{\}\}$) to their single canonical models is bijective, we can also reduce simulation between an Xcerpt query term $q \in$ Xcerpt($\{\{\}\}$) and an Xcerpt data term $d \in$ Xcerpt($\{\}$) to Xcerpt($\{\{\}\}$) subsumption: Let μ be the mapping from query terms in Xcerpt($\{\{\}\}$) to their canonical models. Then q simulates into d if and only if q contains $\mu^{-1}(d)$. Thus we obtain Corollary 8.

Corollary 8 (Complexity of Subsumption for Xcerpt($\{\{\}\}$)). *Subsumption for* Xcerpt($\{\{\}\}$) *is in the same complexity class as Simulation between* Xcerpt($\{\{\}\}$) *query terms and* Xcerpt($\{\}$) *data terms.*

Unfortunately, the complexity of Simulation between Xcerpt($\{\{\}\}$) query terms and Xcerpt($\{\}$) data terms has not yet been determined. Let Xcerpt($\{\{\}\}, |\Sigma| = 1$) be the set of Xcerpt query terms with breadth incomplete subterm specification constructed over a single label only. Subsumption for Xcerpt($\{\{\}\}, |\Sigma| = 1$) – and also Simulation between Xcerpt($\{\{\}\}, |\Sigma| = 1$) query terms and Xcerpt($\{\}$) data terms – is equivalent to the *subtree isomorphism problem*, which has been known to be in P for quite some time, and which has been shown to be solvable in $O(k^{1.376} \cdot n)$ where k is the number of nodes in the embedded tree, and n the number of nodes in the embedding tree [ST97].

Corollary 9 (Complexity of Xcerpt($\{\{\}\}, |\Sigma| = 1$)). *Simulation and subsumption of* Xcerpt($\{\{\}\}, |\Sigma| = 1$) *query terms can be decided in* $O(k^{1.376} \cdot n)$ *where k is the size of the query term and n is the size of the data.*

Subtree isomorphism has also been examined for ordered trees. [M89] obtains an $O(n + m)$ bound for finding an ordered *bottom-up subtree* of size m in an ordered tree of size n by rewriting trees of arity k to binary trees and comparing the Zaks sequence representation of pattern and data tree. A bottom-up subtree t_b of a tree t is a subtree such that for all nodes x and y in t, if x is in t_b and y is a child of x, then also y must be in t_b. Ordered bottom-up subtree matching is equivalent to the Xcerpt query term fragment over a singular alphabet with complete, ordered term specification only, and with the root term qualified as a descendant. We denote this fragment as Xcerpt($[], |\Sigma| = 1, \uparrow$). As a further illustration, the term desc a[a[a[], a[]], a[]] is in Xcerpt($[], |\Sigma| = 1, \uparrow$), but the terms a[], desc a[[ ]] and desc a[b[]] are not.

Figure 11: Embeddings from [Kil92] versus Xcerpt simulation

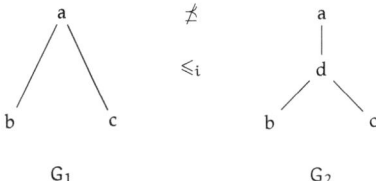

Also [Val02] considers ordered subtree isomorphism over a singular alphabet Σ, but again with a different notion of subtrees than required for Xcerpt([[]]) simulation: If a node n_d in the data tree d is matched by the some node n_p in the pattern tree p, then also all left siblings of n_d must be matched by left siblings of n_p in the same embedding. These kinds of queries are expressible in Xcerpt only in the presence of subterm negation (i.e. the without keyword). Therefore we do not give an upper bound for the complexity of Xcerpt([[]], |Σ| = 1) simulation, but refer to the bound for the larger fragment Xcerpt([[]]) identified below.

Having identified the complexity of simulation and subsumption for Xcerpt({{}}, |Σ| = 1) we now turn to the equivalent problem over an arbitrary alphabet. [Kil92] considers ten different tree inclusion problems, four of which are of interest for Xcerpt simulation and, for the sake of canonical models, also for Xcerpt containment. These are *ordered path inclusion, unordered path inclusion, ordered tree inclusion* and *unordered tree inclusion*. Central to all these problems is the notion of *embeddings*. An embedding as defined in [Kil92] from a pattern tree p to a data tree d is an *injective* function from the nodes of p to the nodes of d, that preserves labels and the ancestor relationship. If there is an embedding from p into d, we write p $\leqslant_i$ q. Embeddings differ from XPath tree matching in that they are required to be *injective*, and from Xcerpt term simulation in that injectivity is treated differently in combination with the Xcerpt descendant modifier, as Figure 11 illustrates. While the Xcerpt query term a{{ desc b, desc c }} does not simulate into the data term a{ d{ b, c } }, there is an injective embedding from G_1 to G_2. Embeddings as defined in [Kil92] are also equivalent to *minor embeddings* (see below). This difference between Xcerpt term simulation and embeddings makes Xcerpt simulation computationally cheaper, without sacrificing much expressivity.

An ordered path inclusion problem is the problem of finding an embedding of an ordered pattern tree p into an ordered data tree d that *respects the order of subtrees in the pattern and the child relationship*. Such an embedding is called an *ordered path embedding* of p in d, and if there is such an embedding, the p is *ordered path included* in d. In Figure 11 G_1 is not ordered path included in G_2, because there is no way of retaining the child relationship in the embedding. Ordered path inclusion is equivalent to Xcerpt([[]]) simulation over an arbitrary alphabet and can be solved in $O(m \cdot n)$.

Corollary 10. *Simulation between an Xcerpt query term* $q \in \mathrm{Xcerpt}([[]])$ *and an arbitrary Xcerpt data term* d *is in* $O(n \cdot m)$, *where* m *is the size of* q, *and* n *the size of* d.[8]

Unordered path inclusion as defined in [Kil92] is the problem of finding an embedding that respects the child relationship, but not necessarily the order relationship. Unordered path inclusion is equivalent to $\mathrm{Xcerpt}(\{\{\}\})$ simulation over an arbitrary alphabet and can be solved in $O(m^{\frac{3}{2}} \cdot n)$ where m is the size of the pattern tree and n the size of the data tree.

Corollary 11. *Simulation between an Xcerpt query term* $q \in \mathrm{Xcerpt}()$ *and an arbitrary Xcerpt data term* d *is in* $O(m^{\frac{3}{2}} \cdot n)$, *where* m *is the size of* q, *and* n *the size of* d.

In combination with Corollary 8 we have that Subsumption for $\mathrm{Xcerpt}()$ is in $O(m^{\frac{3}{2}} \cdot n)$, where m is the size of the subsuming pattern, and n the size of the subsumed pattern. But what about the ordered case? To find an upper bound for the complexity of $\mathrm{Xcerpt}([[]])$ subsumption, we must first introduce canonical models for query terms in $\mathrm{Xcerpt}([[]])$. We give Corollary 12 without proof. In combination with Corollary 10 we have that $\mathrm{Xcerpt}([[]])$ subsumption can be decided in $O(m \cdot n)$ where m and n are the sizes of query and data term, respecitvely.

Definition 78. *Given a query term* $q \in \mathrm{Xcerpt}([[]])$, *the set of canonical models of* q *is the singular set* $\{d\}$ *where* d *is obtained from* q *by substituting double square brackets by single ones.*

Corollary 12. *Given two Xcerpt query terms* $q_1, q_2 \in \mathrm{Xcerpt}([[]])$, q_1 *subsumes* q_2 *if and only if* q_1 *simulates into the single canonical model of* q_2.

Having fixed the complexity of simulation and subsumption for $\mathrm{Xcerpt}([])$, $\mathrm{Xcerpt}(\{\})$, $\mathrm{Xcerpt}([[]])$, $\mathrm{Xcerpt}(\{\{\}\}, |\Sigma| = 1)$ and $\mathrm{Xcerpt}(\{\{\}\})$ we now additionally take into account the descendant axis.

Besides path inclusion problems, [Kil92] also elaborates on the complexity of tree inclusion problems. In contrast to path inclusion problems, the direct children of a node n_p in the pattern tree mapped to a node n_d of the data tree need not be direct children of n_d, but may be descendants. (Un)fortunately, tree ordered and unordered tree inclusion as defined in [Kil92] does not coincide with $\mathrm{Xcerpt}([[]], \mathrm{desc})$ and $\mathrm{Xcerpt}(\{\{\}\}, \mathrm{desc})$ simulation. This is unfortunate in the sense that we cannot transfer the complexity results from (un)ordered tree inclusion problems to Xcerpt simulation and subsumption, but fortunate in the sense that the unordered tree inclusion is NP-complete [KM95], and $\mathrm{Xcerpt}(\{\{\}\}, \mathrm{desc})$ may fall into a lower complexity class. Indeed, simulation for the fragment of $\mathrm{Xcerpt}(\{\{\}\}, \mathrm{desc})$ which is constructed over a *singular alphabet*, is in P, as the following discussion shows.

[MT92] considers the complexity of finding graph isomorphisms, homomorphisms and homeomorphisms for graphs with bounded tree-width. Graphs with a maximum tree-width of 1 are ordinary trees, and can be seen as Xcerpt query or data terms without references. Among others, [MT92] considers the relations $\leqslant_h$ for *homeomorphic*

---

8 Simulation between $\mathrm{Xcerpt}([[]])$ and $\mathrm{Xcerpt}()$ is always false, and can thus be solved in constant time.

Figure 12: Homeomorphic and minor embeddings.

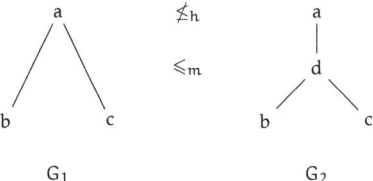

embedding and $\leqslant_m$ for *minor embedding*. For two graphs H and G, H $\leqslant_h$ G holds iff G is isomorphic to a graph that can be obtained from H by subdividing its edges. On the other hand H $\leqslant_m$ G holds iff H is isomorphic to a graph that can be obtained from G by contracting edges.[9] Figure 12 illustrates the difference between homeomorphic and minor embeddings.

Note that the homeomorphic embedding in [MT92] is different from the *tree homeomorphism problem* and the *tree homeomorphism matching problem* considered in [GKM07]. A homeomorphic embedding is by definition an injective function, whereas [MT92] does not have an injectivity requirement.

There is no homeomorphic embedding of G_1 in G_2 in Figure 12, since G_2 cannot be obtained from G_1 by subdividing edges. There is, however, a minor embedding from G_1 in G_2, since G_1 can be obtained from G_2 by edge contraction – in this case by deleting the edge between a and d, thereby making b and c direct children of a. Finding homeomorphic embeddings between graphs is in P, while finding minor embeddings is NP-complete, as shown in [MT92]. What does this tell us about Xcerpt term simulation and subsumption?

In the following, we denote the set of Xcerpt query terms with breadth complete, order incomplete term specification, with descendant subterms only (i.e. each subterm must be qualified by a descendant construct) and unary alphabet Σ by Xcerpt($\{\}$, desc, $|\Sigma| = 1$).

With each Xcerpt term t (no matter if it is a query or data term) we associate the tree tree(t): tree(t) contains a node for each subterm of t, and there is an edge between two nodes x and y in the tree, iff the subterm represented by y is a subterm of the term represented by x. Note that this mapping is not bijective, since we do not distinguish between descendant and child subterms. Thus the tree G_1 in Figure 12 might represent the Xcerpt query term q := a{{ desc b, desc c }} and the tree G_2 might represent the Xcerpt data term a{ d{ b, c } }. Due to the injectivity requirement in Xcerpt term simulation, q does not simulate into d, which is in line with subtree homeomorphism, but not with minor embeddings.

Corollary 13. *Given an Xcerpt query term* q $\in$ Xcerpt($\{\{\}\}$, desc, $|\Sigma| = 1$) *and an Xcerpt data term* d $\in$ Xcerpt($\{\}$), q *simulates into* d, *iff there is a homeomorphic embedding from the tree of* q *into the tree of* d.

---

[9] Loops and multiple-edges resulting from edge-contraction are deleted. In the case of trees, neither loops nor multiple edges can be introduced.

With the complexity results in [MT92], we immediately obtain an upper bound for $q \in \text{Xcerpt}(\{\}, \text{desc}, |\Sigma| = 1)$ simulation:

Corollary 14 (Complexity of $\text{Xcerpt}(\{\{\}\}, \text{desc}, |\Sigma| = 1)$). *Complexity of $\text{Xcerpt}(\{\{\}\}, \text{desc}, |\Sigma| = 1)$ simulation is in P.*

This result indicates that also $\text{Xcerpt}(\{\{\}\}, \text{desc})$ simulation may be in P, whereas the NP-hardness result for minor embeddings over trees indicates that it might also be NP-complete. The NP-hardness proof for minor tree embeddings is by a reduction from the satisfiability problem and requires mappings which are not valid Xcerpt term simulations and therefore cannot be trivially transferred to Xcerpt. We leave the complexity of $\text{Xcerpt}(\{\{\}\}, \text{desc})$ simulation as future work and return to the complexity of $\text{Xcerpt}(\{\{\}\}, \text{desc}, *)$ subsumption.

Theorem 15 (Canonical models for $\text{Xcerpt}(\{\{\}\}, \text{desc})$). *Let q and q' be Xcerpt query terms in $\text{Xcerpt}(\{\{\}\}, \text{desc})$.[10] Let $\mathcal{M}(q)$ be the singular set $\{d\}$ consisting of the term d obtained from q by substituting all double curly braces by single ones and substituting all descendant modified terms desc t by $z\{\{t\}\}$ where z is a fresh symbol not occurring in q and q'. Then $\mathcal{M}(q)$ is a set of canonical models for q with respect to q'.*

Proof. In Lemma 15 we show that extended ground query term simulation and query term subsumption are identical. Moreover we can show that q' simulates into q if and only if q' simulates into d: In extended ground query term simulation (Definition 80) descendant subterms of the subsumed query must be matched by descendant subterms of the subsuming query. In the canonical model d, descendant edges of q are represented by subterms with label z. Since z does not occur in q', and since q' does not include wild cards or regular expressions, subterms with label z in d must also be matched by descendant subterms in q'. It follows that q' subsumes q if and only if q' simulates into d.
□

Since the number of nodes in a tree is one plus the number of its edges, the size of the canonical model of a term q in $\text{Xcerpt}(\{\{\}\}, \text{desc})$ is in $O(2 \cdot n)$ where n is the number of subterms in q: In the worst case, every subterm in q is a descendant subterm, and a new subterm with label z is introduced in the construction of d. For this reason, the deciding subsumption for $\text{Xcerpt}(\{\{\}\}, \text{desc})$ is not much harder than deciding simulation for this same fragment of Xcerpt. Unfortunately, a tight complexity bound for simulation of $\text{Xcerpt}(\{\{\}\}, \text{desc})$ has not yet been determined.

Having identified canonical models for Xcerpt query terms with descendant modifiers, we now additionally take into account label wild cards (*).[11] The following example shows that we cannot simply procede in the same way as for $\text{Xcerpt}(\{\{\}\}, \text{desc})$.

Example 46 (Canonical models for $\text{Xcerpt}(\{\{\}\}, \text{desc}, *)$). *Consider the two query terms $q_1 := a\{\{\text{desc b}\}\}$ and $q_2 := a\{\{*\{\{b\}\}\}\}$. Obviously, q_2 does not subsume q_1. However, the set $\{d\}$ with $d := a\{z\{b\}\}$ is not a set of*

---

[10] Without loss of generality, we assume that q and q' are not of the form desc t. If they are, we can reduce containment between q and q' to containment between $a\{\{q\}\}$ and $a\{\{q'\}\}$ for an arbitrary label a.
[11] In Xcerpt label wildcards are written /.*/. We introduce the * notation to emphasize that not arbitrary regular expressions are allowed, but only label wildcards.

canonical models for q_1, *since with* q_2 *containing a label wild card, it simulates with* d. *On the contrary, the data term* a{z{z{b} } }, *which is matched by* q_1, *but not by* q_2, *can be used to show that* q_2 *does not contain* q_1.

In general, for query terms $q_1 \in$ Xcerpt({{}}, desc, *) and $q_2 \in$ Xcerpt({{}}, *), a discriminating data term d of q_1 and q_2, i.e. a data term that simulates with q_1 but not with q_2, can be obtained from q_1 as follows: Let w be the length of the longest sequence of directly nested subterms with label * in q_2 – we call w the *star depth* of q_2 (e.g. the Xcerpt term a{{*{{*{{b, c}}, d}} }} has star depth 2). (i) substitute all label wildcards (*) in q_1 by a fresh label z, (ii) substitute double curly braces in q_1 by single ones, and (iii) substitute each descendant modified subterm desc t in q_1 by the subterm s := *{{. . . *{{t}} . . .}}, where s contains exactly $w+1$ label wildcards. In the case that q_2 is also from Xcerpt({{}}, desc, *), i.e. may contain descendant constructs, we cannot find singular sets of canonical models, as the following example shows.

Example 47 (Canonical models for Xcerpt({{}}, desc, *)). *Consider again the query terms* q_1 := a{{desc b}}. q_2 := a{{*{{b}} }} *does not subsume* q_1, *and we can test this by including the discriminating data term* d_1 := a{z{z{b} } } *in the set of canonical models of* q_1. *Given the third query term* q_3 := a{*{desc b} }, *we see that* q_3 *does not subsume* q_1, *but it simulates into* d_1. *Hence we must include a second data term* d_2 := a{b} *in the set of canonical models of* q_1. *Indeed, the set* $\{d_1, d_2\}$ *is a set of canonical models for* q_1 *with respect to any other query term that has star depth at most 1.*

Theorem 16 (Canonical models for Xcerpt({{}}, desc, *)). *Let* $q, q' \in$ Xcerpt({{}}, desc, *) *be Xcerpt query terms. Let* $s = s_1, \ldots, s_j$ *be the longest sequence of subterms in* q' *such that all* s_i *are labeled with a* * *and such that* s_{i+1} *is a direct subterm of* s_i, *and all* s_i *are not modified by the descendant construct* desc. *Let* z *be a symbol not occurring in* q *or* q' *and* d *the number of descendant edges in* q. *Furthermore, given a sequence of* d *integers* $u_1, \ldots, u_d \in \{1, \ldots, j+1\}$ *let* $m[u_1, \ldots, u_d](q)$ *denote the data term obtained from* q *by substituting the ith descendant modifier by a sequence of* u_i *intermediate child terms labeled* z, *by substitution of* z *for any label wildcard in* q, *and by substitution of single curly braces for double ones. Then*

$$\mathcal{M}(q, q') = \{m[u_1, \ldots, u_d] \mid u_1, \ldots, u_d \in \{1, \ldots, j+1\}\}$$

is a set of canonical models of q *with respect to* q'.

The proof is analogous to the one in [MS02]. Note that these canonical models for Xcerpt({{}}, desc, *) are not guaranteed to be minimal – i.e. there may be subsets of $\mathcal{M}(q, q')$ that are sufficient for checking subsumption of q by q', as in Example 47. To check that an Xcerpt query term q' does not subsume q, we can guess the d numbers $u_1, \ldots, u_d$, construct $m[u_1, \ldots, u_d](q)$, and verify that q' does not simulate with $m[u_1, \ldots, u_d](q)$. Hence we have that if simulation of Xcerpt({{}}, desc, *) is in P, then subsumption for Xcerpt({{}}, desc, *) is in Co-NP.

We say that p is subsumed by the union of $q_1, \ldots, q_n$, if for any data term d with $p \preceq d$, there is an $i \in \{1, \ldots, n\}$ such that $q_i \preceq d$.

Lemma 13 (Subsumption by unions of terms). *Let* $p, p_1, \ldots, p_n$ *be Xcerpt query terms in* Xcerpt({{}}, desc, *). *Then there exist query terms* $q, q' \in$ Xcerpt({{}}, desc, *) *such that* $p \subseteq p_1, \ldots, p_n$ *if and only if* $q \subseteq q'$.

The proof of Lemma 13 is analogous to the one in [MS02]. Just note that each node in the patterns q and q' constructed in [MS02] has siblings with distinct labels, such that injectivity is not an issue in the proof.

Theorem 17 (Co-NP hardness of Subsumption for Xcerpt({{}}, desc, *)). *Given two query terms* $q_1, q_2 \in$ Xcerpt({{}}, desc, *), *deciding if* q_2 *subsumes* q_1 *is Co-NP hard.*

Again, the proof is analogous to [MS02]. Observe that each node in the patterns A and C_i constructed in this proof has siblings with distinct labels, enforcing an injective mapping of the child subterms of the patterns to subterms of the data.

Theorem 18 (NP Completeness of Simulation for Xcerpt({{}}, LV) and Xcerpt({{}}, ref)). *The Xcerpt query term fragments* Xcerpt({{}}, LV) *with double curly braces and label variables, and* Xcerpt({{}}, ref) *with double curly braces and references is NP-complete.*

Proof. We first show NP-completeness for simulation of Xcerpt({{}}, LV) with Xcerpt({}) data terms.

IN NP: Let $d \in$ Xcerpt({}) be an Xcerpt data term with unordered term specification only, and $q \in$ Xcerpt({{}}, LV) an Xcerpt query term with unordered incomplete term specification and label variables. If q simulates into d, then we can guess a mapping from the variables in q to the nodes of d. Then $\sigma(q)$ is ground and we can check in polynomial time if $\sigma(q)$ simulates into d.

NP-HARD: We show NP hardness of Xcerpt({{}}, LV) simulation by a reduction from the Clique problem. Let $G = (V, E)$ with $E \subseteq V \times V$ a symmetric relation, be an undirected unlabeled graph. We construct an Xcerpt({}) data term $d(G)$ from G as follows: the root of $d(G)$ is labeled r. For each node n in V, $d(G)$ has a direct subterm s with label n. If (x, y) is in E, then the subterm with label x in $d(G)$ has a subterm with label y, which has no children. These are all subterms of $d(G)$. This construction is exemplified in Figure 13.

Now G has a clique of size 3, if and only if the query term

```
q := r{{ var X₁{{ var X₂{{ }}, var X₃{{ }} }},
        var X₂{{ var X₁{{ }}, var X₃{{ }} }},
        var X₃{{ var X₁{{ }}, var X₂{{ }} }}
     }}
```

simulates with $d(G)$. In general, G contains a clique of size n if the query term $q(n)$ simulates with $d(G)$ where $q(n)$ is the term $r\{\{X_1\{\{\overline{X} \setminus X_1\}\}, \ldots, X_n\{\{\overline{X} \setminus X_n\}\}\}\}$, where $\overline{X} \setminus X_i$ denotes the sequence of query terms $X_1\{\{\}\}, \ldots, X_{i-1}\{\{\}\}, X_{i+1}\{\{\}\}, \ldots, X_n\{\{\}\}$. $d(G)$ contains $|V| + 2|E| + 1$ subterms, and $q(n)$ contains $O(n^2)$ subterms.

Since the simulation of an unordered query term q with an unordered data term d is the same as simulation of q with the ordered version of d, also simulation between Xcerpt({{}}, LV) and Xcerpt([]) is NP-complete.

To complete the proof of Theorem 18, we now show that simulation between Xcerpt({{}}, ref) query terms and Xcerpt({}, ref) data terms is NP-complete. This is achieved by a reduction *to and from* the subgraph isomorphism problem.

Figure 13: Representation of an undirected graph as an Xcerpt({}) data term for the proof of Theorem 18

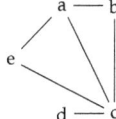

```
r { a{ b, c, e },
    b{ a, c },
    c{ a, b, d, e },
    d{ c }, e{ a, c } }
```

NP-HARD: Given an arbitrary directed graph G, we can obviously encode this graph as a data term d in Xcerpt({}, ref), where the edge (x, y) is in E, if and only if the subterm of d corresponding to y is a child of the subterm of d corresponding to x. Moreover, given an undirected graph, we can encode it as an Xcerpt({}, ref) data term by duplicating edges. We can encode unlabeled graphs by simply giving each subterm in d the same label σ. Given a second undirected graph H we can encode it as a query term q in Xcerpt({{}}, ref) in the same manner. Now q simulates into d if and only if H is isomorphic to a subgraph of G.

IN NP: Simulation between Xcerpt({{}}, ref) and Xcerpt({}, ref) is reduced to subgraph isomorphism in a very similar manner. Observe that there is a one-to-one correspondance of Xcerpt terms in Xcerpt({}, ref) or Xcerpt({{}}, ref) over a singular alphabet and unlabeled directed graphs. Moreover, there is a one-to-one correspondance of Xcerpt terms in Xcerpt({}, ref) or Xcerpt({{}}, ref) over an arbitrary alphabet and labeled directed graphs. Hence a query term q in Xcerpt({{}}, ref) simulates into a data term d in Xcerpt({}, ref) if and only if the directed labeld graph corresponding to q is isomorphic to a subgraph of the directed, labeled graph corresponding to d. Also directed subgraph isomorphism is NP-complete [AHU74], and thus in NP.

Alternatively, one can encode simulation between Xcerpt({{}}, ref) query terms and Xcerpt({}, ref) data terms in first order logic. By Fagin's theorem (see e.g. [Imm83]) we can conclude that this kind of simulation is in NP.

Again, NP completeness holds also for simulation between query terms in Xcerpt({{}}, ref) and Xcerpt([], ref) for the same reason as above.

□

Table 8 summarizes the complexity results for Xcerpt query term simulation and subsumption presented above. Note that simulation and subsumption for Xcerpt({{}}, desc) is in the same complexity class and subsumption for Xcerpt({{}}, desc) is Co-NP complete, if simulation for this fragment is in P.

Figure 14: Simulation for Xcerpt({{}})

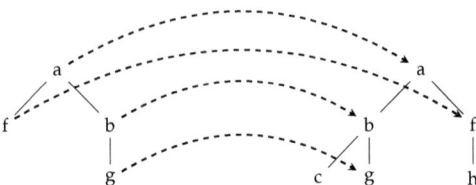

Table 8: Complexity of Simulation and Subsumption for Xcerpt fragments. (m is the size of the query term; n is the size of the data for simulation and the size of the subsumed query term for subsumption.)

Fragment	Simulation	Subsumption
Xcerpt({})	$O(n)$	$O(n)$
Xcerpt([])	$O(n)$	$O(n)$
Xcerpt([], $\|\Sigma\| = 1, \uparrow$)	$O(n+m)$	$O(n+m)$
Xcerpt({{}}, $\|\Sigma\| = 1$)	$O(m^{1.376} \cdot n)$	$O(m^{1.376} \cdot n)$
Xcerpt({{}})	$O(m^{3/2} \cdot n)$	$O(m^{3/2} \cdot n)$
Xcerpt([[]])	$O(m \cdot n)$	$O(m \cdot n)$
Xcerpt({{}}, desc)	?	?
Xcerpt({{}}, desc, ∗)	?	CoNP hard
Xcerpt({{}}, LV)	NP-complete	NP-hard
Xcerpt({{}}, ref)	NP-complete	NP-hard

8.6 FUTURE WORK IN THE AREA OF XCERPT QUERY TERM SUBSUMPTION

Starting out from the problem of improving termination of logic programming based on rich kinds of simulation such as simulation unification, this section investigates the problem of deciding simulation subsumption between query terms. A rewriting system consisting of subsumption monotone query term transformations is introduced and shown to be sound and complete. By convenient pruning of the search tree defined by this rewriting system, the decidability of simulation subsumption is proven, and an upper bound for its complexity is identified. Subsequently upper and lower bounds for the complexity of subsumption for various less expressive fragments of Xcerpt are studied.

Future work includes (a) a proof-of-concept implementation of the rewriting system, (b) the development of heuristics and their incorporation into the prototype to ensure fast termination of the algorithm in the cases when it is possible, (c) further study of the complexity of the problem in absence of subterm negation, descendant constructs, deep-equal, and/or injectivity, (d) the implementation of a backward chaining algorithm with tabling, which uses subsumption checking to avoid redundant computations and infinite branches in the resolution tree, and (e) the adaptation of the rewriting system to XPath in order to decide subsumption and to derive complexity results for the subsumption problem between XPath queries.

9
SUMMARY AND FUTURE WORK

This work describes how rule languages must be adapted to allow user-friendly and format-versatile integration, transformation and deduction of semi-structured data on the Web. It describes XCERPT^{RDF} as an example of a format-versatile rule language with rich unification, presents a model-theoretic formalization of RDF containers, collections and reifications, introduces the expressive, yet efficient RDF path query language RPL, and sketches use-cases for format versatile querying. Moreover it provides a three-valued well-founded semantics for rule languages with rich unfication and Xcerpt in particular, establishes the decidability of subsumption between Xcerpt query terms in general, and the complexity for simulation and subsumption for several fragments of Xcerpt query terms.

Future work is centered around the following topics:

IMPLEMENTATION OF XCERPT^{RDF}: Both a subsumption based evaluation algorithm for rule languages with rich unification[Pop] and the RDF path query language RPL are thoroughly implemented. Nevertheless, many aspects of XCERPT^{RDF} have only been partially realized. While there is a parser for XCERPT^{RDF}, the language still lacks a full-fledged evaluation-engine, including an implementation of XCERPT^{RDF} simulation unification.

RICH UNIFICATION LANGUAGES: This thesis extends Xcerpt to the format versatile language XCERPT^{RDF}. In the last years, microformats have quickly spread over many web sites, especially over social networking sites. Therefore query and construct patterns for microformats should be integrated into XCERPT^{RDF} to obtain an even more powerful language. For querying Wikipedia, patterns for directly querying Wikipedia pages (instead of their HTML serializations) markup would be useful.

USE CASES: There seems to be an infinite number of use-cases for format versatile querying on the Web. A particularly interesting use-case is the transformation of RDF information from the Infoboxes on Wikipedia pages to plain RDF data, as has been done for the DBPedia project[ABK+08].

XCERPT QUERY TERM SUBSUMPTION: Several theoretical questions centered around the complexity of subsumption between Xcerpt fragments remain open, and practical aspects (heuristics, implementation) deserve further attention and promise interesting research results. These ideas are sketched in Section 8.6.

SEMANTICS OF XCERPT PROGRAMS: As mentioned in Section 7.4, the semantics for Xcerpt programs with both grouping constructs and negation has not yet been formally specified. Still, the reduction of grouping constructs to negation seems to be an intuitive and promising approach to such a unified semantics. For this aim a general transformation algorithm for elimination of grouping constructs could be specified. Subsequently the results of this algorithm should be checked for compliance with the intuitive semantics for several example programs.

Part IV

APPENDIX

PROOFS RELATED TO XCERPT QUERY TERM SUBSUMPTION

A.1 NON-GROUND SIMULATION BETWEEN XCERPT^{XML} QUERY TERMS

For the proof of Theorem 13 the simulation relation between pairs of query terms and data terms is extended to pairs of query terms (Definition 80). Furthermore the transitivity of this extended simulation relation is shown (Lemma 14). From the transitivity of extended simulation follows the equivalence of subsumption and extended simulation (Lemma 15).

Extended query term simulation is defined to mirror the subsumption relationship – in fact Lemma 15 shows their equivalence. In extending query term simulation to allow entire query terms to the right of the $\preceq$ symbol, we have to take into account negated subterms, descendant constructs and incompleteness in breadth. The idea is that negated subterms in the first term must be mapped to negated subterms in the second term, such that the positive version of the image subterm subsumes the positive version of the original subterm. Moreover, the mappings must be descendant preserving in addition to being injective or bijective.

Definition 79 (Descendant preserving mappings). *Let q_1 and q_2 be query terms. A mapping π from $\text{Child}(q_1)$ to $\text{Child}(q_2)$ is descendant preserving, if for all $q_1^i \in \text{Child}(q_1)$ holds: if $\pi(q_1^i)$ is of the form $\text{desc}\ \ldots$, then also q_1^i is of the form $\text{desc}\ \ldots$.*

Definition 80 (Extended ground query term simulation). *Let q_1 and q_2 be query terms. q_1 simulates into q_2 (short $q_1 \preceq q_2$) if there is a relation $\mathcal{S}$ that satisifies the following conditions:*

1. $q_1\ \mathcal{S}\ q_2$

2. *If $q\ \mathcal{S}\ q'$ then $\mathcal{L}(l(q')) \subseteq \mathcal{L}(l(q))$.*[1]

3. *If $q\ \mathcal{S}\ q'$ and $ss(q) = \text{complete}$ then $ss(q') = \text{complete}$.*

4. *If $q\ \mathcal{S}\ q'$ and q is not of the form $\text{desc}\ q''$, then there is an injective, descendant preserving mapping $\pi : \text{Child}^+(q) \to \text{Child}^+(q')$ such that for all $q_i \in \text{Child}^+(q)$ holds $q_i\ \mathcal{S}\ \pi(q_i)$.*

    Depending on the subterm specification of q and q', the following additional requirements must be fulfilled:

    a) *If $ss(q) = \text{complete}$, then the mapping π must be bijective.*

    b) *If $ss(q) = \text{incomplete}$ and $ss(q) = \text{complete}$, there must not be a a $q_i \in \text{Child}^-(q)$ and a $q_j \in \text{Child}^+(q') \setminus \text{range}(\pi)$ such that $\text{pos}(q_i) \preceq q_j$.*

    c) *If $ss(q) = \text{incomplete}$ and $ss(q') = \text{incomplete}$, then, besides the mapping π, there must be a (not necessarily injective) mapping σ from $\text{Child}^-(q)$ to $\text{Child}^-(q')$ such that $\text{pos}(\sigma(q_i)) \preceq \text{pos}(q_i)$ for all $q_i \in \text{Child}^-(q)$.*

---

[1] As in Section 8, $l(q)$ denotes the label of the query term q, and $\mathcal{L}(e)$ the language defined by the regular expression e

5. if $q = \text{desc } q_1 \, \mathcal{S} \, q'$ then $q_1 \, \mathcal{S} \, q'$ or $q_1 \, \mathcal{S} \, q_2$ for some $q_2 \in \text{SubT}^+(q')$. Note that q' may itself be a query term with a descendant modifier.

Extended ground query term simulation is extended to *extended non-ground query term simulation* by taking into account variables.

Definition 81 (Extended non-ground query term simulation). *Let q_1 and q_2 be query terms. q_1 simulates into q_2 if there is a substitution σ : $\text{Vars}(q_1) \to \mathcal{Q}$, such that for all substitutions τ : $\text{Vars}(q_2) \to \mathcal{D}$, $\sigma \circ \tau(q_1) \preceq \tau(q_2)$.*

Lemma 14 (Transitivity of extended ground query term simulation). *Extended ground query term simulation is transitive.*

Proof. Let q_1, q_2 and q_3 be query terms such that $q_1 \preceq q_2$ by a relation $\mathcal{S}_{1,2}$ and $q_2 \preceq q_3$ by a relation $\mathcal{S}_{2,3}$. For the transitivity of $\preceq$ we have to show $q_1 \preceq q_3$. We show that the relation $\mathcal{S}_{1,3} := \{(a,c) \mid a \, \mathcal{S}_{1,2} \, b \wedge b \, \mathcal{S}_{2,3} \, c\}$ fulfills the requirements from Definition 80.

The proof is by structural induction over q_1.

INDUCTION HYPOTHESIS : $\preceq$ is transitive.

INDUCTION BASE : q_1 is of the from $a\{\!\{\,\}\!\}$, $a\{\,\}$, $\text{desc } a\{\!\{\,\}\!\}$ or $\text{desc } a\{\,\}$.

1. Since $q_1 \, \mathcal{S}_{1,2} \, q_2$ and $q_2 \, \mathcal{S}_{2,3} \, q_3$, $q_1 \, \mathcal{S}_{1,3} \, q_3$.

2. $\mathcal{L}(q_3) \subseteq \mathcal{L}(q_1)$ follows from the transitivity of the subset relationship.

3. if $ss(q_1)$ is complete then $ss(q_2)$ must be complete and hence also $ss(q_3)$ is complete.

4. This requirement is trivially fulfilled, since q_1 does not have any children. The empty mapping is, of course, injective and descendant preserving.

    a) the empty mapping is also bijective
    b) $\text{Child}^-(q_1)$ is empty.
    c) σ is the empty mapping and trivially fulfills $\text{pos}(\sigma(q_i)) \preceq \text{pos}(q_i)$

5. If q_1 is of the form $\text{desc} \ldots$ then $q_1 \, \mathcal{S}_{1,2} \, q_2^s$ for some subterm q_2^s of q_2. Analogously, q_2^s is mapped to some subterm q_3^s of q_3. Hence $q_1 \, \mathcal{S}_{1,3} \, q_3^s$ holds.

INDUCTION STEP : We assume that the induction hypothesis holds for the children of q_1. We distinguish by the subterm specifications of q_1, q_2 and q_3. From $ss(q_1) = \text{complete}$ follows $ss(q_2) = \text{complete}$ and from $ss(q_2) = \text{complete}$ follows $ss(q_3) = \text{complete}$. Hence the only possible combinations are the following:

1. $ss(q_1) = ss(q_2) = ss(q_3) = \text{complete}$
2. $ss(q_1) = \text{incomplete}, ss(q_2) = ss(q_3) = \text{complete}$
3. $ss(q_1) = ss(q_2) = \text{incomplete}, ss(q_3) = \text{complete}$
4. $ss(q_1) = ss(q_2) = ss(q_3) = \text{incomplete}$

We only prove the first and the last, most complex combination. The others can be shown analogously.
Assume $ss(q_1) = ss(q_2) = ss(q_3) = $ complete.

1. Conditions 1, 2, 3 are shown as in the induction base.
2. Condition 4: Since $q_1 \preceq q_2$ there is an injective mapping $\pi_{1,2}$ from $Child^+(q_1)$ to $Child^+(q_2)$, and a bijective mapping $\pi_{2,3}$ from $Child^+(q_2)$ to $Child^+(q_3)$. The mapping $\pi_{2,3} \circ \pi_{1,2}$ is both bijective and descendant preserving and by induction hypothesis, $q_i \delta \pi_{2,3} \circ \pi_{1,2}(q_i)$ holds for all $q_i \in Child^+(q_1)$.
3. Condition 5 is shown as in the induction base.

Now assume $ss(q_1) = ss(q_2) = ss(q_3) = $ incomplete.

1. Conditions 1 and 2 are shown as in the induction base.
2. Condition 3 does not apply.
3. The first part of condition 4 is shown as in the case for $ss(q_1) = ss(q_2) = ss(q_3) = $ complete, by stating that the composition of two injective, descendant-preserving mappings is itself injective and descendant-preserving.

    Additionally, one must show (c), the existence of a (not necessarily injective) mapping σ from $Child^-(q_1)$ to $Child^-(q_3)$ that fulfills $pos(\sigma(q_i)) \preceq pos(q_i)$ for all $q_i \in Child^-(q_1)$. By induction hypothesis, the mapping $\sigma_{2,3} \circ \sigma_{1,2}$ fulfills this condition.
4. Condition 5 is shown as in the induction base.

□

Lemma 15 (Equivalence of ground query term simulation and subsumption). *Let q_1 and q_2 be two ground query terms. $q_1 \preceq q_2$ if and only if q_1 subsumes q_2.*

Proof. ⇒: Let q_1 and q_2 be query terms such that $q_1 \preceq q_2$. Let q' be an arbitrary query term such that $q_2 \preceq q'$. From the transitivity of $\preceq$ follows that $q_1 \preceq q'$. Hence q_1 subsumes q_2.
⇐: Let q_1 and q_2 be query terms such that q_1 subsumes q_2. Then for all data terms q' with $q_2 \preceq q'$ holds $q_1 \preceq q'$. From the reflexivity of $\preceq$ follows $q_2 \preceq q_2$ and hence $q_1 \preceq q_2$. □

A.2 PROOF OF COMPLETENESS OF THE REWRITING SYSTEM

Before giving the formal proof, some notation is introduced to abbreviate the presentation and improve readability:

- $|q|$ is a shorthand for $|Child(q)|$
- $|q|^+$ is a shorthand for $|Child^+(q)|$
- $|q|^-$ is a shorthand for $|Child^-(q)|$
- A *simulating mapping* π from a set of terms S to a set of terms T satisfies $t_p \preceq \pi(t_p)$ for all positive terms t_p in S and cannot be extended to a mapping $\pi': S \to T$ such that $pos(t_n) \preceq \pi'(t_n)$ for some negated term in S.

INDUCTION HYPOTHESIS: If q_1 subsumes q_2, then there is a sequence of subsumption monotone query term transformations that transforms q_1 into q_2.

INDUCTION BASE: q_1 does not have any subterms, i.e. q_1 is of the form $a\{\{\ \}\}$ or $a\{\ \}$. If q_1 is of the form $a\{\ \}$ then it does not subsume any other query term and the induction hypothesis is trivially fulfilled with the empty transformation sequence. Let q_1 therefore be of the form $a\{\{\ \}\}$.

1. $label(q_2) \not\preceq label(d)$. Substitute $label(q_1) := label(q_2)$ (Equation 8.10). Note that since q_1 subsumes q_2, $label(q_1)$ must subsume $label(q_2)$, and therefore the substitution of $label(q_2)$ for $label(q_1)$ in q_1 is a subsumption monotone query term transformation.

2. $label(q_1) \preceq label(d)$

    a) $ss(q_2) = \text{complete}$.
        i. $|d| > |q_2|$. Then set $ss(q_1) := \text{complete}$ (Equation 8.1).
        ii. $|d| \leqslant |q_2|$. Then insert $Child^+(q_2)$ as children into q_1 by Equations 8.4 and 8.8.
    b) $ss(q_2) = \text{incomplete}$
        i. There is no injective simulating mapping π from $Child^+(q_2)$ to $Child^+(d)$. Then insert $Child^+(q_2)$ as children into q_1 by Equations 8.4 and 8.8.
        ii. There is an injective simulating mapping π from $Child^+(q_2)$ to $Child(d)$, but it can be extended to a mapping $\pi' : Child(q_2) \to Child(d)$ such that $pos(q_2^i) \preceq \pi'(q_2^i)$ for some $q_2^i \in Child^-(q_2)$. Then insert q_2^i as child into q_1 (Equations 8.4 and 8.8).

INDUCTION STEP: Now we assume that the assumption holds for all children of q_2 and prove that it then holds for q_2 itself. Let again q_1 and q_2 be two query terms such that q_1 subsumes q_2 and d a data term such that $q_1 \preceq d$, but $q_2 \not\preceq d$.

1. $label(q_2) \not\preceq label(d)$. Apply the same transformation as in the corresponding case of the induction base.

2. $label(q_2) \preceq label(d)$.

    a) $ss(q_2) = \text{complete}$
        i. $|d| < |q_2|$. Then insert variables into q_1 until $|q_1|^+ = |q_2|$.
        ii. $|d| > |q_2|$. Then set $ss(q_1) := \text{complete}$.
        iii. $|d| = |q_2|$. Since q_2 does not simulate into d, there is no bijective mapping π from $Child^+(q_2)$ to $Child(d)$ such that $q_2^i \preceq \pi(q_2^i)$ for all $q_2^i \in Child^+(q_2)$.
            A. $ss(q_1) = \text{complete}$. Then there is a bijective mapping σ from $Child^+(q_1)$ to $Child^+(q_2)$ such that q_1^i subsumes $\sigma(q_1^i)$ for all $q_1^i \in Child^+(q_1)$ (Lemma 10). Then replace all $q_1^i \in Child^+(q_1)$ in q_1 by $\sigma(q_1^i)$. This step is valid by induction hypothesis and Equation 8.9. The resulting query term q_1' no longer simulates into d.

A.2 PROOF OF COMPLETENESS OF THE REWRITING SYSTEM

    B. $ss(q_1) =$ incomplete. Then there is an injective mapping σ from $\text{Child}^+(q_1)$ to $\text{Child}^+(q_2)$ such q_1^i subsumes $\sigma(q_1^i)$ for all $q_1^i \in \text{Child}^+(q_1)$ (Lemma 10). Then replace all $q_1^i \in \text{Child}^+(q_1)$ in q_1 by $\sigma(q_1^i)$ and insert variables until $|q_2|^+ = |q_1|^+$. This step is valid by induction hypothesis and Equations 8.9 and 8.4. The resulting query term q_1' no longer simulates into d.

b) $ss(q_2) =$ incomplete

    i. $|d| < |q_2|^+$. See the corresponding case for $ss(q_2) =$ complete.

    ii. $|d| = |q_2|^+$.

        A. There is no injective, simulating mapping π from $\text{Child}^+(q_2)$ to $\text{Child}(d)$. Since q_1 subsumes q_2 there is an injective mapping σ from $\text{Child}^+(q_1)$ to $\text{Child}^+(q_2)$ such that q_1^i subsumes $\sigma(q_1^i)$ for all $q_1^i \in \text{Child}^+(q_1)$ (Lemma 10). Then replace the subterms in q_1 by their images under σ.

        B. There is an injective, simulating mapping π from $\text{Child}^+(q_2)$ to $\text{Child}(d)$, but this mapping can be extended to π' such that $pos(q_2^i) \preceq \pi'(q_2^i)$ for some $q_2^i \in \text{Child}^-(q_2)$.

        Since q_1 subsumes q_2 there is an injective mapping σ from $\text{Child}(q_1)$ to $\text{Child}(q_2)$ such that q_1^i subsumes $\sigma(q_1^i)$ for all $q_1^i \in \text{Child}^+(q_1)$ and $\sigma(q_1^i)$ subsumes $pos(q_1^i)$ for all $q_1^i \in \text{Child}^-(q_1)$ (Lemma 10). Then replace the subterms in q_1 by their image under σ. These transformations are subsumption monotone.

BIBLIOGRAPHY

[AB94] Krzysztof R. Apt and Roland N. Bol. Logic programming and negation: A survey. *Journal of Logic Programming*, 19/20:9–71, 1994. (Cited on page 146.)

[AB07] Ben Adida and Mark Birbeck. RDFa primer 1.0 embedding RDF in XHTML. W3C working draft, W3C, October 2007. (Cited on page 63.)

[ABB+07] Uwe Assmann, Sacha Berger, François Bry, Tim Furche, Jakob Henriksson, and Jendrik Johannes. Modular web queries — from rules to stores. In *Proceedings of International Workshop on Scalable Semantic Web Knowledge Base Systems 2007*, volume 4805/2007 of *LCNS*, 2007. (Cited on page 85.)

[ABCC03] Enrico Augurusa, Daniele Braga, Alessandro Campi, and Stefano Ceri. Design and implementation of a graphical interface to XQuery. In *SAC '03: Proceedings of the 2003 ACM symposium on Applied computing*, pages 1163–1167, New York, NY, USA, 2003. ACM. (Cited on page 66.)

[ABE09] Faisal Alkhateeba, Jean-François Baget, and Jerome Euzenat. Extending SPARQL with regular expression patterns. *Journal of Web Semantics*, pages 28–42, 2009. (Cited on page 129.)

[ABK+08] S. Auer, C. Bizer, G. Kobilarov, J. Lehmann, R. Cyganiak, and Z. Ives. DBpedia: A nucleus for a web of open data. In *Proceedings of 6th International Semantic Web Conference, 2nd Asian Semantic Web Conference (ISWC+ASWC 2007)*, pages 722–735. November 2008. (Cited on page 187.)

[ABS00] Serge Abiteboul, Peter Buneman, and Dan Suciu. *Data on the Web: from relations to semistructured data and XML*. Morgan Kaufmann Publishers Inc., San Francisco, CA, USA, 2000. (Cited on page 64.)

[Adi08] Ben Adida. hGRDDL: Bridging microformats and RDFa. *Journal of Web Semantics*, 6(1):54–60, 2008. (Cited on page 63.)

[AGH04] Renzo Angles, Claudio Gutierrez, and Jonathan Hayes. RDF query languages need support for graph properties. Technical report, Universidad de Chile, 2004. (Cited on page 119.)

[AHU74] A. V. Aho, J. E. Hopcroft, and J. D. Ullman. *The Design and Analysis of Computer Algorithms*. Addison-Wesley, Reading, Mass., 1974. (Cited on pages 175 and 183.)

[AKKP08] Waseem Akhtar, Jacek Kopecky, Thomas Krennwallner, and Axel Polleres. XSPARQL: Traveling between the XML and RDF worlds – and avoiding the XSLT pilgrimage. In

Manfred Hauswirth, Manolis Koubarakis, and Sean Bechhofer, editors, *Proceedings of the 5th European Semantic Web Conference*, LNCS, Berlin, Heidelberg, June 2008. Springer Verlag. (Cited on pages 41, 44, and 63.)

[Apt88] Krzysztof R. Apt. Introduction to logic programming. Technical report, University of Texas at Austin, Austin, TX, USA, 1988. (Cited on page 5.)

[Apt92] Krzysztof R. Apt. A new definition of SLDNF-resolution. Technical report, CWI (Centre for Mathematics and Computer Science), 1992. (Cited on page 5.)

[AQM+97] S. Abiteboul, D. Quass, J. McHugh, J. Widom, and J.L. Wiener. The Lorel query language for semistructured data. *International Journal on Digital Libraries*, 1(1):68–88, 1997. (Cited on page 129.)

[BBB+04] Sacha Berger, François Bry, Oliver Bolzer, Tim Furche, Sebastian Schaffert, and Christoph Wieser. Xcerpt and visXcerpt: Twin query languages for the semantic web. In *Proceedings of 3rd International Semantic Web Conference, Hiroshima, Japan (7th–11th November 2004)*, LNCS, 2004. (Cited on pages 3 and 66.)

[BBC+07] Scott Boag, Anders Berglund, Don Chamberlin, Jérôme Siméon, Michael Kay, Jonathan Robie, and Mary F. Fernández. XML path language (XPath) 2.0. W3C recommendation, W3C, January 2007. http://www.w3.org/TR/2007/REC-xpath20-20070123/. (Cited on pages 12 and 66.)

[BBF+06] Sacha Berger, François Bry, Tim Furche, Benedikt Linse, and Andreas Schroeder. Vorführung von Xcerpt und visXcerpt, Anfragesprachen für das Web. In Stefan Brass and Alexander Hinneburg, editors, *Grundlagen von Datenbanken*, page 12. Institute of Computer Science, Martin-Luther-University, 2006. (Cited on page 3.)

[BBFS05] James Bailey, François Bry, Tim Furche, and Sebastian Schaffert. Web and semantic web query languages: A survey. In *Reasoning Web, First International Summer School 2005*, volume 3564 of *LNCS*. Springer-Verlag, 2005. (Cited on page 66.)

[BBSW03] Sacha Berger, François Bry, Sebastian Schaffert, and Christoph Wieser. Xcerpt and visXcerpt: From pattern-based to visual querying of XML and semistructured data. In *Proceedings of 29th Intl. Conference on Very Large Data Bases, Berlin, Germany (9th–12th September 2003)*, 2003. (Cited on page 3.)

[BC99] Angela Bonifati and Stefano Ceri. Comparative analysis of five XML query languages. *CoRR*, cs.DB/9912015, 1999. informal publication. (Cited on page 66.)

[Bec04] David Beckett. RDF/XML syntax specification (revised). W3C recommendation, W3C, February 2004. (Cited on pages 5, 21, 22, and 23.)

[BEE+07] François Bry, Norbert Eisinger, Thomas Eiter, Tim Furche, Georg Gottlob, Clemens Ley, Benedikt Linse, Reinhard Pichler, and Fang Wei. Foundations of rule-based query answering. In Grigoris Antoniou, Uwe Aßmann, Cristina Baroglio, Stefan Decker, Nicola Henze, Paula-Lavinia Patranjan, and Robert Tolksdorf, editors, *Reasoning Web*, volume 4636 of *Lecture Notes in Computer Science*, pages 1–153. Springer, 2007. (Cited on pages 4, 8, and 146.)

[Ber08] Sacha Berger. *Regular Rooted Graph Grammars - A Web Type and Schema Language*. Dissertation/Ph.D. thesis, Institute of Computer Science, LMU, Munich, 2008. PhD Thesis, Institute for Informatics, University of Munich, 2008. (Cited on page 15.)

[BFB+05] François Bry, Tim Furche, Liviu Badea, Christoph Koch, Sebastian Schaffert, and Sacha Berger. Querying the Web reconsidered: Design principles for versatile web query languages. *Journal of Semantic Web and Information Systems (IJSWIS)*, 1(2), 2005. (Cited on pages 15 and 63.)

[BFL06] François Bry, Tim Furche, and Benedikt Linse. Data model and query constructs for versatile web query languages: State-of-the-art and challenges for Xcerpt. In José Júlio Alferes, James Bailey, Wolfgang May, and Uta Schwertel, editors, *PPSWR*, volume 4187 of *Lecture Notes in Computer Science*, pages 90–104. Springer, 2006. (Cited on page 15.)

[BFL07] François Bry, Tim Furche, and Benedikt Linse. Simulation subsumption or déjà vu on the Web (extended version). Technical Report PMS-FB-2008-01, University of Munich, 2007. (Cited on pages 145 and 173.)

[BFL+08a] François Bry, Tim Furche, Clemens Ley, Benedikt Linse, and Bruno Marnette. RDFLog: It's like datalog for RDF. In *Proceedings of 22nd Workshop on (Constraint) Logic Programming, Dresden (30th September–1st October 2008)*, 2008. (Cited on pages 4, 30, 48, 80, and 122.)

[BFL+08b] François Bry, Tim Furche, Clemens Ley, Benedikt Linse, and Bruno Marnette. Taming existence in RDF querying. In Diego Calvanese and Georg Lausen, editors, *RR*, volume 5341 of *Lecture Notes in Computer Science*, pages 236–237. Springer, 2008. (Cited on page 4.)

[BFL08c] François Bry, Tim Furche, and Benedikt Linse. Simulation subsumption or déjà vu on the Web. In Diego Calvanese and Georg Lausen, editors, *RR*, volume 5341 of *Lecture Notes in Computer Science*, pages 28–42. Springer, 2008. (Cited on page 15.)

[BFL+09a] François Bry, Tim Furche, Benedikt Linse, Alexander Pohl, Antonius Weinzierl, and Olga Yestekhina. Four lessons in versatility or how query languages adapt to the web. In *Semantic Techniques for the Web, The Rewerse Perspective*, volume 5500 of *Lecture Notes in Computer Science*. Springer, 2009. (Cited on page 15.)

[BFL+09b] François Bry, Tim Furche, Clemens Ley, Benedikt Linse, Bruno Marnette, and Olga Poppe. SPARQLog: SPARQL with rules and quantification. In Roberto De Virgilio, Fausto Giunchiglia, and Letizia Tanca, editors, *Semantic Web Information Management: A Model-based Perspective*, chapter 12. Springer-Verlag, 2009. (Cited on pages 34 and 122.)

[BFL09c] Francois Bry, Tim Furche, and Benedikt Linse. Model theory and entailment rules for RDF containers, collections and reification. forthcoming, 2009. (Cited on page 15.)

[BFL09d] Francois Bry, Tim Furche, and Benedikt Linse. The perfect match: RPL and RDF rule languages. In *Proceedings of the third international conference on Web reasoning and rule Systems*. Springer, 2009. (Cited on page 15.)

[BFLL07] François Bry, Tim Furche, Clemens Ley, and Benedikt Linse. RDFLog—taming existence - a logic-based query language for RDF. Research report, University of Munich, 2007. (Cited on pages 30 and 80.)

[BFLP08] François Bry, Tim Furche, Benedikt Linse, and Alexander Pohl. XcerptRDF: A pattern-based answer to the versatile web challenge. In *Proceedings of 22nd Workshop on (Constraint) Logic Programming, Dresden, Germany (30th September–1st October 2008)*, pages 27–36, 2008. (Cited on page 15.)

[BFLS06] François Bry, Tim Furche, Benedikt Linse, and Andreas Schroeder. Efficient evaluation of n-ary conjunctive queries over trees and graphs. In Angela Bonifati and Irini Fundulaki, editors, *WIDM*, pages 11–18. ACM, 2006. (Cited on page 15.)

[BFS00] Peter Buneman, Mary F. Fernandez, and Dan Suciu. UnQL: a query language and algebra for semistructured data based on structural recursion. *VLDB Journal: Very Large Data Bases*, 9(1):76–110, 2000. (Cited on page 66.)

[BG04] Dan Brickley and Ramanatgan V. Guha. RDF vocabulary description language 1.0: RDF schema. W3C recommendation, W3C, February 2004. http://www.w3.org/TR/2004/REC-rdf-schema-20040210/. (Cited on page 20.)

[BHK+09] Harold Boley, Gary Hallmark, Michael Kifer, Adrian Paschke, Axel Polleres, and Dave Reynolds. RIF core dialect. W3C working draft, W3C, July 2009. (Cited on pages 3 and 57.)

[BHLT06] Tim Bray, Dave Hollander, Andrew Layman, and Richard Tobin. Namespaces in XML 1.0 (second edition), 2006. W3C Rec. 16 August 2006. (Cited on pages 22, 68, and 117.)

[BK93] Anthony J. Bonner and Michael Kifer. Transaction logic programming. In *ICLP*, pages 257–279, 1993. (Cited on page 49.)

[BK04] Jeen Broekstra and Arjohn Kampman. SeRQL: An RDF query and transformation language. August 2004. (Cited on page 80.)

[BK09a] Harold Boley and Michael Kifer. RIF basic logic dialect. W3C working draft, W3C, July 2009. http://www.w3.org/TR/2008/WD-rif-bld-20080730/. (Cited on page 57.)

[BK09b] Harold Boley and Michael Kifer. RIF framework for logic dialects. W3C working draft, W3C, July 2009. http://www.w3.org/TR/2008/WD-rif-fld-20080730/. (Cited on page 57.)

[BKvH02] Jeen Broekstra, Arjohn Kampman, and Frank van Harmelen. Sesame: A generic architecture for storing and querying RDF and RDF Schema. In *Proceedings of the first International Semantic Web Conference (ISWC 2002)*, number 2342 in Lecture Notes in Computer Science, pages 54–68. Springer Verlag, Heidelberg Germany, 2002. (Cited on page 11.)

[BL98] T. Berners-Lee. Notation 3. Technical report, W3C, 1998. (Cited on page 24.)

[BMS07] Henrik Björklund, Wim Martens, and Thomas Schwentick. Conjunctive query containment over trees. In Marcelo Arenas and Michael I. Schwartzbach, editors, *DBPL*, volume 4797 of *Lecture Notes in Computer Science*, pages 66–80. Springer, 2007. (Cited on page 164.)

[Bol05] Oliver Bolzer. Towards data-integration on the semantic web: Querying RDF with Xcerpt. Diplomarbeit/diploma thesis, Institute of Computer Science, LMU, Munich, 2005. (Cited on pages 15 and 85.)

[BPSM+06] Tim Bray, Jean Paoli, C. M. Sperberg-McQueen, Eve Maler, and François Yergeau. Extensible markup language (XML) 1.0 (fourth edition), 2006. (Cited on pages 79 and 104.)

[BS02] François Bry and Sebastian Schaffert. The XML query language Xcerpt: Design principles, examples, and semantics. In Akmal B. Chaudhri, Mario Jeckle, Erhard Rahm, and Rainer Unland, editors, *Web, Web-Services, and Database Systems*, volume 2593 of *Lecture Notes in Computer Science*, pages 295–310. Springer, 2002. (Cited on pages 15 and 171.)

[BvH+04] Sean Bechhofer, Frank van Harmelen, Jim Hendler, Ian Horrocks, Deborah L. McGuinness, Peter F. Patel-Schneider, and Lynn Andrea Stein. OWL Web Ontology Language Reference. Technical report, W3C, 2004. (Cited on pages 49 and 51.)

[BW01] S. Tabet H. Boley and G. Wagner. Design rationale of RuleML: A markup language for semantic web rules. In I. F. Cruz, S. Decker, J. Euzenat, and D. L. McGuinness, editors, *Proc. Semantic Web Working Symposium*, pages 381–402, Stanford University, California, 2001. (Cited on page 55.)

[CB94] Peter Cholak and Howard A. Blair. The complexity of local stratification. *Fundam. Inform.*, 21(4):333–344, 1994. (Cited on page 141.)

[CBHS05a] Jeremy J. Carroll, Christian Bizer, Pat Hayes, and Patrick Stickler. Named graphs, provenance and trust. In *WWW '05: Proceedings of the 14th international conference on World Wide Web*, pages 613–622, New York, NY, USA, 2005. ACM. (Cited on page 36.)

[CBHS05b] Jeremy J. Carroll, Christian Bizer, Patrick J. Hayes, and Patrick Stickler. Named graphs, provenance and trust. In Allan Ellis and Tatsuya Hagino, editors, *WWW*, pages 613–622. ACM, 2005. (Cited on page 105.)

[CCD$^+$98] S. Ceri, S. Comai, E. Damiani, P. Fraternali, S. Paraboschi, and L. Tanca. XML-GL: a graphical language for querying and restructuring XML documents. 1998. (Cited on page 66.)

[CDD$^+$04] Jeremy J. Carroll, Ian Dickinson, Chris Dollin, Dave Reynolds, Andy Seaborne, and Kevin Wilkinson. Jena: implementing the semantic web recommendations. In *WWW Alt. '04: Proceedings of the 13th international World Wide Web conference on Alternate track papers & posters*, pages 74–83. ACM Press, 2004. (Cited on page 11.)

[CKW93] Weidong Chen, Michael Kifer, and David S. Warren. HiLog: A foundation for higher-order logic programming. *Journal of Logic Programming*, 15(3):187–230, 1993. (Cited on pages 3, 49, and 58.)

[CM77] Ashok K. Chandra and Philip M. Merlin. Optimal implementation of conjunctive queries in relational data bases. In *STOC*, pages 77–90. ACM, 1977. (Cited on page 4.)

[CP06] Juan Carlos and Axel Polleres. SPARQL rules. Technical report, Universidad Rey Juan Carlos, 2006. (Cited on page 41.)

[CRF00] Donald D. Chamberlin, Jonathan Robie, and Daniela Florescu. Quilt: An XML query language for heterogeneous data sources. In Dan Suciu and Gottfried Vossen, editors, *WebDB (Selected Papers)*, volume 1997 of *Lecture Notes in Computer Science*, pages 1–25. Springer, 2000. (Cited on page 66.)

[CT04] John Cowan and Richard Tobin. XML Information Set (second edition). Technical report, W3C, 2004. (Cited on page 22.)

[CW96] Weidong Chen and David Scott Warren. Tabled evaluation with delaying for general logic programs. *Journal of the ACM*, 43(1):20–74, 1996. (Cited on page 164.)

[dav06] GRDDL primer. Technical report, W3C, 2006. (Cited on page 63.)

[DB08] Tim Berners-Lee David Beckett. Turtle - terse RDF triple language, 2008. (Cited on page 35.)

[dB09] Jos de Bruijn. RIF RDF and OWL compatibility. W3C working draft, W3C, jul 2009. (Cited on page 57.)

[DFF+98] Alin Deutsch, Mary F. Fernández, Daniela Florescu, Alon Y. Levy, and Dan Suciu. XML-QL. In *QL*, 1998. (Cited on page 66.)

[Dij82] Edsger Wybe Dijkstra. On the role of scientific thought (EWD447). In *Selected Writings on Computing: A Personal Perspective*, pages 60–66. 1982. (Cited on page 71.)

[dSMPH09] Christian de Sainte Marie, Adrian Paschke, and Gary Hallmark. RIF production rule dialect. W3C working draft, W3C, 2009. (Cited on page 57.)

[DSN03] S. Decker, M. Sintek, and W. Nejdl. The modeltheoretic semantics of TRIPLE. *Proceedings of the International World Wide Web Conference*, 2003. (Cited on pages 53 and 55.)

[DT01] Alin Deutsch and Val Tannen. Containment and integrity constraints for XPath fragments. In *In KRDB*, 2001. (Cited on page 13.)

[Eck08] Michael Eckert. *Complex Event Processing with XChangeEQ: Language Design, Formal Semantics and Incremental Evaluation for Querying Events*. Dissertation/Ph.D. thesis, Institute of Computer Science, LMU, Munich, 2008. PhD Thesis, Institute for Informatics, University of Munich, 2008. (Cited on page 15.)

[EFK+00] Thomas Eiter, Wolfgang Faber, Christoph Koch, Nicola Leone, and Gerald Pfeifer. DLV - a system for declarative problem solving. *CoRR*, cs.AI/0003036, 2000. informal publication. (Cited on page 146.)

[Est08] Olga Estekhina. Well-founded semantics and local-stratification for xcerpt, institute of computer science, lmu, munich. Projektarbeit/project thesis, 2008. (Cited on page 157.)

[EV03] J. Euzenat and P. Valtchev. An integrative proximity measure for ontology alignment. In A. Doan, A. Halevy, and N. Noy, editors, *Proceedings of the 1st Intl. Workshop on Semantic Integration*, volume 82 of *CEUR*, 2003. (Cited on page 63.)

[EV04] J. Euzenat and P. Valtchev. Similarity-based ontology alignment in OWL-lite. In R. López de Mántaras and L. Saitta, editors, *Proceedings of the 16th European Conference on Artificial Intelligence (ECAI-04)*, pages 333–337. IOS Press, 2004. (Cited on page 63.)

[FHW78] S. Fortune, J.E. Hopcroft, and J.C. Wyllie. The Directed Subgraph Homeomorphism Problem. 1978. (Cited on page 130.)

[FLB+06] Tim Furche, Benedikt Linse, François Bry, Dimitris Plexousakis, and Georg Gottlob. RDF querying: Language constructs and evaluation methods compared. In *Reasoning Web, Second International Summer School 2006*, volume 4126 of *LNCS*. 2006. (Cited on page 71.)

[Fur08a] Tim Furche. *Implementation of Web Query Languages Reconsidered: Beyond Tree and Single-Language Algebras at (Almost) No Cost*. Dissertation/doctoral thesis, Ludwig-Maxmilians University Munich, 2008. (Cited on pages 78 and 142.)

[Fur08b] Tim Furche. *Implementation of Web Query Languages Reconsidered: Beyond Tree and Single-Language Algebras at (Almost) No Costs*. Dissertation/Ph.D. thesis, Institute of Computer Science, LMU, Munich, 2008. PhD Thesis, Institute for Informatics, University of Munich, 2008. (Cited on page 15.)

[Gan07] Fabien Gandon. GRDDL use cases: Scenarios of extracting RDF data from XML documents. W3C working group note 6 april 2007, W3C, 2007. (Cited on page 63.)

[GHM03] Claudio Gutiérrez, Carlos A. Hurtado, and Alberto O. Mendelzon. Formal aspects of querying RDF databases. In Isabel F. Cruz, Vipul Kashyap, Stefan Decker, and Rainer Eckstein, editors, *SWDB*, pages 293–307, 2003. (Cited on page 21.)

[GHM04] Claudio Gutiérrez, Carlos A. Hurtado, and Alberto O. Mendelzon. Foundations of semantic web databases. In Alin Deutsch, editor, *PODS 04: Proceedings of the twenty-third ACM SIGMOD-SIGACT-SIGART symposium on Principles of Database Systems*, pages 95–106. ACM, 2004. (Cited on page 28.)

[GKM07] Michaela Götz, Christoph Koch, and Wim Martens. Efficient algorithms for the tree homeomorphism problem. pages 17–31, 2007. (Cited on page 179.)

[GL88] M. Gelfond and V. Lifschitz. The stable model semantics for logic programming. In *Proceeding of the Fifth Logic Programming Symposium*, pages 1070–1080, 1988. (Cited on pages 5 and 146.)

[GM06] Lars Marius Garshol and Graham Moore. ISO 13250-2: Topic Maps — Data Model. International standard, ISO/IEC, 2006. (Cited on page 63.)

[GP91] Douglas N. Gordin and Alexander J. Pasik. Set oriented constructs: From rete rule bases to database systems. In James Clifford and Roger King, editors, *SIGMOD Conference*, pages 60–67. ACM Press, 1991. (Cited on pages 16 and 17.)

[Hay04] Patrick Hayes. RDF semantics. Technical report, W3C, February 2004. (Cited on pages 14, 24, 25, 26, 27, 28, 29, 90, and 94.)

[Hen01] J. Hendler. Agents and the Semantic Web. *IEEE INTELLIGENT SYSTEMS*, pages 30–37, 2001. (Cited on page 16.)

[HHK95] Monika Rauch Henzinger, Thomas A. Henzinger, and Peter W. Kopke. Computing simulations on finite and infinite graphs. In *FOCS*, pages 453–462, 1995. (Cited on page 141.)

[HPSB+04] Ian Horrocks, Peter F. Patel-Schneider, Harold Boley, Said Tabet, Benjamin Grosof, and Mike Dean. SWRL: A semantic web rule language combining OWL and RuleML. Draft version, DARPA DAML Program, December 2004. http://www.daml.org/rules/proposal/. (Cited on page 55.)

[HU79] John E. Hopcroft and Jeffrey D. Ullman. *Introduction to Automata Theory, Languages and Computation*. Addison-Wesley, 1979. (Cited on page 144.)

[Imm83] Neil Immerman. Languages which capture complexity classes. In *STOC '83: Proceedings of the fifteenth annual ACM symposium on theory of computing*, pages 347–354, New York, NY, USA, 1983. ACM. (Cited on page 183.)

[Isho2] Masayasu Ishikawa. XHTML 1.0 in XML schema. W3C note, W3C, September 2002. http://www.w3.org/TR/2002/NOTE-xhtml1-schema-20020902/. (Cited on page 5.)

[Kay84] Martin Kay. Functional unification grammar: A formalism for machine translation. In *COLING-84*, pages 75–78, Stanford, CA, 1984. (Cited on page 65.)

[Kay85] M. Kay. Parsing in functional unification grammar. In D.R. Dowty, L. Karttunen, and A.M. Zwicky, editors, *Natural Language Parsing: Psychological, Computational, and Theoretical Perspectives*, pages 251–278. Cambridge University Press, Cambridge, 1985. (Cited on page 65.)

[Kay07] Michael Kay. XSL transformations (XSLT) version 2.0. W3C recommendation, W3C, January 2007. http://www.w3.org/TR/2007/REC-xslt20-20070123/. (Cited on page 66.)

[Kc06] Rohit Khare and Tantek Çelik. Microformats: a pragmatic path to the semantic web. In *WWW '06: Proceedings of the 15th international conference on World Wide Web*, pages 865–866, New York, NY, USA, 2006. ACM Press. (Cited on page 63.)

[Kif05] M. Kifer. Nonmonotonic reasoning in FLORA-2. *Lecture Notes in Computer Science*, 3662:1, 2005. (Cited on page 49.)

[Kil92] Pekka Kilpeläinen. Tree matching problems with applications to structured text databases. 1992. (Cited on pages xvii, 177, and 178.)

[KJ07] Krys Kochut and Maciej Janik. SPARQLeR: Extended SPARQL for semantic association discovery. In Enrico Franconi, Michael Kifer, and Wolfgang May, editors, *ESWC*, volume 4519 of *Lecture Notes in Computer Science*, pages 145–159. Springer, 2007. (Cited on pages 42, 43, 119, and 120.)

[Kla07] Vanessa Klaas. Who's who in the world wide web: Approaches to name disambiguation. Diplomarbeit/diploma thesis, Institute of Computer Science, LMU, Munich, 2007. (Cited on page 87.)

[Klu88a] Anthony Klug. On conjunctive queries containing inequalities. *Journal of the ACM*, 35(1):146–160, 1988. (Cited on page 4.)

[Klu88b] Anthony C. Klug. On conjunctive queries containing inequalities. *Journal of the ACM*, 35(1):146–160, 1988. (Cited on page 164.)

[KLW95a] M. Kifer, G. Lausen, and J. Wu. Logical foundations of object-oriented and frame-based languages. *Journal of the ACM*, 42(4):741–843, 1995. (Cited on page 58.)

[KLW95b] Michael Kifer, George Lausen, and James Wu. Logical foundations of object oriented and frame based languages. *Journal of the ACM*, 42(4):741–843, 1995. (Cited on page 49.)

[Kly04] J. J. Carroll G. Klyne. Resource description framework (RDF): Concepts and abstract syntax. Technical report, W3C, 2004. (Cited on pages 19 and 20.)

[KM95] Pekka Kilpelainen and Heikki Mannila. Ordered and unordered tree inclusion. *SIAM Comput.*, 24(2):340–356, 1995. (Cited on page 178.)

[KMA$^+$98] Craig A. Knoblock, Steven Minton, José Luis Ambite, Naveen Ashish, Pragnesh Jay Modi, Ion Muslea, Andrew Philpot, and Sheila Tejada. Modeling web sources for information integration. In *AAAI/IAAI*, pages 211–218, 1998. (Cited on page 63.)

[KMA$^+$04] G. Karvounarakis, A. Magkanaraki, S. Alexaki, V. Christophides, D. Plexousakis, M. Scholl, and K. Tolle. RQL: A functional query language for RDF. In P. M. D. Gray, L. Kerschberg, P. J. H. King, and A. Poulovassilis, editors, *The Functional Approach to Data Management: Modelling, Analyzing and Integrating Heterogeneous Data*, LNCS, pages 435–465. Springer-Verlag, 2004. (Cited on pages 52 and 80.)

[Koc05] Christoph Koch. On the complexity of nonrecursive XQuery and functional query languages on complex values. *CoRR*, abs/cs/0503062, 2005. informal publication. (Cited on page 164.)

[KP88] Phokion G. Kolaitis and Christos H. Papadimitriou. Why not negation by fixpoint? In *PODS*, pages 231–239. ACM, 1988. (Cited on page 146.)

[Kub04] Marek Kubale. *Graph Colorings*. American Mathematical Society, 2004. (Cited on page 12.)

[Len02] Maurizio Lenzerini. Data integration: A theoretical perspective. In *PODS '02: Proceedings of the twenty-first ACM SIGMOD-SIGACT-SIGART symposium on Principles of Database Systems*, 2002. (Cited on page 63.)

[LP84] As La Paugh and Ch Papadimitrou. The even-path problem for graphs and digraphs. *Networks(New York, NY)*, 14(4):507–513, 1984. (Cited on page 130.)

[LS93] Alon Y. Levy and Yehoshua Sagiv. Queries independent of updates. In *VLDB '93: Proceedings of the 19th International Conference on Very Large Data Bases*, pages 171–181, San Francisco, CA, USA, 1993. Morgan Kaufmann Publishers Inc. (Cited on page 4.)

[LW06] Sergey Lukichev and Gerd Wagner. G.: Visual rules modeling. In *In: Sixth International Andrei Ershov Memorial Conference Perspectives Of System Informatics*, pages 467–673. LNCS, Springer, 2006. (Cited on page 3.)

[M89] Erkki Mäkinen. On the subtree isomorphism problem for ordered trees. *Information Processing Letters*, 32(5):271–273, 1989. (Cited on page 176.)

[Mar04a] Massimo Marchiori. Towards a people's web: Metalog. In *Web Intelligence*, pages 320–326. IEEE Computer Society, 2004. (Cited on page 56.)

[Mar04b] M. Marx. Conditional XPath, the first order complete XPath dialect. In *Proceedings of the twenty-third ACM SIGMOD-SIGACT-SIGART symposium on Principles of Database Systems*, pages 13–22. ACM New York, NY, USA, 2004. (Cited on page 48.)

[Mar05] M. Marx. Conditional XPath. *ACM Transactions on Database Systems (TODS)*, 30(4):929–959, 2005. (Cited on page 48.)

[May04] Wolfgang May. XPath-logic and XPathLog: A logic-programming style XML data manipulation language. *Theory Pract. Log. Program.*, 4(3):239–287, 2004. (Cited on page 6.)

[McB04] Brian McBride. Rdf vocabulary description language 1.0: RDF schema, 2004. (Cited on pages 75 and 94.)

[Mil71] Robin Milner. An algebraic definition of simulation between programs. In *IJCAI*, pages 481–489, 1971. (Cited on page 141.)

[MM04] Frank Manola and Eric Miller. RDF primer, W3C recommendation. Technical report, W3C, 2004. (Cited on pages 14, 74, 90, 92, 94, and 96.)

[MS02] Gerome Miklau and Dan Suciu. Containment and equivalence for an XPath fragment (extended anstract), 2002. (Cited on pages 12, 174, 181, and 182.)

[MT92] Jiří Matoušek and Robin Thomas. On the complexity of finding iso- and other morphisms for partial k-trees. *Discrete Mathematics*, 108(1-3):343–364, 1992. (Cited on pages 178, 179, and 180.)

[MT08] Jonathan Marsh and Richard Tobin. XML base (second edition). W3C proposed edited recommendation, W3C, March 2008. http://www.w3.org/TR/2008/PER-xmlbase-20080320/. (Cited on page 22.)

[MW95] A.O. Mendelzon and P.T. Wood. Finding Regular Simple Paths in Graph Databases. *SIAM Journal on Computing*, 24:1235, 1995. (Cited on pages 129 and 130.)

[NM00] Natalya Fridman Noy and Mark A. Musen. PROMPT: Algorithm and tool for automated ontology merging and alignment. In *AAAI/IAAI*, pages 450–455, 2000. (Cited on page 63.)

[NS02] Frank Neven and Thomas Schwentick. XPath containment in the presence of disjunction, DTDs, and variables. In *ICDT '03: Proceedings of the 9th International Conference on Database Theory*, pages 315–329, London, UK, 2002. Springer-Verlag. (Cited on page 12.)

[Ogb05] Chimezie Ogbuji. Versa: Path-based RDF query language, 2005. (Cited on page 119.)

[OMD01] David Orchard, Eve Maler, and Steven DeRose. XML linking language (XLink) version 1.0. W3C recommendation, W3C, June 2001. http://www.w3.org/TR/2001/REC-xlink-20010627/. (Cited on page 104.)

[OMFB02] Dan Olteanu, Holger Meuss, Tim Furche, and François Bry. XPath: Looking forward. In Akmal B. Chaudhri, Rainer Unland, Chabane Djeraba, and Wolfgang Lindner, editors, *EDBT Workshops*, volume 2490 of *Lecture Notes in Computer Science*, pages 109–127. Springer, 2002. (Cited on page 163.)

[PAG06] Jorge Pérez, Marcelo Arenas, and Claudio Gutierrez. Semantics and complexity of SPARQL. In Isabel F. Cruz, Stefan Decker, Dean Allemang, Chris Preist, Daniel Schwabe, Peter Mika, Michael Uschold, and Lora Aroyo, editors, *International Semantic Web Conference*, volume 4273 of *Lecture Notes in Computer Science*, pages 30–43. Springer, 2006. (Cited on pages 12, 33, 39, and 40.)

[PAG08] Jorge Pérez, Marcelo Arenas, and Claudio Gutierrez. nSPARQL: A navigational language for RDF. In Amit P. Sheth, Steffen Staab, Mike Dean, Massimo Paolucci, Diana Maynard, Timothy W. Finin, and Krishnaprasad Thirunarayan, editors, *International Semantic Web Conference*, volume 5318 of *Lecture Notes in Computer Science*, pages 66–81. Springer, 2008. (Cited on pages 41, 119, 123, 126, 130, 131, and 133.)

[Pan04] Jeff Z. Pan. *Description Logics: Reasoning Support for the Semantic Web*. PhD thesis, 2004. (Cited on page 32.)

[PBK09] Axel Polleres, Harold Boley, and Michael Kifer. RIF datatypes and built-ins 1.0. W3C working draft, W3C, July 2009. (Cited on page 58.)

[Pep00] Steve Pepper. The TAO of topic maps. 2000. (Cited on page 63.)

[PFH06] Axel Polleres, Cristina Feier, and Andreas Harth. Rules with contextually scoped negation. In York Sure and John Domingue, editors, *ESWC*, volume 4011 of *Lecture Notes in*

Computer Science, pages 332–347. Springer, 2006. (Cited on pages 21 and 105.)

[PH03a] Jeff Pan and Ian Horrocks. RDFS(FA) and RDF MT: Two semantics for RDFS. In Dieter Fensel, Katia Sycara, and John Mylopoulos, editors, *Proc. of the 2003 International Semantic Web Conference (ISWC2003)*, number 2870 in Lecture Notes in Computer Science, pages 30–46. Springer, 2003. http://www.cs.man.ac.uk/~horrocks/Publications/download/2003/HoPa03b.pdf. (Cited on page 31.)

[PH03b] Jeff Z. Pan and Ian Horrocks. RDFS(FA): A DL-ised sublanguage of RDFS. In *International Workshop on Description Logics 2003*, pages 95–102, 2003. (Cited on page 31.)

[Poh08] Alexander Pohl. RDF Querying in Xcerpt: Language Constructs and Implementation. Deliverable I4-Dx2, REWERSE, 2008. (Cited on pages 15 and 58.)

[Pol07] Axel Polleres. From SPARQL to rules (and back). In Carey L. Williamson, Mary Ellen Zurko, Peter F. Patel-Schneider, and Prashant J. Shenoy, editors, *WWW*, pages 787–796. ACM, 2007. (Cited on pages 36, 40, 41, 47, 48, and 122.)

[Pop] Olga Poppe. Subsumption-based resolution for rule languages with rich unification http://www.pms.ifi.lmu.de/publikationen/. diploma thesis, University of Munich. (Cited on pages 5 and 187.)

[PP90] H. Przymusinska and T. C. Przymunsinski. Weakly stratified logic programs. *Fundam. Inf.*, 13(1):51–65, 1990. (Cited on page 153.)

[Prz88] Teodor C. Przymusinski. On the declarative semantics of deductive databases and logic programs. In *Foundations of Deductive Databases and Logic Programming.*, pages 193–216. Morgan Kaufmann, 1988. (Cited on page 146.)

[PS04] Peter F. Patel-Schneider. A proposal for a SWRL extension to first-order logic. Proposal, DARPA DAML Program, November 2004. http://www.daml.org/2004/11/fol/proposal. (Cited on page 56.)

[PSF02] Peter F. Patel-Schneider and Dieter Fensel. Layering the Semantic Web: Problems and directions. In *First International Semantic Web Conference (ISWC2002)*, Sardinia, Italy, June 2002. (Cited on page 31.)

[Pö5] Paula-Lavinia Pătrânjan. *The Language XChange: A Declarative Approach to Reactivity on the Web*. Dissertation/Ph.D. thesis, Institute of Computer Science, LMU, Munich, 2005. PhD Thesis, Institute for Informatics, University of Munich, 2005. (Cited on page 15.)

[RC97] R. Ramesh and Weidong Chen. Implementation of tabled evaluation with delaying in prolog. *IEEE Trans. Knowl. Data Eng.*, 9(4):559–574, 1997. (Cited on page 5.)

[Ros90] Kenneth A. Ross. Modular stratification and magic sets for DATALOG programs with negation. In *PODS*, pages 161–171. ACM Press, 1990. (Cited on page 146.)

[RR06] David Recordon and Drummond Reed. OpenID 2.0: a platform for user-centric identity management. In *DIM '06: Proceedings of the second ACM workshop on Digital identity management*, pages 11–16, New York, NY, USA, 2006. ACM. (Cited on page 87.)

[SCF+07] Jérôme Siméon, Don Chamberlin, Daniela Florescu, Scott Boag, Mary F. Fernández, and Jonathan Robie. XQuery 1.0: An XML query language. W3C recommendation, W3C, January 2007. http://www.w3.org/TR/2007/REC-xquery-20070123/. (Cited on pages 7 and 66.)

[Scho4a] Sebastian Schaffert. *Xcerpt: A Rule-Based Query and Transformation Language for the Web*. PhD thesis, University of Munich, 2004. (Cited on pages 15, 17, 109, 115, 142, 156, 157, 158, 163, and 165.)

[Scho4b] Thomas Schwentick. XPath query containment. *SIGMOD Record*, 33(1):101–109, 2004. (Cited on pages 11, 12, 164, and 165.)

[SD01] Michael Sintek and Stefan Decker. TRIPLE - an RDF query, inference and transformation language. Technical report, DFKI, 2001. (Cited on pages 53 and 54.)

[Shm87] O. Shmueli. Decidability and expressiveness aspects of logic queries. In *PODS '87: Proceedings of the sixth ACM SIGACT-SIGMOD-SIGART symposium on Principles of Database Systems*, pages 237–249, New York, NY, USA, 1987. ACM. (Cited on page 4.)

[SMB+08] Andy Seaborne, Geetha Manjunath, Chris Bizer, John Breslin, Souripriya Das, Ian Davis, Steve Harris, Kingsley Idehen, Olivier Corby, Kjetil Kjernsmo, and Benjamin Nowack. SPARQL/Update: A language for updating RDF graphs. W3C Member Submission, W3C, July 2008. http://www.w3.org/Submission/2008/04/. (Cited on page 41.)

[SP08] Andy Seaborne and Eric Prud'hommeaux. SPARQL query language for RDF. W3C recommendation, W3C, January 2008. http://www.w3.org/TR/2008/REC-rdf-sparql-query-20080115/. (Cited on pages 7, 35, and 80.)

[SS04] Simon Schenk and Steffen Staab. Networked graphs: A declarative mechanism for SPARQL rules, SPARQL views and RDF data integration on the Web. In *Proceedings of the 17th International World Wide Web Conference*, Beijing, China, 2008-04. (Cited on pages 41 and 122.)

[SSW93] Konstantinos F. Sagonas, Terrance Swift, and David Scott Warren. The XSB programming system. In *Workshop on Programming with Logic Databases (Informal Proceedings), ILPS*, page 164, 1993. (Cited on page 146.)

[ST97] R. Shamir and D. Tsur. Faster subtree isomorphism. In *ISTCS '97: Proceedings of the Fifth Israel Symposium on the Theory of Computing Systems (ISTCS '97)*, page 126, Washington, DC, USA, 1997. IEEE Computer Society. (Cited on page 176.)

[Sti05] Patrick Stickler. Concise bounded description. http://www.w3.org/Submission/CBD/, June 2005. (Cited on pages 34 and 39.)

[ter04] Herman J. ter Horst. Extending the RDFS entailment lemma. In Sheila A. McIlraith, Dimitris Plexousakis, and Frank van Harmelen, editors, *International Semantic Web Conference*, volume 3298 of *Lecture Notes in Computer Science*, pages 77–91. Springer, 2004. (Cited on page 30.)

[ter05a] Herman J. ter Horst. Combining RDF and part of OWL with rules: Semantics, decidability, complexity. In Yolanda Gil, Enrico Motta, V. Richard Benjamins, and Mark A. Musen, editors, *The Semantic Web - ISWC 2005*, number 3729 in Lecture Notes in Computer Science, pages 668–684, Heidelberg, 2005. Springer Verlag. (Cited on pages 29, 30, and 31.)

[ter05b] Herman J. ter Horst. Completeness, decidability and complexity of entailment for RDF schema and a semantic extension involving the OWL vocabulary. *Journal of Web Semantics*, 3(2-3):79–115, 2005. (Cited on pages 92, 93, 94, and 99.)

[tL07] Balder ten Cate and Carsten Lutz. The complexity of query containment in expressive fragments of XPath 2.0. In *PODS '07: Proceedings of the twenty-sixth ACM SIGMOD-SIGACT-SIGART symposium on Principles of Database Systems*, pages 73–82, New York, NY, USA, 2007. ACM. (Cited on page 12.)

[TS86] Hisao Tamaki and Taisuke Sato. OLD resolution with tabulation. In Ehud Y. Shapiro, editor, *ICLP*, volume 225 of *Lecture Notes in Computer Science*, pages 84–98. Springer, 1986. (Cited on pages 5 and 164.)

[Ull00] Jeffrey D. Ullman. Information integration using logical views. *Theor. Comput. Sci.*, 239(2):189–210, 2000. (Cited on pages 4 and 63.)

[Val02] Gabriel Valiente. *Algorithms on Trees and Graphs*. Springer-Verlag New York, Inc., Secaucus, NJ, USA, 2002. (Cited on page 177.)

[VD03] Jean-Yves Vion-Dury. Xpath on left and right sides of rules: toward compact xml tree rewriting through node patterns. In *DocEng '03: Proceedings of the 2003 ACM symposium on Document engineering*, pages 19–25, New York, NY, USA, 2003. ACM. (Cited on page 6.)

[vRS91a] A. van Gelder, K. Ross, and J.S. Schlipf. The well-founded semantics for general logic programs. *Journal of the ACM*, 18:620–650, 1991. (Cited on pages 150 and 151.)

[vRS91b] Allen van Gelder, Kenneth A. Ross, and John S. Schlipf. The well-founded semantics for general logic programs. *Journal of the ACM*, 1991. (Cited on pages 5 and 146.)

[W3C07] W3C. Gleaning resource descriptions from dialects of languages (GRDDL). W3C recommendation, W3C, September 2007. (Cited on page 63.)

[WL03] Fang Wei and Georg Lausen. Containment of conjunctive queries with safe negation. In Diego Calvanese, Maurizio Lenzerini, and Rajeev Motwani, editors, *ICDT*, volume 2572 of *Lecture Notes in Computer Science*, pages 343–357. Springer, 2003. (Cited on pages 4 and 164.)

[YKZ02] G. Yang, M. Kifer, and C. Zhao. Flora-2: User's Manual. *Department of Computer Science, Stony Brook University, Stony Brook*, 2002. (Cited on page 49.)

[YKZ03] Guizhen Yang, Michael Kifer, and Chang Zhao. Flora-2: A rule-based knowledge representation and inference infrastructure for the semantic web. In Robert Meersman, Zahir Tari, and Douglas C. Schmidt, editors, *CoopIS/DOA/OD-BASE*, volume 2888 of *Lecture Notes in Computer Science*, pages 671–688. Springer, 2003. (Cited on pages 49 and 51.)

I want morebooks!

Buy your books fast and straightforward online - at one of world's fastest growing online book stores! Environmentally sound due to Print-on-Demand technologies.

Buy your books online at
www.morebooks.shop

Kaufen Sie Ihre Bücher schnell und unkompliziert online – auf einer der am schnellsten wachsenden Buchhandelsplattformen weltweit! Dank Print-On-Demand umwelt- und ressourcenschonend produziert.

Bücher schneller online kaufen
www.morebooks.shop

KS OmniScriptum Publishing
Brivibas gatve 197
LV-1039 Riga, Latvia
Telefax: +371 686 204 55

info@omniscriptum.com
www.omniscriptum.com

Printed by Books on Demand GmbH, Norderstedt / Germany